FANTASIA IMPROMPTU
& FINIS

Benjamin DeCasseres

Fantasia Impromptu & FINIS

by
Benjamin DeCasseres

Underworld Amusements

isbn: 978-0-9885536-6-8

Edited and prepared by Kevin I. Slaughter
for Underworld Amusements
WWW.UNDERWORLDAMUSEMENTS.COM

Cover art by Josh McAlear
JOSHMCALEAR.COM

Half-title/spine illustration by Josh Latta
JOSHLATTA.COM

Thanks to Pól Cullivan *for frontispiece portrait, and* Erin Latta.

Fantasia Impromptu & FINIS *is the fourth in a series of books*
collecting and reviving the writings of Benjamin DeCasseres.
Other titles:
Anathema! Litanies of Negation
IMP: The Poetry of Benjamin DeCasseres
The Sublime Boy: The Poems of Walter DeCasseres
Forthcoming:
New York Is Hell: Thinking and Drinking in the Beautiful Beast

A website devoted to Benjamin DeCasseres
BENJAMINDECASSERES.COM

EDITOR'S NOTE

DeCasseres (1873-1945) began a diary-like collection of notes and reminiscences in December 1925. In January 1936 he began self-publishing a series of booklets through the Blackstone Publishers' called "The DeCasseres Books". He planned on releasing one booklet a month indefinitely. In 1937 the first of the sections from his diary was published. The published writings cover the time period from December of 1925 through June of 1927, though as of the late 1930's he was still maintaining his journals with the full intention of publishing them in their entirety.

DeCasseres was in a period of great productivity, and he was being rewarded. Before his entries begin, in 1925, both his book on Huneker (Joseph Lawren, 1925) and his *Mirrors of New York* (Joseph Lawren, 1925) were published. During the year and a half that this selection covers, he discusses three books being released. His *Forty Immortals*, a collection of biographical sketches, was the first. The collection of his brother's poetry, published as *The Sublime Boy,* was released as well as his wife's *The Boy of Bethlehem.* All three of these books came under the imprint of The Seven Arts, but *Forty Immortals* seems to have originally been published by Joseph Lawren.** It is noted by art

---

* Blackstone Publishers may be DeCasseres' own imprint, though there are at least three known booklets published under that name that are not by or about DeCasseres. Two are short collections of poetry, and the subject matter of the third can possibly be derived from the title: *Orthod Oxen of Science: Synoptic conspectus of author's Unitary Theory.* That George F. Gillette, the author, is prone to both zany wordplay AND overturning the basis of known physical laws does lend credibility to the idea that DeCasseres might have printed it.

** The copy in my personal collection has a dustjacket by The Seven Arts, but the spine is imprinted Joseph Lawren. On the title page, a legend for the Seven Arts is pasted over Joseph Lawren.

The DeCasseres Books

Book No. 13

Fantasia Impromptu:
The Adventures of an
Intellectual Faun

(Part 1)

By

BENJAMIN DeCASSERES

Fifty Cents

The DeCasseres Books

Book No. 15

Fantasia Impromptu:
The Adventures of an
Intellectual Faun

(Part 2)

By
BENJAMIN DeCASSERES

Fifty Cents

The DeCasseres Books

Book No. 17

Fantasia Impromptu:
The Adventures of an
Intellectual Faun
(Part 3)
By
BENJAMIN DeCASSERES

Fifty Cents

The DeCasseres Books

Book No. 19

Fantasia Impromptu:
The Adventures of an
Intellectual Faun
(Part 4)
By
BENJAMIN DeCASSERES

Fifty Cents

The DeCasseres Books

Book No. 21

Fantasia Impromptu:
The Adventures of an
Intellectual Faun
(Part 5)
By
BENJAMIN DeCASSERES

Fifty Cents

The DeCasseres Books

Book No. 23

Fantasia Impromptu:
The Adventures of an
Intellectual Faun
(Part 6)
By
BENJAMIN DeCASSERES

Fifty Cents

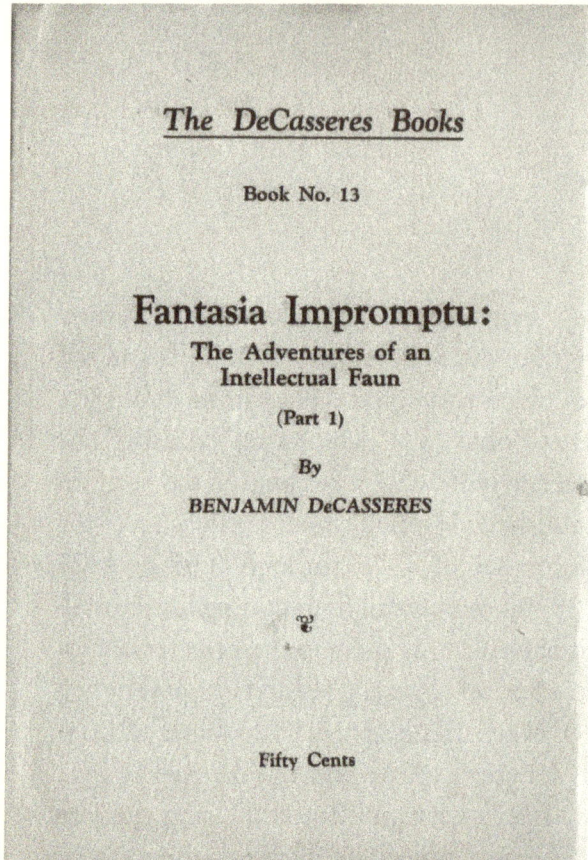

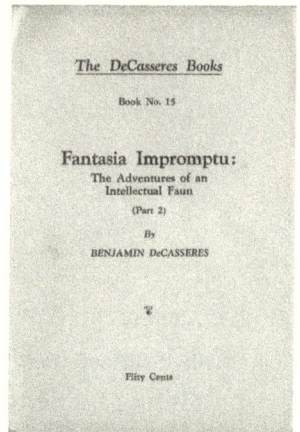

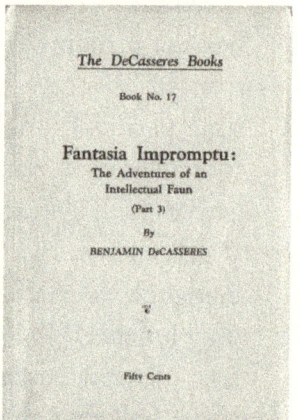

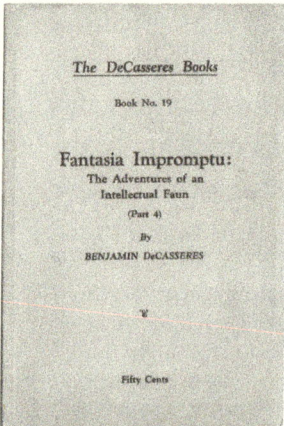

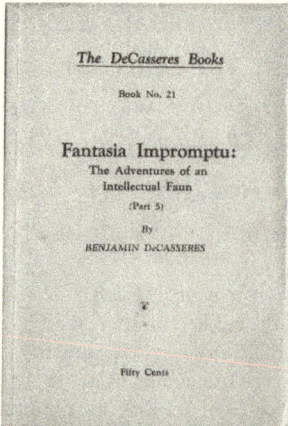

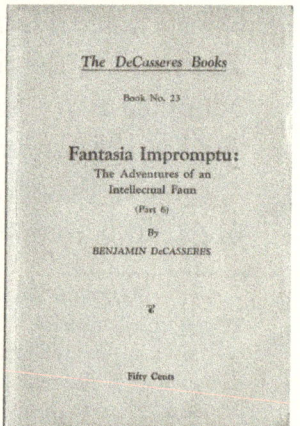

The covers of all six released excerpts from Fantasia Impromptu.

historian Randy J. Ploog that Joseph Lawren was Benjamin's friend Foranado's lawyer* and that Lawren paid for the original printing of *The Shadow-Eater* (Gotham Book Mart, 1915).

Anathema! Litanies of Negation would be published shortly after these excerpts end, in 1928, but he discusses it frequently as he had send out the manuscript to a number of people.

Chameleon: Being a Book of My Selves (Lieber & Lewis, 1922) was his second book to be published, and throughout his *Fantasia* he makes mention of responses to it.

Fantasia Impromptu was a resource for his professional work. About a year after he'd written a reminiscent about shutters, he cribbed much of it for part of a newspaper article (facsimile reproduced on the following page). The second section, transcribed below, can be read in original form on page 122.

The magic of shutters!

There are a few houses left with shutters in New York. I love to linger in front of the houses around Gramercy Park that still have shutters, some of them always closed as if to shut out the eye of Reality. They are the last vestiges of privacy; they are the last symbols of Mystery left to us.

A house without shutters is like an eye without an eyelid. Dignity, silence, reticence live in houses with shutters. They are breedy with stories. As I lean against the grill of Gramercy Park they evoke in my brain nostalgic old-fashioned reveries. The surrounding apartment houses have the brazen look of courtesans—for they have no shutters.

If I built a house in the city it would have cool, green shutters, like these old houses around Gramercy Park—shutters with perfectly closing slats, so that at high noon on cloudless, sunny days, when New York is lighted up like an operating room, I could produce the perfect illusion of living in the night time for a week, if I so desired.

Shutters have a spiritual quality. The soul of New York began

---

* According to one obituary, Mr. Lawren was a lawyer in Boston for 13 years before moving to St. Petersburg, Florida, where he set up a writer's colony and began publishing books. He moved to Venice in 1949 where he continued the colony and being active in the arts. He died in January of 1954, survived by a son, a sister and his brother Jacob Lebowich.

Magic!

By Benjamin De Casseres

A dull, hot afternoon on 19th Street, between Irving Place and Third Avenue. An old man plants his harp in front of a house in the middle of the block. A beautiful old German sentimental air suddenly fills the street like a barrel of old Falernian wine spilled into a dry brook.

Time turns backward. That harp, with its ancient dream music, has smitten us all with sudden youth. We hang out of the windows like a lot of fishwives, some of us in summer undress. The ragman stops with his cart in the middle of the street. His Ragland has suddenly become Prester John Land. The gutters of his mind are flushed with magic waters. The vegetable man has stopped his bawling, leans against his wagon, his face keyed to faraway dreams, and his apples are now the apples of Hesperides.

Janitors come out of their cellars, cooks from their kitchens and the furnace stokers in a hotel from their hell pits—all like damned souls swarming up into the Empyrean. A chauffeur stops his car in mid-street and rests his wheel. Phaeton has run into a sun! A policeman lays his club down and sits on a step. He has stolen ten minutes from Routine and Reality; he is intruding in a Mansion in the Skies!

It is a ten-minute triumph of Music over Business, a "dissolve" of Matter into Soul.

We shower this old German Prospero of the Harp with silver from our windows—real magic casements to him. And when he leaves we all blink our way back to Reality. The apples look rotten. The rags look cootie-ridden. The janitors, cooks and stokers look ugly and mean. The chauffeur looks like a crook. The cop is once more an avatar of Evil.

The dull hum and murmur of the brazen, inexorable Hell of New York fills the block once more.

* * *

The magic of shutters!

There are a few houses left with shutters in New York. I love to linger in front of the houses around Gramercy Park that still have shutters, some of them always closed as if to shut out the eye of Reality. They are the last vestiges of privacy; they are the last symbols of Mystery left to us.

A house without shutters is like an eye without an eyelid. Dignity, silence, reticence live in houses with shutters. They are breedy with stories. As I lean against the grill of Gramercy Park they evoke in my brain nostalgic old-fashioned reveries. They have a modesty. The surrounding apartment houses have the brazen look of courtesans—for they have no shutters.

If I built a house in the city it would have cool, green shutters, like these old houses around Gramercy Park—shutters with perfectly closing slats, so that at high noon on cloudless, sunny days, when New York is lighted up like an operating room, I could produce the perfect illusion of living in the night time for a week, if I so desired.

Shutters have a spiritual quality. The soul of New York began to change when its shutters began to disappear.

* * *

The magic of gay, unbuttoned, alcoholic laughter!

Suddenly in the evening from a house somewhere in back of me I hear this mad, healthy gayety breaking the dark like an exploding sun, out of which stream Puck, Falstaff, Momus, Gargantua and all the Comic Souls of time. The triumph of Life over Prohibition! The idiotic political speeches on the radios are drowned in a tempest of bawls, guffaws, belly-shaking mirth. It is a hurricane of joviality that must come like divine music to the ears of those tossing on their beds of pain in hospitals, drenching and blowing away the dismal thoughts that open like black parasols in their brains when night comes.

This unmuzzled laughter is the old song of New York! It is the ghost of jolly good fellows and the devil-may-care rogues of the past, overwhelming Fate and Care in festal explosions. It is the Emancipation Proclamation of body and soul burst from the belly of the grape.

Where is now the magic of the old laughter such as we used to tune our evenings to in Maria's, Jack's, Mouquin's and Joel's?—those Mansions of Momus, those cathedrals of healthy unreason. In America the crashing, alcoholic laughter is now taboo in public. We giggle, snicker and simper, and look around us cautiously. The buffoon in us is dead. A pogrom on Seriousness! A pogrom on the Prohibitionists! I shout into my own soul as the joyous magic of a Lost Day gushes the night from somewhere in back of me.

* * *

The lost magic of chimes!

They used to mean rest and meditation. But the chimes in the Metropolitan Tower have now another story. Those who sit under it in Madison Square listen to these chimes to the roar of trolley cars, the infernal squawking of trucks and taxicabs and the cacophonic fury of an age that is eating them alive.

The Metropolitan chimes are tolling 7 A. M. It is a war tocsin. It is not a call to rest and meditation, but a call to a cutthroat struggle. Seven A. M.: Millions of eyes are now slowly opening to the crash of hundreds of thousands of alarm clocks—the chimes of the Industrial Age, the age of standardized human machines. To me, the slow tolling of the bell in the tower sounds more like a death knell than hosannah to another day.

This tower, which presides over that section of New York like a grim muezzin in white, is not satisfied with its satiric musical warning every hour that we are all just sixty minutes nearer oblivion, reincarnation, immortality, or whatever awaits us when we have shuffled off this mortal coil of income tax and cut Scotch, but it must remind us every fifteen minutes with a blondlike tinkle that time is eating us up and we had better put that deal through.

Chimes in the heart of New York. Metropolitan chimes—reminders of a magic as dead as the arts of leisure and thinking.

* * *

Miracle money!

Ah, there is a magic left! A new magic, rather; a magic of sweet torture and bright dreams. Nothing expands our ego to such colossal proportions and button-busting delight as to think, talk and shout money in terms of billions. Never was there such a money souse! We dream, night and day, of miracle money, how to "grab off" a million, how to make "Open Sesame!" work over a lunch table.

Sudden money—all the old magics have dissolved into that. And what began in Hollywood may land us all finally in the Great Kingdom of Magic—the nut house.

Article from The World,
Tuesday, July 17, 1928.

to change when its shutters began to disappear.

In 1938 *Fantasia Impromptu, Part 6* was the last of "The DeCasseres Books" released. The final entry was followed by the parenthetical remark "To be continued in book 25". In all, 23 "The DeCasseres Books" were released, and the following year 25 sets of the complete series were bound together into a three volume collection titled *The Works of Benjamin DeCasseres*. That collection was reprinted once by Gordon Press in 1977.

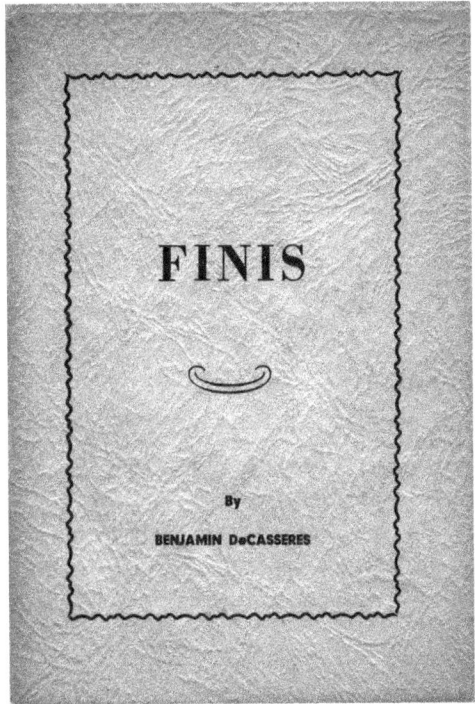

DeCasseres moved back into writing for newspapers. He regularly wrote book reviews and a separate column that focused his efforts on attacking Communism (and the American drift towards it) and writing about general local and world affairs.

The Works of Benjamin DeCasseres, and specifically *Fantasia Impromptu* (Part 6), was the last book DeCasseres was to publish until the 20 page booklet *FINIS* (1945), which was printed "in limited numbers" shortly after his death.

I know nothing of Benjamin's state of mind or health during the last year of his life, though there is nothing written in *FINIS* that should surprise the reader of anything he'd written prior. In the three essays and last "hymn", he pays tribute to "oblivion" as the one true constant in the universe, and the end of all things.

—*Kevin I. Slaughter.*
Baltimore, November, 2015

ix

THIS SIDE OF CARD IS FOR ADDRESS

Mrs. Carmen Henry.
1356 Pearl St.,
Denver, Col.

THE DeCASSERES BOOKS

Book No. 17 (the Third Part of "Fantasia Impromptu: the Adventures of an intellectual Faun") will be issued at the end of September and the series continued thenceforward. Books will not be issued during June, July and August.

I quite understand why these books of sheer literature, satire, humor, philosophy and poetry have not been reviewed by the book-reviewers of the American press—*ex nihilo nihil fit.*

Benjamin DeCasseres

Postcard dated June 19th, 1937 from DeCasseres to Mrs. Carmen Henry announcing the upcoming third installment of Fantasia Impromptu.

BENJAMIN DeCASSERES
593 Riverside Drive
NEW YORK.

HAM GRANGE, S·A·
NOV 21
12—PM
1937

THIS SIDE OF CARD IS FOR ADDRESS

[handwritten address: Mrs. Carmen Henry, 1356 Pearl St., Denver, Colorado]

THE DeCASSERES BOOKS

Book No. 19 of the **DeCASSERES BOOKS**, written and published each month by Benjamin DeCasseres, will be **"FANTASIA IMPROMPTU: THE ADVENTURES OF AN INTELLECTUAL FAUN"** (Part 4). This is part of DeCasseres' 400,000-word intellectual, emotional and spiritual autobiography, begun in 1925. 50 Cents. Make checks or money orders payable to Benjamin DeCasseres, care of the Blackstone Publishers, 118 West 27th Street, New York City.

Back numbers of the **DeCASSERES BOOKS**---literature, poetry, philosophy and epigram---may be had.

Postcard dated November 21st, 1937 announcing the upcoming fourth installment of Fantasia Impromptu.
Includes the personal note:
Dear Mrs. Henry: Thanks - I
think you have said some
real things about woman
Best wishes from both
of us to both of you. Benjamin DeCasseres

xi

I fertilize the eggs of ecstasy, of revolt and of laughter in the sleeping wombs of your *brain*.
—*DeCasseres.*

I who watch myself more narrowly and have my eye continually bent on myself as one that has no great business elsewhere... I'll gladly come back from the other world to give the lie to any one who will shape me other than I was, even though to honor *me*.
—*Montaigne.*

When we look at life it is in ourselves that we look, and we can see life profoundly only on condition of seeing profoundly in ourselves.
—*Charles Morice.*

I write because I wish to make for ideas which are my ideas a place in the world. If I could foresee that these must take from you peace of mind and repose, if in these ideas that I sow I should see the germs of bloody wars and even the cause of the ruins of many generations, I would nevertheless continue to spread them. It is neither for the love of you nor even for the love of truth that I express what I think. No—I sing! I sing because I am a singer. If I use you in this way, it is because I have need of your ears!
—*Max Stirner.*

Fantasia Impromptu

TO THE
THINKERS, POETS, SATIRISTS,
INDIVIDUALISTS, DARE-DEVILS, EGOISTS,
SATANISTS AND GODOLEPTS
OF
POSTERITY

FOREWORD

I began *Fantasia Impromptu: the Adventures of an Intellectual Faun* in December, 1925. It is now about 400,000 words long. My present intention is to print a part of it indefinitely. It will be printed as it was written—that is, from the beginning, page for page.

It is an intellectual, emotional and spiritual autobiography. It is done spontaneously, without calculation. It is a mirror broken into a thousand bits. In each bit an angle, a part of me is shown. The whole cannot be seen, cannot be known. The whole is Elsewhere.

I am blown where the mood listeth. I am honest; therefore I contradict myself. I despise formal logic, formal thought, formal action of any kind. I know there is no logic in the universe of feeling and thought. Logically, the universe is absurd. My inner life is a reflection of the Immanent Absurdity.

Fantasia Impromptu: the Adventures of an Intellectual Faun is, then, the tragicomic spectacle of the Great Absurdity conceived and executed, without any forethought, in terms of my own contradictory and paradoxical life.

—*Benjamin DeCasseres.*

FANTASIA IMPROMPTU

Sleep, Drink and Become Famous.—Lord Byron said he woke up one day and found himself famous (this needs resurrection since Publicity has become confounded with Fame).

The author of *Don Juan* does not tell us how long he had been sleeping while Fame worked for him. It may have been only for a night or it may have been one of those five-day post-Burgundian sleeps of which he speaks in one of his letters.

I, too, slept my way into fame, but more nearly in the manner of Rip Van Winkle than of Lord Byron.

Old Rip after a drastic drinking party up in the Catskills went to sleep for twenty years. He woke up immortal.

The same goddess that presided over the soul of Rip while he slept has been my presiding genius. I grew famous while I slept. I slept all day and worked on a New York newspaper all night (1900 to 1920), and almost precisely at the end of twenty years I was astounded to find out that I was famous not only in my own country but that I was being translated into French by no less a person than Remy de Gourmont, who was writing about me in the *Mercure de France* and *La France*.

At this day and date in my life (1925) I cannot recall clearly or visualize definitely just how I wrote, when I wrote or why I wrote any of the books of essays, satire, epigram, poetry and cosmic drama besides the vast mass of newspaper and magazine articles that has appeared over my name in the last twenty-four years— books and articles that have caused me to be hailed, without solicitation, as "a genius of the very highest order" and the "most revolutionary thinker and ecstatic stylist" that America has yet produced...

It is my belief that neither fame nor success (success of any kind) has anything to do with rules; that it cannot be plotted or planned by an individual; that genius is not necessarily an infinite capacity for taking pains (genius is rather an infinite capacity for giving pain), and that there is in us a power—an imp, a daemon, a fairy goddess, a fatal dark star or a star of destiny, call it what you will—that works with the inexorable fatality of sidereal law.

There is a divinity that shapes our ends—that raises us to glory or hurls us to our private hells—as surely as I know that what was mine has come to me without my raising my hand to get it or willing it.

You may spend your days planning or sleeping; you may spend your days and nights scheming for wealth, or glory, or a woman, or the White House; you may curse the stars or beg God to snare your secret dream for you—it is of no use, for the black doom or the golden glory that is fatally yours comes on with the measured tramp of those gigantic gods of the mountains in Lord Dunsany's play.

Since boyhood I have never hoped for anything, planned anything, wished for anything or lived for anybody or anything. But I have always felt at my side or within me a mysterious, almost material, being, who was using me for its mysterious purpose.

"Through me, not of me," I have whispered with Emerson, and again that profoundest of all fatalistic prayers, "Thy will be done!"

This being—this Alter Ego, this Daemon, this goddess, half ethereal vampire and half angelic harpy—has hammered out my destiny, my fame and my work in sleep, in careless ness, in alcohol and in the most diabolical form of torture—some drudgery that an imaginative creator can be sentenced to—proofreading on a metropolitan daily.

Careless of my health—drinking and carousing at intermittent periods to excess for thirty years—I never have been seriously ill—physically.

A spendthrift since boyhood—throwing money away quicker than I could borrow or make it—I have never wanted for a meal or a roof.

Never having written a single word, prose or verse, in praise of love; sometimes sneering like a libertine at the Grand Passion—the sublimest and most beautiful love came toward me and is mine.

With a genius that is profoundly Latin to my latter atom, I have been accepted and printed in various magazines in an Anglo-Saxon and puritan country. I am a one-call salesman. If I don't succeed at first, I never try again. Forget it!—and take a drink. What is mine cannot be kept from me.

Looking on Fame as the dream of egomaniacs and dotards, I found myself famous, and, astounding to relate, famous when I did not know it myself.

What is the exact moment that a person becomes aware of the fact that he is famous?

I can only relate my own experience of that miraculous minute when Fame, the First Lady of the Planet, taps you on the shoulder and says, with a trace of sly roguery in her voice and just a glint of irony in her eyes:

"You're drafted!"

The first tap came when I had got up unusually early so as to reach a department store just before it closed. The saleswoman picked up her order book to write my name (an unusual and difficult one). I got as far as my first name and the De when she wrote the rest of the name quickly and perfectly. Astounded, I asked her how she knew the rest of the name, as I had never seen her before.

She looked up at me and said, "When you said Benjamin De—I knew the rest. There is only one, and I have read everything you ever had printed—but, really, I thought you would look like Tolstoy!"

It was the first kiss on my lips by the great goddess Fame! I had been tapped on the shoulder and anointed! My ego blew up like a balloon. My vanity burgeoned with swords and roses: I blushed and stammered at the mouthpiece of the Hidden Miracle-Worker like a girl of sixteen receiving her first kiss in public from a famous movie hero. I bleated, I whinnied. I felt like James O'Neill when he mounted the stage rock and shouted "The world is mine!"

I had been multiplying and sowing my ego on the winds while I slept, while I drank, while I drudged! How many persons were there, I wondered, in the world who knew me, persons that I never heard of and never will hear of?

This sudden first consciousness of the multiplication of one's ego in the minds of others is the most astounding moment, I take it, in the life of an artist.

If any artist or public man denies that it is like Falernian wine to a man dying of thirst in the Sahara he is both liar and hypocrite. Nothing stimulates or raises the tide of life to a higher pitch in any soul than this sudden inflation of one's vanity. It is health, wealth and happiness with a single shot of Fortune's needle.

When I left that store and went down the street I believed that every eye was on me, that everybody was looking back at me and saying:

"There goes the famous DeCasseres."

But alas!, I was not universal yet, for that very night the desk sergeant in a west side station-house had the greatest difficulty in getting my name down right when a beneficent cop put myself and another newspaper man away for the night "for safekeeping"...

I come now to the most mysterious part of my legend. I lived for almost twenty years in a medium-sized room on the fourth-floor back of 11 West 39th Street, an old fashioned brownstone front house covered by a vine. (It is now a commercial skyscraper.) It was here that there came to me during my day-sleeps the substance and form of many of my philosophic books, my poetry, my epigrams, satires and super-dramas—almost in the same manner in which Samuel Coleridge brought forth "Kubla Khan," which he saw word for word in a dream right before waking. But I have never used a drug of any kind.

Sometimes whole poems would blaze forth in the sky of my brain and I would leap from my bed to my table and put them down. I have made very few changes in them, either in *The Shadow-Eater, Anathema!* or *Black Suns*. I never planned a poem or sat down in a cold waking state "to write a poem" in my life. They were forged in the black chambers of Sleep by a mysterious Blacksmith.

I have suddenly been awakened in that room (I sometimes stayed in bed sleeping and drowsing for twenty hours at a stretch) from a sound sleep as if someone had tapped me with a heavy finger on the brain.

Like a gorgeous exhibition of fireworks, epigrams, profound thoughts, paradoxes and cosmic visions burst, gyrated, spun and shot across the dark field of my consciousness—many of them gone forever before I could get them on paper, like falling stars glimpsed in all their hallucinating splendor for only a single instant.

I have come to believe that planned thinking and reasoning are of a low psychological order. The creative artist, the overturning genius is always inspired. He knows not what he does. He is possessed by a Spirit. The brain is only a total-adder, a phonograph record, a scoreboard. Creation is ecstasy in the aesthetic as well as in the physical world.

Everything I have written has "occurred to me suddenly" while I was doing something commonplace, while sleeping, while shaving, while evacuating, while putting a semicolon in an advertisement at my desk in the proofroom. I never thought out anything—I do not think anything is worth thinking out. It is all arranged for you and me anyhow. Why be the butt of the gods when you can pal it with them by playing their game, by waiting to see what's next going to happen to you?

The reason why fatalists and pessimists are generally a happy lot and optimists and free-willies are always trying to explain why "things went wrong" is because the former are "in the Know" and the latter are not.

In the last twenty-five years, and especially during my residence on 39th Street, I have—just naturally—done every thing that would tend to shoo fame and literary success from the door.

As hundreds who know me will attest, the landlady and the maid in the house told everybody who called to see me that I was "not in." I had a large sign marked "OUT" hung on my door whenever I was in in case somebody got past by sheer force—which seldom occurred.

I have heard them pound and beat on my door, shouting my name (and in some instances they have torn the sign down) . But I sat tight in my Morris chair reading "Alice in Wonderland" or turned over in my bed uttering a smiling and fraternal "Go to hell!"

Was I anti-social in those long years? Was I a snob, a cad? Everybody who knows me would laugh at the idea. But I had decided that the only place for sociability is the cafe and the barroom. Home is the place for contemplation, creation and sleep. Once I let a poet into my room at 3 o'clock in the afternoon—I was still in bed. He dropped a cigarette in the bed while telling me in basso-alcoholic English what a marvellous poem I had written—"Ingression", which Don Marquis had just published in his column in *The Sun*. The cigarette almost set fire to the bed.

After that if anybody wanted to see me either to negotiate for articles or tell me how "great" I was he had to do it in Mouquin's or Jack's after 10 P.M.

Quite often I would meet writers of all kinds—poets, short-story writers, "inspirationalists", "philosophers"—who had the air of businessmen. They began to scheme at 7 A.M. Always lunch with somebody at 1 o'clock. Dickering, haggling, 'phoning all day.

Almost all of them have "succeeded" in the sense that they have larger bank accounts than I have. But they are all the unhappiest, most harassed looking, most disappointed crew I know. Every one of them has his "great poem", his "great novel," his "great drama" which he never wrote, and never will write, because he got up early, planned too much, always had his door open, his 'phone on the latch and made of himself a public arcade.

The house 'phone at 11 West 39th rang continuously during the day. Half the calls were for me. They were never answered before 5 P.M.

"He's not here," "Gone to Cuba," "He's dead," "He's in the hoosegow," were some of the answers I bribed the maid to fire back. I may have lost hundreds of dollars because of this, but I would not have my inspirational sleeps and my creative laziness disturbed at any price.

I read recently that Gabriele D'Annunzio burns all letters he receives without opening them. I never went as far as that, but for years in the semi-somnambulistic but tremendously *aware* life I led letters meant very little to me.

My mail was shoved under my door every morning, and sometimes I would not gather it up until midnight, an hour at which I often arose to go out and meet "people worth while" (between 1900 and 1920 in New York all the "people worth while" were to be seen after midnight) . I cut them (the letters) open and shook them down for possible checks. I threw the other letters aside, to be read at leisure, and sped away to a café or a barroom to get the checks cashed.

That, I held, must be the way "business" was done on Olympus...

Mine is a disordered, anarchic, explosive mind. But there is really no such thing as anarchy or disorder either in the material or mental world. Earthquakes and sudden thunderstorms, actual or physical, are as cosmically legal as Los Angeles sunshine.

I have tossed out my books helter-skelter. I have written poems and essays without any conscious knowledge of "theme." But they possessed a unity profounder than I knew. In the years of unwitting creation I found I had been making poems and books that fell into ordered wholes and mass-themes. There were group-ideas and linked super-reasonings and themes of which I was never conscious until I began to grope around to arrange them for publication.

Thus all the poems in *The Shadow-Eater*—tossed into a drawer as they were written as if my hand were a planchette on a Ouija board—I found linked by one theme: the ever lasting protest of Man against the brutality of "the gods." The unity that had guided me in the essays in *Chameleon* was the spirit of pagan scepticism. The *pensées* in *The Muse of Lies* (written over a period of ten years) all sounded the note of the universality of illusion. The super-dramas and stories in *The Eternal Return* were strung on the thread of fourth dimensional satire. The laughing pixies in my blood unified *The Elect and the Damned* into a new method of literary criticism. And so with all the others.

Character and imagination, not "solid plugging" and knowledge, create. I never had any "education." I never studied anything. I emit because of organic necessity.

"Where did you learn to write that way?" "How did you learn all those beautiful word-mosaics?" "What college did you go to?" Such questions! Great writing, great art, is merely the art of putting down, painting or composing with sound-waves sincerely what you feel, not what you know. Genius is merely the highest form of sincerity. Art is the laughter of Knowledge.

Plans? Only fools and politicians plan.

I was born with a nature that believes so firmly in Fatality and the omnipresence of a Will that I have always felt that to plan anything was a form of blasphemy.

It is, moreover, comic. It is a straw's belief that it shapes the course of a stream or the belief of the weathervane that it causes the veering of the winds.

No man brings anything to pass in his life. He is a puppet. But the Immanent Jester endows him at birth with a belief in the freedom of the will. That is what constitutes the Divine Comedy of Life.

On the eve of my twenty-first birthday I gave a party in a wine-cellar in Philadelphia to a crowd of young pessimists and poets; in fact, to all of those whom I could find who believed that the greatest thing in life was to be a rolling stone, a drifter, an epicurean. None of us had any principles. This was not a pose—but an inherent trait of our natures; a philosophic certainty founded on sensibilities in which the reaction to life was humorous and cynical.

Plans—no! Desires—yes! At twenty-one I desired to travel, to read, to know, to dissect—to get rid of all that planning that parents, society and religion had done for me before my birth; to become the spectator of the drama of my life, to record my driftings—and to satirize humanity and the gods. Amiel was a "failure." He put it all down on paper and his failures made him immortal in his Journal.

I have nothing to regret. I have never aimed to do anything in particular, never made any plans, never "went after anything." I lived spontaneously—unto the day. I let circumstance, heredity and environment have their way with me. As I always hoped for the worst, I was never disappointed; on the other hand, every day surprised me with pleasures that came with the tang of the unexpected.

Only the epicurean pessimist gets one hundred per cent out of life. All things build a road to his door.

Happiness is the aim of fools. *Experience* is the way, the truth and the life.

Carelessness is the great secret of life.

To the prudent come all ills. They may live long, but they die before birth spiritually, mentally and emotionally.

God is a comedian; and when you realize that, all veils are lifted.

I guessed that secret at fifteen. My life since then has been merely an excursion of verification.

If a book is not an appetizer for a good meal on my own brain, then it is not *my* book.

What difference is there between the frenzied worship of Life (Nietzsche, for instance) and the frenzied worship of Life Everlasting (Jesus, for instance)?

Whims.—To obey my whims gives me more pleasure than sticking to my principles (my principles are merely prolonged and ossified whims—all principles are). I suppose this is true of everyone. Thoreau condemns a life without principles. Emerson praises whims, and says principles can go hang. I prefer Emerson's way. To obey every whim is a form of freedom.

There is genius in whim because it arises from the subconscious, because it is untutored, because it is unreasonable. Whims are moods in action. A general principle is a jail. Whim is jail-delivery.

Last night as I was about to jump into bed in my nightgown (to hell with pajamas!) I was seized by a sudden desire to read a few lines of Montaigne. I went into the next room in my "nighty," and in my bare feet stood reading before the bookcase something from the Essays—I do not even recall what lines they were or what the essay was about. After reading about five lines I put the book back and went to bed. I felt immensely satisfied—just why, I do not know. Why Montaigne—and no one else—at that precise moment? Why not Shakespeare, Pascal or Rabelais? That's the beauty, charm and magic of whim—we do not know why the little sprite orders us to do so-and-so.

I think we are all whims in the brain of God, who makes us and unmakes us in his "nighty" just before he blows out the light of a star or two.

To be Read After or Before My Death.—After reading all the hogwash of the broken-down critics, impotent minds and no-toriety-seekers who nuzzle in Poe and Baudelaire and Verlaine and others under the guise of "doing a biography in the new manner," I feel a whim to put these facts down about myself for those who may be curious about me after (or before) my death:

Ladies and Gentlemen of Posterity:

I drank a great deal before my fiftieth year. I was not a steady drinker, but a periodical drinker—gay, Rabelaisian, brilliant. After every bout, which lasted probably from two to four days, I would remain completely sober for several weeks, sometimes months.

My favorite drink (until prohibition was fastened on us by Oil and Steel and the churches) was imported (Bohemian) beer.

I was always a gentleman when drunk—tender, sentimental, sometimes "blasphemous," and often very noisy.

I never wrote a line in my life while under the influence of drink. Everything I put on paper has been written while deadly sober.

I never used a drug or narcotic of any kind in my life stronger than bromides (for the nerves).

I have never been insane at any time.

I was always a man's man—liking the companionship of he-males and "regular fellows."

I never was in absolute want—but often needed a dollar to "tide me over" for a day or so.

In my early days I preferred harlots to the old coaxing and waiting game. Pay and get out. If you can't conquer a woman in an hour, she isn't worth bothering about.

The two words that have most completely and continually obsessed me since puberty have been *suicide* and *God*. The two words that have obsessed me least have been *love* and *money*. (But after my forty-fifth year the word *money* took the place of *suicide*—and now it is the most important word in the world to me. It means freedom, fame and happiness *now*—but alas!—and also a lack!)

My Hypocrisy.—"You write for posterity, Mr. DeCasseres," a publisher said to me the other day after giving my books the kick in the pants. Then, by God! I will!, thought I. "Liar!" whispered my Comic Imp in my ear.

It is not through fear that my eyes lower before you, but because I do not want you to see yourself.

Science the Crab.—Does Science travel backward? Is its work simply the materialization, the mechanization of the ancient mystics, poets, soothsayers and the "nuts"? I believe so.

Science is always second-hand. It is merely a verifier. A superstition is said to be a false belief. Well, so are all the postulates of science. I am no enemy of science—their fairy tales are to me the most fascinating in existence; the fairy tale of the electron, the fairy-tale of the atom, the fairy-tale of the germ, the fairy-tale of history, the fairy-tale of the phonograph, of the radio, of the telephone, of the motion-picture, of the great murder-engines of war, etc.

Science conceived as a vast network of superstitions is far more fascinating to me than the "scientific destruction of superstitions," which simply cannot be done. I rather like the idea that Jesus was born of Mary the Virgin. Whether it is "true" or "false" is of no consequence. It's a beautiful fairy-tale, and will recur again and again when the names of Jesus and Mary are no more and when the superstition that the Earth is round or spheroid ana that there are no inhabitants of the space between us and, say, the Moon have been demolished—quite demolished by another superstition, called "a scientific verity."

The machine-made mind and the mystical-imaginative mind are the Sancho Panza and the Don Quixote who ought to be inseparable. But they will not travel together because the machine-made ("cash-down") mind refuses to play the part of a servant even to a reckless adventurer and sublime boob like Don Quixote. Being without imagination and the mys tical sense, it has a tragic inferiority complex masked under an air of arrogant superiority, for the scientific, machine-made mind knows secretly that all it does is based on the imagina tion, and it also knows that Don Quixote, and not Sancho Panza, is the eternal core of life on this planet. Don Quixote knows the value of his Sancho, and would not lose him for the world; but Sancho is forever forbidden to know the greatness, the grandeur and the magic of Don Quixote.

Sancho Science must serve forever the Quixotic ruler of the world, the imaginative, mystical, intuitional psyche of Man.

Stendhal: "I write for the happy few." A beautiful instance of the sublimation of self-pity into pride.

Satan's Valedictory.—Satan appeared to me and said (he looked melancholy, depressed, had lack-lustre eyes, and—god of gods!— his goatee and eyebrows were graying!): "Since the advent of the scientific spirit, the decline in the belief in God, the disappearance of the virgin, the break-up of the churches and the universal rise of the cynical spirit even in young boys and girls life on earth has lost its savor for me. The romance of soul-potting is gone. There is nobody left to damn, since no one cares a damn. You all laugh at me—just as you all laugh at God, virginity, virtue, honesty and all the good old traits that were meat and nuts to me. You all beat me at my own game. You've all stolen my bag of tricks. You call me 'Sate', yank me by the goatee, kick me in the derriere, tell me I'm 'old stuff'.

"I ask God every night to resurrect, get back on the job, put the fear of Him in your hearts by some great world-catastrophe. Ah! what pickings, what sport, during the 'Dark Ages'! The whole world today has wise-cracked my job away. I'm out of work and I have not where to lay my epigrams. There are no longer any ears to whisper into: they laugh and show me a trick worth two of mine.

"I spend my evening under my lamp reading of my salad days in the pages of Milton, Marlowe, Goethe and Calderon. The Catholic Church still gives me now and then a handful of sinners to work on, but they're scurvy stuff. If God doesn't wake up soon, I myself will have to re-invent all the good old ideals of honesty, virtue, belief and duty so that I can resume my ancient sport."

And Satan sank into my armchair, read the *Atlantic Monthly* for a bit—and went sound asleep.

There never was a Diogenes who went around with a lantern looking for an honest woman.

Nostalgic Tears.—A distant note of music that sounds almost like an echo—such as I am hearing now in this New York apartment—awakes in me lost emotions of childhood, or something before childhood from I know not where; something nostalgic, vibrant of lost moods, of twilight, of undiscovered lands, of tears for something nameless, of yesterdays forever passed away, of a baby in a nightgown, of sudden wakings in the silent night when I was a child when I heard the distant, long-drawn-out shriek of a locomotive that sounded as if it came from a country of gnomes—

For You and Him.—A wife and her lover should always have a portrait of the husband *at the head* of the bed. As she cannot see it, she will not experience any *ill-timed* remorse. The lover, looking at it, will rise to titanic deeds.
My life is like this cigar I am smoking: all chewed up at one end, a little fire and a great deal of ashes at the other.
The more profoundly I see the inherent humor in all life, the less I laugh!

Evolution.—After a famous man dies he passes out of the realm of the emotions and prejudices into the aesthetic realm —or at least he should. Nero, Jesus, Benedict Arnold should be considered as drama—and drama only.

His Punching-Bag.—Nietzsche has consumed many pages telling us what he owes to the ancients. But he owes more to Jesus than any thinker in the Christian era.

Courage by Incantation.—I know a man who always has to charge himself with an epigram or a motto when he has someone to confront in the practical world. Absolutely fearless and never considering consequences when his ideas are attacked, he wilts when he has to do business with the swine of the practical Broadway variety. Before entering the office of the man he had to confront he repeated, for years, a phrase with Bio. Von Stroheim in "Foolish Wives". The movies always fascinate me. They are an anodyne to my restless, keyhole-peeping mind. They stop thought. We walk home—up Fifth Avenue. We are rich—shop-window rich. What gorgeous ties I cannot afford to buy! What walking-sticks! Stop in to get a pair of shoes I had had mended.

Home. Back to my "den." Read the letters of Abelard and Heloise. Rather dull compared to *our* love-letters, which may be published some day. Bio goes shopping for supper. Will it be fish or meat? Read some of Balzac's "Physiology of Marriage". Entertaining. Yawn. Yawn. Yawn. Wonder whether the evening papers are up yet. Let Bio in. It's fish. In kitchen. Bio and I get into violent discussion about Spinoza and Christ—can they be reconciled? Bio says yes. I bawl no. Going hot and heavy when dumbwaiter buzzer starts. "Garbage!" Symbolic of our discussion? Shall I take a drink of rye? Guess not.

Dinner at 7 o'clock. Lie down on couch afterward. Curse life, etc. When will my books be published? When will I have some real money for my own magazine? Will I ever see Europe? Shall I get drunk? Or commit suicide? Long meditation on the mystery of personal identity. Bio comes in and kisses me in the dark. Off the couch at 8. Read the evening papers. Same slop. Cigar. Wash face and hands.

Fifth Avenue bus. Prowl through a second-hand bookstore at Twelfth street. Sam Loveman, who is employed there, hands us a personally conducted tour. Sam was a friend of Bitter Bierce and George Sterling. Presents me with a copy of *The Brethren of Joseph*, almost forgotten play in verse by Charles Wells. Introductions by Swinburne and Watts-Dunton.

Back home, 10:30. Read Swinburne's introduction, bits of play. Very beautiful in parts. Joseph, father of Parsifal. But how could that be? The immaculate phallus? Holy Ghosting? Midnight. 'Phone rings. "The boys are over at the Tavern, Ben—let's make a night of it!" "Go to hell! I want my stomach for breakfast." Stinking prohibition (bitter, venomous, murderous revery on the blue-snooted hypocrites of the Middle West and South). Eat a banana. Bio calls from bed room, "Time for bed, my busted Bacchant!" In bed. Bio and I both pray to the god who invented sleep and the sense of humor. I drowse off dreaming of Carmel-by-the-Sea, fame, death, Swinburne, money, harems, beer.

Be thine own palace, or the world's thy jail.—*John Donne.*

Everything tends to become a counterfeit of itself.

In genius each idea feeds every other idea.

The lovely body of Creation now rides in the hearse of Criticism.

A woman's first love is her mirror; her last is God.

Duse said of Rossetti: "His eyes had the feverish pursuit of a thing that his chin and his jaw could not follow."

Thought is an absinthe that eats certain men hollow. All ultimate knowledge is negative knowledge.

A Postponed Revelation.—I read biographies and autobiographies in order to find in the famous and great of the earth justifications for my own shortcomings, transgressions, perversities and stupidities. Am I thinking of Rousseau, Goethe, Amiel when reading their confessions? No. I'm seeking myself, hoping they will say something that will cause me to mutter to myself, "Just like me!" or "How much alike we are!"
But how stale, superficial and cowardly I find all "confessions", biographies and autobiographies compared to one day's glance in my own soul! James Joyce did something tremendously daring in the unpunctuated meditations of Mrs. Bloom in "Ulysses"—but he hadn't the courage to give us his *own* private thoughts. Frank Harris is just *bourgeois,* if not a downright liar. He doesn't confess anything—he just relates commonplaces. He never had an extraordinary psychic adventure, or any other kind of adventure.
I have not the courage to put down all my secretest dreams, cravings, visions—both alcoholic and sober. They are—or were—astounding, especially those experienced under the influence of alcohol (not drunk, however, when I have no memory) .

Lucky Me!—I cannot say that I have ever taken pains to "create" or, in fact, do anything. Anything that takes much time and trouble is not worth doing. I am either inspired or I am a bore. All my best writing is pure inspiration; bubbles out of me whence I know not. I do not think—I see. Things "come to me". I never go toward anything. This law of my being applies in the practical as well as in the intellectual sphere. To fail, I have only to plan.

Morning of an Intellectual Faun.—Up at ten. The usual. Delicious feeling of bodilessness in hot bath. Mental and psychical well-being. Thoughts, idle thoughts, float on the top of my consciousness like beautiful pond-lilies. How chaste the belly looks through clear water! Is there anything better than physical well-being?, I ask myself. Divine, lazy, luscious, languorous fifteen minutes! Cold shower. Bang! The real world again! Sharp and definite angles of reality. Hilarious, dynamic, Dionysian ten minutes of cold water and hard towel. Bowels perfect. Brain as clear as the eye of God and little children.

Shave. Thoughts bound through brain like the wild play of fauns in a thicket, like the sports of dryads in star-lit pools. I catch a fine thought by the tail. Presto! It's gone! Tumult of visions. Panorama of hopes, rising, falling. The pomp of consciousness. Superb ten minutes. Brain too swift for paper. Besides, I'm shaving. Ought to have a rapid-fire shorthand secretary in the bathroom with me. Is God a monist? I'd like to be a humorist like "Bugs" Baer. An emotion revives in me—the first sex feeling. The divine feel of her chubby hand! Did the Yankees win the pennant last year? Does Elie Faure prove his thesis that War is the mother of Art? How can I make ten thousand dollars?

Breakfast. 11:30. A two-thousand word introduction to my brother Walter's poems after twenty-six years of postponement! I *do* get some things done! Bio orders me to get a manicure and a bottle of cream.

Noon. I'll take a walk. Button off my overcoat. God-damn the riveters!

Hail, Demagogues!—In a sense, all who create artistically — however remote from popular standards and rewards—are demagogues. They desire an audience—even if it is a "happy few" (that smug and insipid phrase of Stendhal). All creators desire to sway other minds.

I desire an audience every day. Not finding my thoughts, my intellectual wares, salable, I write to myself and Bio in this book. I am auto-demagogic. I am my own Demosthenes, my own Danton, my own Bryan. I am (dead or alive) trying to reach and sway your emotions and intellect in this book (and my other books) without regard to whether I am right or wrong. *I desire to sway.*

I differ from the common gutter-and-soapbox blatherskite in the qualities of the wares I hawk, but not in fundamental motive.

Time is a glow-worm that reveals to us how deep we are in darkness.

Hell or a Circus.—Life, the universe—at least to me—is either a black tragedy or a grotesque farce. There is no middle ground. God is either an Aeschylus or a Rabelais, a Hamlet or a Puck. My mood is either unrelievedly tragical or bitterly fantastical, diabolically gay. My God varies between these two extremes. Indifference is inconceivable. It is a mask of glass that conceals nothing.

Sexual felicity is the foundation of mental health. Asceticism is the father of dreams, but fornication is the sap of creation.

The Great Moment.—The profoundest moment in the history of the universe was not the moment in which God said "Let there be light," but the moment in which He first laughed at what He had created. Or when he looked Satan in the face for the first time and they both winked slyly at one another. That was the birth of humor—the Eternal Substance of the intellectual world.

What is progress?—the victory of humor over dogma.

The maxims of Confucius are of as much value to an extraordinary man as a cook-book is to an astronomer.

The Tricks of Elohim.—God made of life an impenetrable mystery in order to flatter Man and give him a sense of dignity, so that *Homo* could repeat to himself with profound seriousness, "I am a great Mystery!"

Scale of Values.—If Newton, Copernicus, Darwin and Einstein had never lived, it would make no difference to me. Johann Strauss and his hundred and twenty-five waltzes are worth the whole lot of them.

The End of a Peep-Show.—The sublimest spectacle of which I can conceive is an interplanetary war carried on by the Earth, Mars, Jupiter and Venus. This will occur some day—soon after we exchange kisses and salutations by radio. This war will probably set up forces that will cause the whole solar system to founder, bust up, decompose and may even cause a cosmic conflagration which will amuse God and Satan for a kalpa or two. And that will be the end of the old starry peep-show, ladies and gentlemen of the current age and posterity. The only ones who will escape will be those beings who have the luck to be admitted to other dimensions.

The Tickle of Anonymous Letters.—I suppose everyone has thought of writing an anonymous letter. Most of us (oh, yes, you too, you hypocritical reader of these lines) have thought of it many times. Those who protest loudest against even the thought of it have been tempted oftener than anyone else. The anonymous letter is as deadly as the handkerchief of

Desdemona in the hands of Iago. I have known three or four deaths I could have caused by a ten-line note. I know others (women) that I could have fired with murderous rage by a five-line note. And, my dears, I need only have held myself strictly to the truth (except in one instance, where I could foresee a beautiful and dramatic murder by dropping a poisonous lie in her ear).

I have refrained, like millions of others, through mixed motives—a sense of honor, conscience, cowardice, pride, pity; but, above all, the fear of being found out, which is the supreme motive for the non-execution of all "bad deeds." There is nothing more cowardly than the anonymous letter, and that, I think, is the second most powerful motive, added to the fact that if we are discovered our cowardice is laid bare.

But there will always be something fascinating in rolling the idea over on the tongue of our mind—to sit back like a god and set in motion a drama or tragedy or comedy of our creation and be the only spectator who knows what the play is about and who the author is; in fact, being able to give the play a new twist at any moment by further letters; to play on nerves and hearts and brains of human beings like a skilled organist—the organ in this instance being a type writer.

There are more anonymous ("poison-pen") letter-writers than we are aware of. You, reader of these lines, are probably visualizing now, at this minute, the persons that you have itched for years to bludgeon with — a little word, a little word! Like the first soft, sweet, silent thought of murder in the brain of Macbeth—

Aviating with God.—By an act of will I can inflate my consciousness until it hovers like a disembodied intelligence over the planet. It is something like the opening of a titanic transparent parasol in the hands of a nameless and ineffable power in my own soul.

It is my daily flight over humanity. I can take the flight at any moment; it is not an isolated or sporadic phenomenon. My consciousness can follow the Earth easily and gracefully in its three movements. This is so natural and ordinary to me that there is very little thrill in it.

But it is such a release, such a pleasurable feeling, and it so grows in vividness and intensity with the years that I must continually record it. It also dovetails in with my off-and on dreams for years of flying toward golden constellations and standing outside the Earth, seeing it revolve, lifeless, ice-clad, with an unspeakable pity in my heart.

Poetic images are the magic keyholes through which the locked-in spirit may escape.

Image.—This curious image came into my mind while listening to one of Chopin's Nocturnes: I crawl toward my Vision on the skinned knees of hope, dragging with me the corpses of my yesterdays.

A practical man should have knuckles in his eyes; a poet should have them in his images.

Fantasia.—My dreams are the most grotesque conceivable, especially just before waking after a night of alcohol. This morning I saw a stupendous file of the damned moving on the horizon of the universe; socketted in their skulls were frozen giants that reached to the zenith. This dissolved into the Sun, which gradually turned into a golden coffin standing upright from nadir to zenith. Then I suddenly saw a vast hall in which John L. Sullivan was playing a Chopin waltz on the teeth of Satan. Now the universe turned into a vast champagne goblet and in it seethed the consciousness of God. In the center of the goblet rose and fell a dead fly—the human race.

To almost any American "thinker": the feet of your thoughts are always asleep.

Criticism.—The only sound basis of criticism: What did a man do and did he do it well or poorly according to *his own standards,* not yours? Do not tell me what he might have done, what he didn't do, what he was "capable of," what he might have done if he hadn't drank, don-juaned or committed suicide.

Now, there is another kind of criticism which is personal reaction to a play, a novel, a poem or a picture. Dreiser, for instance, may be perfect according to Dreiserian standards. I have no doubt his dream and his work are in perfect harmony. But I consider Dreiser a bore, and I simply can't read him.

I believe, at bottom, there is nothing but personal criticism. "Scientific criticism" is generally vapid because it is the attempt to do away with the emotional bias of the person who undertakes it, which simply cannot be done. When you approach a writer, poet or thinker, you are not approaching a theorem. You are dealing with something alive that must upset you, entrance you or leave you indifferent. It is possible afterward to sit down and write a cold, formal, analytical *critique,* but it will ring false or stamp the writer as a mere intellectual weighing machine. Almost all American critics are of this school—the Nunkey-Donkeys I call them.

A case in point. I received a letter from a critic about my book on Huneker. He regrets it was not a "criticism" instead of an "appreciation." Well, if he wants an archaeological excavation of the whys and wherefores of the work of Huneker, why doesn't he do it himself? As I only write appreciations or excoriations (I'm not a plumber), the only thing I care about knowing is this: is the appreciation, or excoriation, well written?

In the case of my Huneker book, I think it is done so well (both as an appreciation of a beloved friend and as prose) that no one could have done it better in the same space, or probably any space. My critic says he "suffered from my presupposed idea of what you were going to do. I'll do no more advance guessing."

This critic has laid bare in those two sentences the whole trouble with our "critics." He expected me to write a nunkey-donkey criticism of Huneker's work, whereas I spilled my personality into Huneker's and we collaborated on my book about him.

Our Four Gifts.—The sex ecstasy, the transfigurating power of music, the ethereal levitations of wine, the cataleptic heav ens of abstractions. I remain on earth—in this stinking cesspool—only because of those four gifts.

A Week's Sheaf of Thoughts Amorous, Cynical and Poetical.—My soul is a heaven laden with lightnings with no space in which to discharge... She left me forever when my desire had just begun to peck at her eyes... Her eyes kept open house; her heart, free bed and board. I did not enter... We have all the Christian vices except the most dangerous—chastity... Her eyes were like a box of new-born kittens... Her eyes always seemed to be holding their breath... Her tongue moulded the molten silver of her voice into words that sang like swords... Life: water flowing through a shadow... A woman's eyes are the grammar of her thoughts... Desire circulates in her eyes like a snake in a tank... Her eyes were two grey breasts with tiny nipples of light... Her eyes were two great hothouses, with secret walks lost in perfumes... There are a thousand ships of hope burning on the ocean of my past... I am sieving the sunlight in my brain for the golden gnats that stung to madness the brains of Blake and Nietzsche... How many of my great epigrams died with my cigarette and how many great poems lay drowned in highballs!... The first and last woman: Madame Diable... To reach the point where you have the illusion that you can *choose your illusion*—that is freedom... The brain is a star that thinks... Like God, the Artist wastes time by making things that die... Time is the humor of God... An exquisite conscience is nature's masterwork of decadent art... Genius is planetary consciousness—sometimes sidereal consciousness.

Fantasia Impromptu

The Eternal Enemy.—"The Public: a thing I cannot help looking upon as an Enemy, and which I cannot address without feelings of Hostility"—John Keats. Engrave that, O poets, thinkers, artists, on your hearts! Carve it on your brains!

The Seductions of Contact.—Personal contact generally smashes a generalization all to Hinders. Had I met George Sand, been her lover, or just played around with her, all my prejudices against women writers might have melted and I might even have lost my unaccountable aversion for the old "ink-giving cow," as Nietzsche calls her.

Philosophers and thinkers need broadening by personal contact. Suppose, for instance, Spinoza had fallen in with Nell Gwyn, would we have had the marvellous "Ethics"? I fear "personal contact" would have smashed many sublime generalizations.

Suppose Sarah Bernhardt had seduced Nietzsche—this opens vast areas of speculation and fantasy.

Or, again, does personal contact have very little effect on powerful and original minds? Suppose Tiberius and Jesus had met—suppose Victor Hugo and Napoleon the Third had divided the same *cocotte* in their youth—suppose—but that word "suppose" is the most luring, the most tantalizing in the language! It leads everywhere—to the moon, to Domdaniel, to the fourth dimension. *Suppose* is the mother of all comedy and tragedy. *Suppose* is the protagonist of the future. *Suppose* is a satire on reality. (I delight in this sauntering, care-free style of mine—going nowhither, everywhither.) I started with generalizations, got into fantastic speculations about Sarah Bernhardt and Nietzsche, then fell into a reverie on the infinitudes in the word "suppose," which leads me back into the same hole "I cum out of," as Br'er Rabbit says—which is that that word "suppose" is the greatest of all generalizations. It can make millions of personal and ideational contacts without affecting in the least its eternal gayety, its infinite freedom and its protean possibilities.

The Flow and Ebb of My Mind.—When my friend M. thinks, I can almost see his brain flap like a stricken bird... Immorality is the fairyland of the inhibited. It is the postponed Great Adventure of the Puritan... The panther of Curiosity crouches on the horizon of my least thought... In Spinoza the immeasurable entities of the higher mathematics become corporate and carnate... The born thinker lives in a kind of frozen delirium... All summits are cemeteries... Leconte de Lisle and Emerson are of those poets who sucked iced milk from those frozen nipples of heaven—the stars... Old age: the crippled squirrel of Memory winding its slow way down the leafless trunk of the Past.

Spotlight!—All conversation is demagogic—each one tries to out-rant, out-epigram, out-wisecrack, out-rhetoric the other. We all fight for the middle of the floor, the spotlight. And who is that hypocrite off in the corner who is trying to draw attention to himself by his humility, his silence, his aloofness? Can it be you—or me?

Chopin.—It rained a black spring rain all afternoon. I put on the Paderewski, Godowsky and DePachmann Chopin records. Divine Ariel! Exquisite and marvellous Frederic! A universe exhales in thy music. Thou wert Israfel and Uriel. Thou dost discorporate me. With thee I float through matter into essence. Bubbles of ether. Moths of gold. The waltz of my soul down the corridors of sea-drowned temples. Ecstasies that my ear cannot receive, my nerves cannot support! Thanks for life!—for Chopin!

Spring Song.—Spring is in the air and the orgiastic impulse is in my blood. Vague ecstasies. Trailing memories of lost existences. Pan. Priapus. Wine, wine, wine. Wild dances. Liszt. "Carmen". Hymen. Ravished virgins. Hymns to the Sun. Blood-lust. Wine, wine, wine. Dionysus. Women, women, women. Buds. Passionate longing for the formless. God. Resurrection. Vine-leaves, vine-leaves, vine-leaves trailing from hard, red-nippled breasts. Goats, satyrs. Longing for union with the Eternal. Christ. Easter. Mystical chants. Sap, semen. Epileptic dances. Bush-calls. Grass, grass, grass, green and flesh-tickling grass. Walt Whitman. Sappho. The sun-gods. Phalluses of gods that crash into the mystical clefts of Mother-Earth. Skunk-cabbage. Seed catalogs. Moving.

Yes, 'tis spring!

Science is mystical!—for does it not actually *believe* in matter without being able to prove its existence?

The Other Fellow.—The transition from "moral indignation" to the ironic outlook—the passage from Tragedy to Humor, from Don Quixotism to Pucketry, from Sir Galahad to Falstaff—this I call "ascent." I now reserve the "tragic outlook" only for those things that are really tragical in my own life. All that is tragical in the world and does not touch me personally I see with the laughing eye and ironic smile.

And this itself is ironical, for I know perfectly well that many are doing that unto me which I doeth unto them; that is, the world is laughing at *my* tragedies as I smile at theirs. And I find that just. It is so hard not to believe that *my* tragedy is *the tragedy*, that *my* comedy is *the comedy*.

My Gorgeous Nirvana.—There is no finer bit of mental adventure than to pass a sleepless (but restful) night. To lie on the pillow for hours, the body in a state of perfect equilibration, so perfectly equilibrated that it has ceased to exist for consciousness, with the brain pouring ideas, swarming with images and visions: that brings me nearer to the sources of the ultimate illusion (and hence the ultimate Reality) than any other experience. The will is dead. The veils of purpose are rent. All inhibitions evaporate. My consciousness becomes a gigantic luminous aquarium where marvellous fish swish and dive and glitter—

fish that swim up gracefully and easily from the subconscious depths *and talk*.

All rules and regulations—all logic—are non-existent. All the traffic cops have gone to sleep. The cores of the self, the kernels of the ego, bob like corks on the waters of thought, Truth walks the waters naked and serpent-crowned. My soul is lighted to its last taper. I know the "silence of eternity", and that still more enigmatical silence, the silence of conscious thought. Sleepless, restful hours after midnight—the ecstasy, the terror, the charm, the magic of them!

I Do Not Look Like A Book.—Some writers' works are closely allied to their private lives, while in others there is no relation between what they have put on paper and their everyday lives. One could guess fairly well the kind of men D'Annunzio and Shaw are, for instance, in their works. Nothing whatsoever can be known of the man Shakespeare from his plays. Walt Whitman's "Leaves of Grass" is literally the man. Reading Poe's tales and poems would convey no idea whatsoever of the daily life of that genius.

My own work has absolutely nothing to do with my daily life. My practical side and my psychic-intellectual side are as completely dissevered as two stars. Everybody that meets me is astounded that "I do not look like my writings." It is curious how a certain style or mode of thought will build up in a reader's mind a fictitious physiognomy of the writer. Those who have read *The Shadow-Eater*, *Chameleon* and others of my serious essays and poems are astounded on meeting me that I do not "look like Tolstoy", that I am not "old looking", that I have not "sunken cheeks" and "fierce, hungry eyes," to quote some of them.

The paradoxical nature of my being insists on the most violent contrasts. The ironical nature of my dæmon is perpetual and inexhaustible. My body records sensations, my mind records ideas and visions. It was only after my forty-fifth year that I discerned a *rapprochement* between the two—that my sensations were beginning to influence my ideas, and *vice versa*. When the unification is complete (if ever) I will father "harmless satire," "cute paradoxes" and reach that state of serene equilibration known as the "sane genius."

And Some Days I Love to Write Lines for Poems I'll Never Write.—The far Meccas of the mysterious caravans of my thought... Thoughts like giant centurions that crucify the emotions and the will... The Ghettos of the brain... Kisses that rustle like dry and withered leaves in the stripped parks of Memory... The muted memories of the dead... The chemical restlessness of the dead... The veiled miracle of the brain... The sombre legions of the inflexibly dead... The opaque veils of his laughter... The dying planet of his brain lit by the scarlet sun of alcohol... The stark belly of the dawn... My brain is a golden matchbox, and when I strike the match of a thought on it a star is born!... The boreal brains of the dead... The taut banners of his pride... The suns, monstrous illuminated fish swimming in the Aquarium of Space... Eyes like wet air... His thoughts wore boots... The hot stench of her clamorous love... The stiff politeness of the dead... His laughter was like a syringe of vitriol... As ancient as tomorrow... The Moon—dead in its sarcophagus of air... A black ghost rose in the moon of my memories.

The Evil That Is Woman.—In many religions and religious allegories woman is depicted as the Spirit of Evil, the destroyer.
This is woman's greatness. She is the lyrical, colorful element in creation. She is the germ of dualism. She ought to glorify it. She is chaos, anarchy, disorder, lure; she is the disrupter. Before the Madonna (an idea of comparatively recent origin) was the Vampire, the whore, the provoker. Both Eve and Helen might say to the Madonna, "Before you were I am!"
But Mary herself, having brought Jesus into the world, was the instrument of the so-called Evil Forces immanent in the

Universe—for has there been a mightier destroyer, a greater disrupter than Jesus?—Written on Yom Kippur, 1925.

"Dear" and "Deary".—When I meet a husband and wife for the first time I try to look past their masks to find how far their hatred of one another has progressed, try to guess at the secret erotic dreams of the wife and wonder how clever the husband is in covering up the adventures of his secret tumescences. Those wives who come to the house and always refer to the absent husband as "that dear", "that darling of mine" are generally dreaming secretly of murdering him.
It is the secret antagonisms of the sexes that attract one to the other so powerfully. I have only desired to rape those women that I have instantaneously disliked.

Saving Up.—If we refrain habitually from doing acts that will give pain to another but which give us pain because we haven't performed them, we shall some day take our revenge on that person in another way—in another series of acts. There is, therefore, in the long run no such thing as a "thwarted desire."

No atheist can prove that there is no God; but he can easily prove that God is evil or that God and Devil are one.

Desire Is God.—What, dominantly, perpetually lures the Spirit, the Essence, back into bodies? It must be the senses—and, above all, the sex-call. In the Infinite we desire the finite; in the finite, we seek the Infinite again. God and Eros —systole and diastole.
After thirty-five years of thought and meditation, I still believe Desire to be metaphysical, to be the mysterious Substance, to be the ultimate generalization for man. Schopenhauer—and the Buddhists—are eternally right!

Verbal Obsessions.—Why does that line, "the sunken gardens of memory," haunt me? It has been buzzing at my brain like a

Tinker Bell for many hours. Who wrote it? Did I write it? There is certainly nothing extraordinary in it. But it sets me to thinking of the mysterious obsession, from time to time, of certain lines of poetry, ditties, phrases, names. Generally the morning after a night of moderate drinking (ah! those headacheless "hang-overs" that spawn the golden fish, when the brain and blood sing, when the consciousness is an aviary of nightingales, thrushes and larks!), these lines take possession of me. Is it a vestige of the shibboleth, the war-cry, the slogan? Is it a verbal materialization of a persistent and dominant mood? Or a form of logomania?

(I am a Logocrat. Words are to me like the scale to Chopin. like colors on a palette to a painter, like the jingle of gold coin to a miser. Pure Beauty has no substance. It is all form, the Logos reverberating through the void of eternity.) What is the great poet's gift?—mirages and sunken gardens. Pastels of colored words. His truth is perpetual evanescence.

The Chameleon Child.—I had never heard of her. She lived in Los Angeles. I lived in New York. My *Chameleon* fell into her hand. It set her brain on fire. It gave her great emotional up-swirls. She lived with the book during all of her pregnancy. She desired that the child should be imbued with the music, mysticism and fire of the book. She spoke of the coming one as "The Chameleon-child." She called it at birth my "cosmic son". It was born in my month, April, as she desired.

The boy is a superb piece of mechanism, three years old now. It may turn out to be a shoe-salesman or a Turkish bath rubber.

Alcoholic Periodicity.—I have been reading Havelock Ellis' fascinating study of sexual periodicity in the male. He quotes many examples. I have not experienced it; at least, I did not take note of it. But I have since my eighteenth year been subject to alcoholic periodicity, which always struck me as being very peculiar. Was it a perversion of sex-periodicity? I used to call it laughingly "my monthlies." The need of a good souse used to overwhelm my whole organism about every three weeks with an imperious command. It was not a "thirst", a "craving" (I hate the taste of all alcoholic drinks except beer and sparkling Burgundy) . It was a desire to free myself of something, a healthy call to get rid of something. It had to be obeyed.

The psychology and physiology of this in relation to Ellis' theory of male sexual periodicity (which is a vestige, I be lieve, of the time when the sexes were hermaphroditic) would be very interesting.

Theme: the External Universe and the Poets.—Keats and Shelley and Poe seem never to have been aware of an external universe: complete internalization of the cosmos; perfect types of ethereal introverts. Shakespeare and Hugo and Goethe have firm grips upon the external universe; macrocosm and microcosm blend perfectly. Whitman is the most perfect type of externalization. He even sees himself objectively. Baude laire never loses contact with the earth. Verlaine is semi-ethereal. Omar is Shakespearean. In D'Annunzio the very soil of Italy kisses the stars. Francis Thompson is not so far removed from mundane things. He is always on solid ground.

The Time-Dissolvers.—In speaking of the great geniuses of the earth the present tense should always be used, for are they not the highest manifestation of the timeless *Presence?*

The Decay of Surprise.—The prevalence of universal *ennui* as a consequence. The "kick", the tingle and thrill that are everywhere being hunted for. Millions of Columbuses, practical, emotional, intellectual and sexual Columbuses, with no more Americas to conquer and explore.

The Bright Door.—The Bright Door as the symbol of Death. The Bright Door as the comforting suicide-idea in everybody's life. The Bright Door in the middle of a darkened stage, which is Life, in whose depths I hear whispering, which is the unintelligible buzz of Life, and wherein I see endless shadows come and go and dissolve into one another, which is Life's senseless movement.

My Psychic Families.—To feed and raise and keep the peace among my family of opposing entities is a problem. I am six or seven well-defined persons in one—not exactly persons but arcs of persons. They all have their inhibitions which they desire to throw off, but, curious to relate, in my psychic family one entity is the inhibition of another entity. The Cynic inhibits the Idealist, the Idealist inhibits the Pig, the Pig inhibits the Sentimentalist, the Sentimentalist inhibits the Ruthless Money-Maker, the Ruthless Money-Maker inhibits the Pure Contemplator—and so on.

My aesthetic-sexual nature is always at war with my ascetic-intellectual nature. Sometimes there is a sudden cessation of the war of the entities in me and they fall on one another in another kind of war—called Love. They go on a frenzied copulatory debauch. In my house are many incests.

One of my entities is a Mystic—and on her belly I have often found her two sons, Pig and Art. My Cynic and my Idealist are brother and sister (twins) , but how often have I caught them *flagrante delicto* on the lounges of the tower of Pure Contemplation!

A rare, a bizarre family, a family that keeps me poor, for they feed off of my flesh and blood and brain—and my *will!*

Youth is the time for lustful thoughts; middle-age for solid love; old age for erotic day-dreams.

The Stupid Circle.—Having reached the point of absolute scepticism, I am ready to believe anything, no matter how absurd. Indifference breeds belief. The eternal return with in the cage of the skull.

"Futilitarian".—I came across the word "Futilitarian" and also "Futilist" the other day. Both fine words that sum up a frame of mind or a whole philosophy (or absence of it) of the world. Whatever is is futile. It is neither good nor bad —it is just useless. But, paradoxically, as the sense of futility deepens and broadens in me sensation grows keener.

Is futility a return to first principles? Like absolute scepticism, "Futilism" may be the point at which the worm turns on ultra-intellectualism and resumes its ecstatic life in the earth.

Pathos and Sex.—Pathos is related to voluptuousness. Here again opposites flow subtly, indefinably into one another. The tearless pathos in some of the music of Chopin, the pathos of an old Vienna waltz played by Kreisler—these awake perfumes, languishing women, desires for sobbing unions.

Pathos is the sigh of the Inevitable, and the sigh is sexual.

My Imagination.—An imagination such as mine is the pre paratory school for gods and demons. There are curriculums of diabolism and ethereal fornications, courses in all the vices and all the virtues.

Only music could evoke my imagination to an outsider—and that music has not been composed, and probably never will be. Its melodies and harmonies, dissonances, crescendos and decrescendos are immanent in the breath of Brahm.

The God of Spinoza is like Narcissus—he can only fall in love with his own reflections.

My Greatest Work.—There has been fecundating in my brain for many years a History of the Human Imagination. I am writing it all the time with the many-colored pencils of my ideas on the paper of my consciousness. This book will be a gorgeous work of the imagination about the Imagination.

Shall I conceive the Imagination in terms of the Platonic philosophy? Shall I begin by evoking the Imagination as an eternal Idea, as a sublime abstraction that exists independently of the mind of man but which functions through it? Shall I conceive it as one of the "Modalities" of Spinoza's God? Or shall I conceive it as something that has evolved gradually and slowly like Reason and Love? Temperamentally, the Platonic-Spinozistic idea appeals to me.

I believe all that is exists as ideas in a Universal Mind. We, with all our attributes, are only incarnations. I have never felt any conflict between Idealism and Realism—between Plato and Aristotle, between Spinoza and the materialists. While Imagination reposes eternally in the Essence, Shakespeare, Blake, Beethoven and Aeschylus appear and disappear according to certain immutable laws of birth and decay.

My book must, then, be the history of an Idea eternally vibrating in the brain of God and its epiphanies in certain individuals of the human race from the earliest times to the present. It will be the history of the gods on earth. It must be a Ninth Symphony of words dedicated to Art.

The Book of Ecstasy.—I contemplate a book on Ecstasy. Sexual, literary, religious, philosophical, artistic, musical, alcoholic, mathematical, cosmic, open-air, sadic, ironic ecstasy. Ecstasy as seizure, possession, concentration. Ecstasy as a form of catalepsy, the hypostatic union, craving for the Absolute. Ecstasy as the law of life. Ecstasy in death. The physiology of ecstasy. The psychology and metaphysics of ecstasy.

Is ecstasy founded entirely on the sex-act? Is all ecstasy a variation of the sex-spasm? I believe so. Trace the God-ecstasy of Spinoza and the sex-ecstasy of Sappho, tie them one to another; marry Spinoza and Sappho, for instance. Spinoza was a dervish of the Mystical Reason, Sappho was a dervish of eroticism. They embrace on the bed of the eternal Idea of Ecstasy.

The Book of Ecstasy and the History of the Imagination are being developed for a twin-birth in the womb of my brain.

Flippancy.—Serious flippancy—which is a form of humorous audacity—is born of a profoundly tragic background. A philosophic flippant is a farcical Aeschylus, a Hamlet whose agonies have turned to saucy defiance just at the suicidal point, a Don Quixote become self-conscious—God, suddenly struck with the witlessness of His enforced eternity and fecundity, doing a jazz on the ruins of his works and winding up a kalpa with a light epigram.

The serious world is in deadly fear of the flippant and the cynic. They are like a great earthquake among the "solid" skyscrapers of New York City. It is laughing lightning—Nietzsche's flippancy, for instance.

As everything tends to create a counterfeit of itself, there is also a false, cheap, artificial flippancy. But real flippancy is as eternal as tragedy. The shade of Aristophanes follows Aeschylus into the very streets of Hell. For every Chopin there is a Heine—sometimes both inhabit the same body.

Flippancy is the Youth born of age.

"The Shadow-Eater."—*The Shadow-Eater* was my great gesture of revolt. It was my Gargantuan evacuation of venom, lava and contempt. It was my ego vomiting itself over worlds, gods, Gods, men and forms. Then came indifference, serenity, calm—the passage to Epicurus and Spinoza and Whitman. Followed by another distention of hate and spleen and cosmic fury embodied in *Anathema!*

Demos the Puppet.—The greatest sport I know of: the cultured, powerful, oracular demagogue swaying the minds (!), emotions and acts of millions of men like a giant swinging a cat by its tail in all directions. Lenin, Wilson, Bryan, Mussolini —all they lacked to make them great was the spirit of Mephistopheles. Machiavelli took himself too seriously. He was himself the dupe of his own cynicism. The great demagogic genius —he who will nearly strangle with suppressed laughter while he moulds millions to his will—is yet to come. Had I daring and will equal to my imagination, I might undertake that role—the very Puck of democracy!

Harmony.—Proof-positive of the death of a man's genius or character—when he is in complete harmony with man and the universe.

The Jew.—"*Diabolique et caressant,*" says Paul Bourget of Heinrich Heine. That's a fine description of the soul of the Jew—diabolically caressing.

The Sex-Hour.—It does not take any study to divine the secret of life—of the machinery of hope, of illusion, of the comic vision, of despair, of ideality, of reality; the machinery of futility, of ecstasy; in a word, of a complete expose of what Emerson calls "God's method." Any intelligent *man* can focalize, visualize and *experience* all of the foregoing in an hour—in that hour of preliminary passionate love-making, possession, redressing and departure. Exultation, decantation, recuperation—sometimes imprecation and lamentation—that is the "method" of Brahma.

Medusa.—Again I write it: to be disenchanted before experience: the tragedy of Gautier, of Flaubert, of Baudelaire—*my* tragedy.
On the white tentacles of the octopus of Reality as it drags me down to death I have tattooed some beautiful images and epigrams in *crimson ink.*

A Slight Oversight.—Browning was right. God's on his throne. But he forgot to say that Satan was on *his* throne also.

The Black Pinions.—An entry in the diary of Baudelaire: "I felt pass over me a gust from the wing of imbecility." That was written in 1862, five years before his death. I know of no more terrible line in any literature.

I, Too.—The above has recalled to me certain momentary —infinitesimal in time—syncopes that I have always been subject to. The brain of genius is a gorgeous flower, exotic to earth. It is only logical it should fade first.

Murder.—The need for murder is profound. Have you slain your man yet—or a woman—or yourself? You hypocrite pacifist! You are a peace-lover because you itch to murder. Your pacifism is your guard, your fear erected into a virtue.

Prayers.—A woman's prayers, like her tears, are a bit of emotional millinery. But there is something awesome in the prayers of a strong man, especially if he is cultured.

To You, Hypocrite!—Why should I write about my "virtues," my generosity, my courtesy, my humanity, etc.? It is my vices, my perversities, my hatreds, my intellectual heartlessness you want to read about, that you wallow in, that you remember—is it not, my dear hypocritical reader?

I am very weak in the presence of a woman with a mischievous air. It is like a love-bite.

Love-Fear.—There is a frozen, cold, bitter, taciturn love as well as its opposite, which is the normal expression of love. It is founded on the brain's hatred of the emotions. Pride is also one of its elements; then there is the fear of appearing ridiculous in one's own eyes. When the ironic eye catches glimpses of one's self in the same postures, attitudes and repeating the same perfervid platitudes that one heard in the play the night before, farcically treated, there is a reticence, a curling up, an introversion of love-expression.

Opiates.—In lieu of adventure, new sensations, variety in the physical life, I read five or six books at once to experience the ecstasy of sudden contrast, surprise and universality.

At present I am reading Chesterton's short stories, which

amuse me and feed my love of paradox; short stories by Henri de Regnier, which satisfy my craving for exquisite prose and Venetian canals and psychic piddling in the hearts of lovers; short stories by Edgar Saltus, from which I get the aroma of nihilistic sophistication and which satisfy my sadistic instincts; the sex essays of Havelock Ellis, where I open the door of the blast-furnaces of passion and satisfy my erotic curiosity; the essays of Paul Bourget, on whose beautiful prose I voyage into the hearts of my favorite poets and novelists and lie gobbled up in abstractions, which I like above all things; the stories of Paul Morand, one of the most brilliant of present-day sophisticates; then there are Huneker, his "Melomaniacs" and "Chopin," which I am re-reading, and Spinoza, Clark Ashton Smith, Baudelaire (who becomes, to me, greater and greater at every reading), Chekhov, Swinburne always, and Chestov, the Russian nihilist. (What a life for a man who secretly dreams of living in one of the lotus—and leprous!—isles of the South Seas with a harem of beautiful native girls, none over twenty!)

My Escapes.—Three illusions that console and last and can always be renewed with no diminution of power *au contraire*. I speak of Literature, Music and Alcohol. Three forms of escaping reality. Sex is only an escape if you are a moderate libertine. The perfect life: Literature (all forms of Art), music, alcohol, with women as a by-product and an orgiastic outlet, not to be taken seriously.

God and Sex.—When a man is God-intoxicated his sex leaves him; he swims in a giant emotionalized abstraction. When a woman is God-intoxicated her sex dilates; she goes into heaven on the point of a mystical phallus. She meets the Bridegroom. Study the difference between Spinoza and Saint Theresa (or Mary-with-child). In Woman, God is an expression of sex perversion.

The Cure-All.—I wonder whether there is a grief in the world that cannot be cured by the appearance in the room of the heart-broken man of an exquisitely beautiful and nude young girl. And the grief-stricken woman? A black-haired, black-eyed, musical voiced, well-set-up young man—not naked, to be sure; but in a purple bathrobe. A woman's grief, too, can always be cured by—tut! tut! I'm a cynic tonight.

Perfect, unruffled love can only exist between two imbeciles.

Chestov.—A thought by Leon Chestov: "The first and essential condition of life is lawlessness. Laws are a refreshing sleep—lawlessness is creative activity." This is beautifully said and it ought not to be lost.

The Threshold.—In many dreams I have had the sensation of dying. On waking I have noted the fact that I did not experience fear but something like ecstatic curiosity. Does the subconscious know that I am merely dreaming?

God couldn't possibly be a female, for he keeps so well and so long the profoundest secrets of life.

Calvary.—"To know all is to forgive all." And to suffer all! There is no hell like universal comprehension. This magic light in the brain gleams with veritable hell-fire.

Perfume of Dreams.—Sometimes on awakening I have thoughts and emotions of such inexpressible magnificence that I feel that during sleep I must have stood on the topmost mountain of the world and drunk the light of all the constellations.

Time may be symbolized by a tear and Space by laughter.

Thighs.—The ugliest thing to me in the world is a straight line. The curve is the mother of surprise, sensuality, beauty, transgression and evanescence.

Mudguards.—The whole activity of the human race consists in

Fantasia Impromptu

the invention of mudguards. Reality is the mud and the guard is the lie-preservative.

Irony is frozen anger.

The Wise One.—The grave, contemplative, Minerva-like being who lives in my psyche, but who has no parley or quar rel with the Other One, my Demon, who really rules me for better or for worse.

Three.—Hamlet, Don Quixote and Bazaroff have been in fiction the most real to me: the sceptic, the idealist, the nihilist. They are one man.

Injections.—Stoicism is the art of suddenly flooding the blood, nerves, heart and emotions with Arctic sea-water. But for great physical pain there has never been found a substitute for the hypodermic injection.

Cynics are the seers of Reality.

Evolution, Again.—All evolution is a growth of wakefulness, a widening and deepening of consciousness—awareness —not a *change* in forms. It is a rising from slumber to insomnia. Intelligence is divided into levels and layers of wakefulness, castes of awareness, circles of apprehension. The mob, the crowd, is half-asleep; they are sleep-walkers. The genius is the highest degree of wakefulness attained on the planet. And so we speak of God as the "unslumbering," "the all-seeing" etc. Every original act, or thought, is a movement toward a completer wakefulness.

Art can only influence artists.

Corn and the Games.—The most beautiful passages in the Old and New Testaments have never had any influence on the masses. Only those passages that *promise* something are of importance to them—or the passages that lift a responsibility from their shoulders.

Puritan Intelligence.—Even the smut-hounds and puritan nuzzlers never speak of "an immoral work of art." However low their intelligence, they know that that is a contradiction in terms. They avoid self-incrimination.

"Immorality" is a secret form of universal hope.

The three most humorous words in the language are "doctor of divinity." What the hell is that?

The "secret of life" lies neither in action nor in art, but in learning how to rise to your feet every time the Referee strokes off "nine!"

You will notice that in the phrase "petty thief," the word that is stressed with contempt is petty, not "thief."

A man may sell his soul to the Devil; but even the Devil knows no woman could do *that*.

The Mystical Destroyers.—There is a holy and sacred emotion in the destruction of sacred things. Iconoclasts, too, have their epileptic frenzies of mystical joy.

The Tongue and the Sphinx.—There are transparent minds, but there are no transparent hearts. The mind may be crystal-clear or as heavily veiled as the events of the next century; but the heart always remains unguessable, unseeable, unpredictable. The heart may know what it wants, but it never knows what it needs.

The more biographers a man has the more he tends to become mythical.

My Egotism.—I desire to see all of my books published in my lifetime, to see them read everywhere, to hear them talked about, wrangled over, written about; to hear my name on every intelligent person's tongue; to be pointed out, to be whispered about. Wherever I go, I wish to sow eyes looking at me as God sows suns. I desire glory, fame, honor, friends, sulky and envious enemies. My heart still bounds with joy at seeing my name in print after twenty-five years of it. And yet there are those who say about me, "He is not human"! And I get a "big" kick out of that, too, for they mean *me!*

"Don't let on," the children say when playing. Idiomatic, universal, profound!

The very core of humor: to curse necessity.

Curses and Prayers.—A curse or prayer is an emotional explosion. It is in the psychic world exactly what a posterial belch is in the physical world. One is always answered as the other is—in the *relief.*

The Puritan Mind.—There is nothing more comic to me than to watch a puritan writer (English or New England) compelling himself to admit in print that vice may be fascinating. An essay on "Voltaire," by Gamaliel Bradford, for instance. "Why not admit it" and "we must admit" and "truth to tell." Bradford is a good, racy writer, but there is the eternal pathos of his puritan morality and his sex-inhibitions. When the puritan mind tries to be ironic—good God!

The Fertilizer.—Keep your imagination always irrigated and fertile with the images of the naked women you have never possessed. Transmute their flesh into ink, music, color, marble.

On Breaking My Elbow.—If I were not a stoic (which I am not), I would have shrieked with pain (which I did).

The Satanic Graces.—Baudelaire speaks somewhere of the "Satanic Graces." What shall I name them? Irony, Perversity, Disillusion!

"The Old Army Game."—To understand all is to forgive all; to

forgive all is to become indifferent; to become indifferent is just what the invisible powers behind Church and State desire of you and me, for they do *not* understand, do *not* forgive—and never sleep. It is on the understanding, the forgiving and the indifferent that tyranny, cruelty and spolia tion of the individual are built. Teach them to forgive one another—then forge their chains.

The Jailer.—Man's whole quarrel on this planet from his first appearance to the finale is with Cause and Effect. He is locked in Logic. His imagination forges many keys to escape. Miracle, poetry, alcohol are some of the names of these keys. The eternal jailers, Cause and Effect, look through the bars at man's child-play and smile at him with the cold mathematical smile of inexorability.

Pleasure has no eyes.

My Core.—Like a great diamond lodged in a drain-pipe, there is an almighty world-dissolving, world-creating Thought that lies in the stupid, redundant coils of my brain. Will the coils wear away the diamond or will the diamond finally cut its way out of the brain?

What I Must Destroy.—Elements in my nature which must be destroyed before I can attain material success and begin the aggressive conquest of my public: the incubus Christ, with his poisonous doctrines; pity as a social theory; the fear of hurting someone else; sympathy with the man I've jostled off a pedestal or out of a job.

For years these poisons have prevented me from functioning in the world of matter, in the practical world. I must dramatize myself, egotize myself literally, and return to the Mosaic law— an eye for an eye and a tooth for a tooth; for, at bottom, I am an Old Testament Jew. I pit Moses against Christ, for it isn't cruelty that is destroying the human race, but *softness, flabbiness.*

Fantasia Impromptu

The Baptismal Fount.—The Mediterranean is holy water—where it washes there are culture and genius and civilization. Poets, vision-makers and ironists should be baptized between Gibraltar and the Orient.

Sex and Art.—Sex is the delectable nuisance in the life of the artist. The term "sex-emancipation" means quite differ ent things to the woman of today and to the artist. In the case of the woman "sex-emancipation" means more sex; to the artist it means less sex and more art.

Art and Love.—Is there a conflict between Art and Love? There must be, for they are irreconcilable opposites, as opposite as blindness and sight. Art sees; Love is blind.

Blind men paint ever-fading dreams on the dark—even as those who see.

The Crystal Screen.—I feel sometimes on awaking that I am about to abolish the time-sense, that *succession* has thinned to the faintest of psychical pulse-beats, that a crystal screen is being lifted between me and Eternal Simultaneity. And by time, I mean Space also, for Time and Space are one.

My Cannibal.—My Dæmon has turned affirmative. His knuckles are pounding the tocsin of action; he has picked up the cymbals of courage; he has uttered Evohé! to life. He is hungry for human power. He wants fresh flesh and brains. His beautiful dreams, on which he lived for so long, have given him diarrhea of the will. He is all leak. He is going to dramatize me. I have only been a curtain-raiser up to date. I hear a roll of drums over the earth through the corridors of the stars. The curtain is rising on my epic. Salute my Daemon, my Familiar, my Astral Self, who is incarnating!

The Artist-Bandit.—Life is only justified in the Artist. He is its ethico-aesthetic excuse for being. He is the Sun, the light-giver, the vision-fabricator, the heat of the soul. And, like the Sun, he has the right to eat up his planets. The Artist and the bandit have always understood one another. It is only the Artist who has a *right to live, to take,* to use everything.

Comedy and Humor.—The comedy of life is one thing, the humor of life is another thing. Comedy is variety. Humor is a unity. Comedy depends on plot, situation. Humor is the eternal plot, the eternal situation itself.

My "Close Friend."—"Now", he said, "we are always going to be close friends, are we not?"
"Friend," I said, "is a sublime word—it may, you know, imply the thrust of my hand in your bank savings—"
He shook my hand hurriedly, mumbled about an appoint ment he had almost forgotten, by Jove! — and hurried away —did my "close friend."

The Romantics.—Christ made a romance of poverty. Messalina made a romance of whoredom. Napoleon made a romance of murder. The art of romanticizing and dramatizing your fatalities—that is all ye need to know, children.

My fatal gift is disillusion, but I have romanticized it. I have dramatized my boredom in words.

Epiphany.—How proud I am of my ignorance! With what honeyed tongue I announce that I do not know! My humility is an Assumption, an Annunciation.

The Borgian Ring.—When I have shaken hands warmly with some critic who has "roasted" my books and said to him "I recognize your sincerity," I have secretly wished that all five fingers on my hand that clasped his had on them the poisoned rings of the Borgias.

In America, the Castrati write the book reviews.

Re-Making the Dead.—I have thought of writing the lives of some great artist—Shelley, Manet, Beethoven, Shakespeare, Chopin, Keats, Sappho, Emerson, Nietzsche, Redon, for instance—directly from a complete inhalation of and meditation on their work without any regard to the facts. Wherever the known facts conflict with my mythus, I shall reject them or flatly deny them. I know there are no "facts" in regard to myself only in so far as I know them and as they appear in my work. It would be a fascinating undertaking—the lives of Shakespeare, Chopin and Verlaine, for instance, as I conceive them to have been from their faces and work alone.

"Influences."—I do not think any writer has ever deeply influenced my style or even my thought. At fifteen I was a profound and melancholy pessimist and by my seventeenth year I had one thought supremely in my mind each day—suicide. I was neither sickly nor in want. I was born a Buddha of enlightened disillusion, as was my brother Walter, who majestically and sublimely walked out of life at the age of 18. The pessismistic writers that I then began to read were only excursions of verification. They did not influence me; I selected them. I have never been conscious of any "influence," but my affinities and enthusiasms are legion.

And if I died tonight (February 8, 1926) what five men of genius, after my brother, would I want to meet above all others? I answer unhesitatingly: Shakespeare, Shelley, Spinoza, Beethoven and Whitman. Then Chopin, Hugo, Nietzsche, Baudelaire, and so on.

To Shock a Pessimist.—All pessimists wish to live to an old age in order to distil from life, to the very end, the exquisite pleasures of verification. If a pessimist should ever discover that he is wrong, the shock would probably kill him.

The Law of My Being.—There goes on in me perpetually a condensation and evaporation and recondensation and re-evaporation of thoughts, emotions and will. I am a miniature of all eternal laws. I duplicate the four seasons every day. The law of the tides is almost an hourly phenomenon in my soul. The curious rhythm of ethereal mathematics, which is the astral body of temporal mathematics, is my ecliptic.

In the evolution of my moods, thoughts, dreams and emotions from the time I rise in the morning until I go to bed at night I repeat the nebular hypothesis. Incandescent, inchoate, bulging with mighty potentials that are dragged from their racial depths during slumber, I arise and begin to whirl off planets—thoughts, concepts, visions and plans for my implacable march on Reality. While bathing, while shaving, while stooling, the loaded sun of my new consciousness flings off Mercuries, Venuses, Neptunes, Jupiters and comets which vanish before I can formulate them, so swift is their flight through my consciousness. As the day goes on, I begin to evaporate. The central sun, the core of the day's consciousness, loses gradually in heat and intensity, evaporates into yawns, belches and general fatigue.

Ticklers.—George Sterling calls me "a Dionysian pessimist," Shaemas O'Sheel calls me "the Laureate of Disillusion," James Huneker called me "that Apocalyptic genius," John McClure, à la Blake, spoke of me as "a fiend or an angel that lives in a cloud," Edgar Saltus, "a Titan in an inkstand;" William Marion Reedy, "another Nietzsche," and so forth.

If you want to get rid of people let them know you are in financial trouble.

The Buzzards.—There are at least six publishers in America waiting patiently for me to die in order to make money on my unpublished books and love-letters, depending on the obituary notices and the rising curiosity that a fresh corpse awakens to give them free preliminary advertising and exploitation.

I regret the future: can pessimism and despair go further?

The Celestial Barn-Stormers.—It would not surprise me to find out (some day) that there was an eternal pattern of life and that every habitable planet in the universe repeated (with scenic variations) the life on every other planet. There may be a Jesus myth, a Prometheus myth, an Original Sin Myth, a Golden Age myth among all planetary peoples. It is probable that the laws of psychic and imaginative evolution do not vary much anywhere. Prometheus and Jesus have probably died billions of times in billions of worlds. Is it not ridiculous to think that we on this planet have been subject to something unique? It is highly probable that the Play is everlastingly the same—with millions of road companies barn-storming the stars.

The War Goes On.—At 52—nearly 53—I am not at peace with God, man, the world, myself, my work or the idea of death. I have experienced "peace" under two—maybe three—conditions only in my life: in the first stages of intoxication, when the inner and outer worlds co-ordinate perfectly, external things taking on the poesy of my own mind, all inhibitions of speech and act being canceled, the physical and mental being fused— then I have attained mental, spiritual and physical peace. Again, in those many hours, days, years passed in the library, in my early years, absorbed in philosophies, metaphysics, poetry and those excursions of the mind in the infinitudes of dilated consciousness and high cerebral emotions—total abolition of time, space, circumstance and knowledge of the physical body; divine junkets into worlds and ages that existed before I was wombed. That was the peace that passed all understanding—complete union with the eternal Idea.

I have found peace also in certain hours and moods with nature, in which the pantheistic rapture of my oneness with the hills, rivers, trees and the heavens transported me to the peace of the Infinite and the Eternal. Also, in rare moments of creational activity, in doing my best work in a fury, in the orgasms of mind. But with the years these anodynes have lost their power.

Cynicism, the critical faculty, the insistent ego, the sex-Tantalus destroy more and more the concentrative powers; and peace, still present somewhat in music, has taken refuge in the dream of personal annihilation.

Emerson.—Twenty-six years after my first reading I am reading Emerson again. I see what a profound influence he has been in my life. How we two tally! He not only lasts, but I find him greater today—in thought, style, profundity, clarity, sublimity and concentrative wisdom—than I did in those younger, molten days.

His apprehension is godlike (literally). He was the Praxiteles, the Angelo of style. Every sentence is a treasure-house. He is the king of the philosophic epigram. All of Stirner, Nietzsche, Ibsen, Maeterlinck and Whitman are in Emerson. He has never been placed high enough. He is one of the eternals. His prose gives me infinite joy. His poetry also is unique, sublime.

The Revolving Mirror.—I have a revolving mirror in my brain wherein each thought, idea, resolution, purpose and aspiration sees itself reflected at a dozen different angles—grotesquely, tragically, practically, ideally, jestingly, negatively, positively, under the aspect of eternity and under the as pect of time.

There is a hidden photographer in me who takes all possible poses of each idea, resolution, purpose and call to action. So all motives to action are immediately split into motives for non-action, and in these sinister gaps my will evaporates. To act one must have unity of motive; but all motives in me burst into opposing units, and the pleasure that might have been had from the action I find in the intellectual joy of examining the debris of the motive.

There is a great pleasure in knowing why one does *not* do a thing.

The Sex-Essence.—That mysterious sex-ecstasy in the blood —is it metaphysical? There is a delirium of sex-restraint, the ecstasy of continence, the sublimation and introversion of the orgasm. The saints, Spinoza, many of the poets know it.

Is the sex-essence in the blood a shadow of one of the Platonic Ideas, the mere counterfeit of a sublimer ecstasy in metaphysical regions? God-intoxication—is it a sublimation of sex-ecstasy; or, is sex-ecstasy a lower form, a faint adumbration of God-intoxication, the prolonged ecstasy of an ethereal union with the Presence? Plato and Aristotle again! I do not know, but I am slightly inclined toward the Platonic explanation.

Our psychic lives, like our bodily lives, seem to be miniatures of a larger Reality. Alcohol, drugs and the ecstasy of killing seem to indicate that we are copies, marionettes, miniatures.

Joy-Rides in the Dark!—We hate physical pain; but no one hates or regrets grief, melancholy, cosmical despair. They are really joy-rides on the other side of the moon.

Three Liars.—Three of us sat around talking until three o'clock this morning—two intellectual materialists and myself. (What am I *anyhow?* A mystical nihilist? A God-intoxicated Satan? A paradoxical idea-juggler? A Bacchic pessimist?)

Well, we all three agreed that we wished to be annihilated at death and looked with horror on the thought of waking up a few hours after death in a condition to identify ourselves.

Of course, we all lied to one another. No one wants to be annihilated. What we meant was that we wanted a good, long, recuperative sleep. I should like to return to this world or voyage through the stars as a disembodied intelligence, a contemplative looker-on. But that would grow tiresome, too. Pah!

The Holy Ghost.—If the Holy Ghost of Irony is with you, you will get as much pleasure out of your failures as out of your triumphs. Elie Faure says we must take everything tragically but nothing seriously. But the instant the tragic is flooded with the boreal light of irony the tragic becomes comic. Irony is, literally, the Holy Ghost of thinkers and sceptics.

I have written so much on irony, defined it so many times, that there scarcely seems anything left to say about it. Still, I am always returning to it, must return to it each day to save my reason, to go on living. In fact, irony has become my sole reason for being. To-day, for instance, I got a check for fifteen dollars from a publisher after he had promised me one hundred and fifty dollars. At first I thought of murder, then an abusive letter; then the whole petty transaction melted into ironic ether in the heavens of my skull. I saw the bilk as the gods would see it. Once again I had verified my profound intuition in regard to the human being in the business sphere, and by a curious twist I found something like satisfaction in the fact that I, a poet, a thinker, had been bilked by a publisher.

If the Holy Ghost of Irony will remain with me, I can survive the murderous foragings of the Imp of the Perverse on my will.

There are no ladders to success; only tightropes.

Evanescing Fish.—Irritating: ideas that come up into my consciousness like rare and gorgeously colored fish for a moment and sink again into the depths before I can get my hook and bait ready.

Intellectual Poetry.—Why is there not more cerebral, intellectual poetry? It is very rare. The brain has its emotions; the intellect has its feelings. Emerson's poetry has always seemed very beautiful to me. Nietzsche's poetry has great passion. Much of Shelley's poetry is intellectual.

What an idea!—that the brain is cold, that cerebral poetry is boreal, that pure thought cannot be lyrical, frenzied! It is astonishing to find so little intellect among what we call the cultured classes. Is culture the very opposite of intelligence?

Pessimism Is Health.—Nietzsche says all the great pessimists were sick. Yes, they were sick of the futility of Nietzsche's way to salvation. They were sick of the vanity of joy, the illusions of Dionysus and the hopelessness of "transvaluing" values.

As a matter of fact, there is nothing more vigorous and red-blooded in all literature than the lamentations, wails and blackguarding of the pessimists—from Solomon to Octave Mirbeau and myself. There is nothing more anaemic and energy-lowering than the writings of the optimists (who are they? They do not survive. Only the pessimists and ironists survive). The great pessimists are not sick men; they are, in fact, so healthy, so superabundant in energy, that they emit mighty lyrical, dramatic and prose protests against being thrust into the straitjacket of three dimensions.

Nietzsche himself was a sick man, but he invented a sublime bluff in the face of the facts. He had the tremendous vigor in his prose of all born sick men.

Remorse.—I live too much within myself. I should live more in (and on) others. Theft, Horatio, theft!

Obvious Woman.—What becomes of the boasted sex-intuition of women when they pick out for lovers and husbands the things we discriminating men see them pick out? Every woman, I suppose, likes to be assaulted by a strong man at some time in her life; or, in lieu of an assault, she takes on something she can assault herself—a pimp, a minor poet, a lapdog, a lounge-lizard.

Woman—a charming, delightful, bewitching and quite necessary bit of bric-a-brac. Her "depth," her "profundity," her "mystery" are, as Nietzsche said, pure fiction. There are, of course, exceptions to this dictum; but ninety-five per cent of all women born of men (and they *are* born of us) are as obvious to a penetrating male mind as a three weeks-old baby.

Man is always in the attitude of raising his hands toward heaven in prayer because he instinctively feels the need of handcuffs.

Elie Faure.—I am reading Elie Faure's *The Dance Over Fire and*

Water. It is a brilliantly written book, all of which I wrote — more concisely and epigrammatically—years ago in *The Muse of Lies, The Crown of Cactus, The Book of Vengeance, Sir Galahad,* all as yet unpublished (1926) because, being an American, I am *naturally* looked upon by publishers as a faker.

I can see the standpoint of the American publishers: an American thinker *must* be a faker of some sort because fake is a national trait. They simply will not believe in the possibility of my existence—as an American. They can, and do, conceive me as a Spaniard or a Frenchman, but as a Philadelphia-born original—*Jamais!*

Faure is out of Nietzsche with little variation. Sometimes he seems a veritable echo of him. There's a lot of Nietzsche in me, too; but it would have been there just the same if there had been no Nietzsche. But not so with Faure. Without Nietzsche, no Faure—that is, as we have him today.

In a Bathtub.—A curious thought came to me while lying in the hot bath this morning (I must some day write an ironic, or comic, history of the influence of the bathroom on cerebration. The minute I enter a bathroom, close the door and engage in shaving, bathing or in any of the other uses for which our modern bathrooms are constructed, thoughts, ideas, images and plans well through me. I believe Montaigne noted the effect of certain necessary morning organic functions on the fecundating power of the brain. Is the answer found in the fact that nowhere are we more alone, nowhere does the ego retire more completely into itself, nowhere is the world more completely shut out than in the bathroom—or, as in Montaigne's time, in the outhouse?)—well, as I was saying to myself, a curious thought came to me: Are sensual delights mental and are mental delights sensual?

I was going to enlarge on this, but it has all flown away—what I was *going* to write—in evolving bathroom psychology in the parenthesis.

Caceres.—The other evening at the house of Kurt Schindler I was shown pictures of my old native Spanish province, Caceres, in a German book called *Unknown Spain.*

A curious feeling of nostalgia came over me. The province is old, old, very old—as I am. It has something of eternity about it and is not susceptible to "progress"—like myself. It is off all beaten tracks—as are my thoughts, my aspirations (what are they, anyway?), my desires.

If I ever get enough money, I will go to Caceres. What a thrill! To find an inn with my name painted outside! To see, maybe, senoritas with coal-black eyes, who dance menaedic dances to crashing, frenzied, sexual music, who bear my name!

Or is it better not to go and retain my illusions about it? "I've never been to Carcassonne—".

Promise or Memory?—That ever-recurring revery in my mind—my core-revery, the persistent thought in my brain: *how to achieve complete control of the visible cosmos in order to re-order all of life on all the stars, or destroy it.* The ultimate dream of the will-to-power in the dream of an egomaniac, myself.

This twenty-year revery is not just a fantasy with me, but has a profound emotional and mystical basis. Is it a promise of future kalpas of time—or a memory?

A Curious Book.—Curious ideas one comes across in old books. I like to ramble through the card index in the New York Public Library, pulling out any drawer and choosing something that looks odd. Yesterday I came across a book in French translated from the Persian—*Celestial Mechanics*, by a Hassoud Ali-Effem. He related a legendary belief among the Persians that a straight, vertical rain came from the goddesses and that a slanting, blowing, wabbly rain came from the gods. A list of these curious books with their curious legends would make a notable, and salable, work.

The Pronoun Test.—The use of the pronoun I in this and other books of mine sometimes costs me a struggle—so hard is it to eradicate the syphilis of Christian humility from my blood.

Don't Kill Goliath!—Certainly "The Antichrist of Nietzsche is a terrific onslaught on Christianity, but it is not justified from the Nietzschean standpoint. For two thousand years this "falsifier of all instincts," this "transvaluer of all natural values," this "corrupter of the sources of all life" has caused the Western world to flounder through corpses, waddle up to its waist in blood and set the Dionysian-satanic tempo of life. Christianity has, paradoxically, been a supreme life-urging force. It is the greatest witness of the incurable "immoralism" of man. The Catholic and Protestant churches have always been militant forces.
Personally, I am bitterly anti-Christian; but I cannot do without Christianity. It is the mother of my irony, my scepticism, my mystical nihilism.
As the Churches today become more and more liberal, life becomes stupider and stupider. We Davids will soon have no Goliaths to slungshot! No Christ, no Nietzsche.

The Venom in Pity.—Nietzsche is, also, all wrong about pity. Pity, in the individual, is an attribute of the will-to-power. There is always a touch of satanism and venom in pity.

Ludwig Laughs.—While I was listening to Beethoven's Fifth at a concert this afternoon why did the unpaid electric light bill bob up in my mind and make me uneasy?

Vision.—I see a long line of pillars which stretch away before me into the infinite. These pillars are slowly falling. A frenzied figure is using all his strength trying to keep a pillar from crushing him. With both of his hands he tries to get the pillar back to an upright position, but it falls slowly, implacably, and just as it is about to crush the ridiculous Samson he dodges from under and attempts the same impossible feat at another column, which falls, falls implacably.

The pillars are Hours and the terrified Samson is Man. He is trying to prevent time from elapsing, and forever and for ever he will continue the struggle until the Hours are fused in Eternity and our little Samson himself retires into the rising and falling eyelashes of Brahm and is drowned in the satanic rays from his eyes. (As I write this Bio is running an electric violet-ray machine up and down my spine to "fit me for my fifty-fourth year," she says.)

Proteus.—The atheist-materialist is a fine study in the paradoxes of God. The atheist-materialist finds profound comfort in his disbelief. "I am your disbelief too," whispers God in his ear.

No one can dodge the ruses of the eternal protean Essence.

Indoor Sports.—The restless, vivacious, feminine culture hound—I have three of them under the magnifying glass of my mind. They fascinate but do not magnetize.

One looks like a saint (a hair-dresser's and beauty-parlor saint) and she prattles of the new Hindu Christ-Incarnation (a beautiful boy who plays tennis, with Annie Besant in the press-box) and other bric-a-brac.

Another curls and uncurls herself like a beautiful snake in the chaise-longe, pulls her dress down incessantly so that I may look at her legs, her knees and get glimpses of her thighs, the while she gabbles of Henry James.

The third plays with the stars, astrologically, and rolls her eyes sextatically when I pronounce the word "cosmos," which I do solemnly with my eyes deep in hers.

Some of the indoor sports of 1926 of the famished, neurotic, ambisextrous Dear Ones.

At a Party.—The wife of a publisher. Every time I looked at her she was looking at some one present (mostly people just introduced) with the most venomous, murderous and contemptuous look that I have ever seen on a woman's face. What a "document" in that woman for a Balzac! What deviltries! What suppressions! What secret plotting! I am getting to be a soul-sampler, a peeper, a connoisseur of "psychological instances"—the periwig and slippers stage of Dionysus.

The Art of Exaggeration.—I always exaggerate, in speech, in writing and even when I tell the truth.

Exaggeration is the art or the instinct of moving a thing from the finite into the infinite. It is the art of putting beautiful hair on the bald spots of life. Whatever is tends to exaggeration.

Exaggeration is growth. "One should never fear exaggerating," says Flaubert. Not how shall I describe a fact, but what shall I do with it is the problem and the pleasure of it. It is the thread of gold on the spool of reality.

Mon Dieu!—A bullet in the brain of us Latins fired by Flaubert: "At bottom I am German." I nearly expired when I read it!

Genius is the poetry of pain.

Time Is My Garden.—All that has gone before me is my raw material, both in a literary and psycho-physical sense.

Whatever is not done for the glorification and exfoliation of your ego is of no value to you or to the world.

Peter Pans.—Is there anything more delightful than the man of fifty who will not grow up? There is something of eternity in the play-instinct. He who has it all of his life partakes of the blood and flesh of the adventurous gods.

I am still boyish-minded. I hate to be a man. To keep the winking beads on the stale beer of life is a miracle, but it *is* done. And the delight of recognition when two men past maturity find in one another the old rowdy, leaping kid of forty years back!

Lyrical Anecdote.—Fatality. I did not want to drink. My wife didn't want me to drink. She insisted that we go to a certain restaurant for dinner. I would never go. I felt that that particular restaurant was a blind for bootleg and moonshine highballs. But I did not tell her so. I was not drinking. And my wife didn't want me to drink and kept me away from the restaurants where they served booze. But she became so insistent about this "nice-looking place" that she finally broke down my opposition and we went in for dinner. As soon as we got seated, six waiters rushed up to me, greeted me as a long-lost brother, thrust whiskey glasses and syphon bottles on us, and we drank. I did not want to drink. My wife did not want me to drink. The food in that place was only a "chaser" for booze.

And so it was ordered by the high gods that I should get drunk that evening in spite of my will and my wife's will. And they used her as the instrument.

I did not want to drink.

My wife didn't want me to drink.

Fatality.

Nowadays we no longer say a woman is pretty or plain. We say she "makes up" well or she doesn't.

Flaubert and Myself—My great difficulty is in trying to write like one not inspired—to write calmly, descriptively, just as one orders a meal in a restaurant. Whenever a thought, idea, vision or fine epigram begins to germinate in my brain, I begin to tremble, fret, feel a hot flush of some fluid in my brain, my blood begins to dance; I feel a "seizure." I feel, potentially at least, epileptic, cataleptic, drunken, fountain like (as I feel now in putting down this more or less important observation of myself).

I do not ever remember having deliberately "manufactured" anything—certainly not my epigrams. (I do not think anything is worth manufacturing.) My God! When I read the way Flaubert worked over his books (his "Correspondence" reads like the confessions of an inventor, not a writer) I get sick in my soul. He gives me a sensation of futile drudgery that reminds me of the days when, as a boy, I used to polish up spittoons in a cigar store for the boss' eye.

How seriously Flaubert took Art! If my books had cost me one-millionth part of the effort that he expended on one chapter alone, I would have said, "God-damn literature! I'm going to be a bartender or a pimp!"

All that I have written has come out with such ease that in reading it over I remember nothing of its creation; just came out like the babies of those husky peasant women of Russia I've read about, who accouch a child while working in the field and go on working again as if nothing had happened.

Nothing had happened, as a matter of fact. What's a baby or a book more or less in the life of the planet? The brain should work like the bowels of a perfectly healthy being or like the organs of those peasant women. Mine does—and when it doesn't I go to a "movie," turn on my phonograph, get drunk or smoke my pipe.

Was Flaubert a Second-Rater?—I do not aim at perfection. I aim at expression. I like Walt Whitman for putting *everything* on paper, like Montaigne and Voltaire. Their common places, platitudes, crudities—is it not all a part of life, a part of all of our lives?

More and more I feel that Flaubert was a second-rater. He was always so damned careful about what he wrote, always "blushing" at his "first youthful experiments." He has a feminine fear of being "caught."

This about Flaubert sounds far different from my glorification of him in "Forty Immortals." What of it? That was *then—and* this is *now*.

Had Flaubert Imagination?—Flaubert in criticizing Victor Hugo's "Les Miserables" asks: "Where is the factory that turns away a girl because she has a child?" This is poor criticism. Whatever is conceivable is *real*. More so in literature than anywhere else.

Fantasia Impromptu

Turning away a girl for that reason is quite probable in certain American towns and in certain towns in England. That's the German in Flaubert—facts, facts, facts, to be "solidly documented," observation, observation, verification, verification (Taine, who is revered by the Germans).

Hugo invented facts to drive home his drama, like Shakespeare. Flaubert had no inspirational imagination. It is true he made marvellous pictures of his facts; but Hugo, Balzac and Shakespeare put wings on facts and flew away with them.

The Untainted.—Flaubert's superstition: science. Hugo's superstition: universal suffrage. All tainted, all tainted. Whitman's superstition: democracy. Shakespeare and Balzac seem to be without superstitions. Also Gautier and Leconte de Lisle.

What is my pet superstition? Immanent Evil, maybe. Shakespeare and Keats are immaculates, for pure Beauty can hardly be called a superstition.

My Caul.—There is always a caul, a veil, a film between me and the external world. It has always enveloped me like a thin mesh, like fleshings. Whenever I come in physical contact with a person it falls over me like a cold flush from my head to my feet. It establishes an impregnable barrier between us immediately. It seems to be something on duty, on guard.

This mysterious I-know-not-what holds me separated in what seems vast, impassable distances from the nearest objects, to set me as a thing apart. It may be compared to an emanation, an aura. It is at once self-defensive and isolating. It says, "Thou shalt not mix!" It is not present to me consciously when alone. In fact, then I am allowed to cross vast spaces and blend with my surroundings—especially in the presence of nature; but let a human intrude on my vision and immediately my whole being flows back to its viewless sockets and there emanate from within—I know not how nor whence—this fine immaterial but adamant casing, these ethereal quills that threaten and isolate.

The King of Terrors is not Death but Ridicule.

Parents.—To be born bodily of parents is not enough to produce love or even respect for them. One must be born spiritually of one's parents. Between my own parents and myself and Walter there was no spiritual, mental or psychical relation whatsoever. They simply meant nothing to us. Cowed by a sense of ancestral duty, I went regularly to see them and sent them all the money I could when they were ill.

Ah, children, children, we are not brave at all. Your parents—allowing for many exceptions—are your natural enemies from the cradle to the grave. If they are not, you belong to the herd; but I do not address the herd. I speak to the differentiated (if I'm speaking or writing to anybody).

The Murder of Birth.—Children of accident may be excused, but to plan deliberately to bring children into the world has always seemed to me a form of murder.

Ladies and Gentlemen of Posterity:—I'd like to be with you to see what your special illusions are in the time in which you live. The eternal transformations of Maya and the eternal transformations of my ashes (from whose atoms I am speaking to you) are a perpetual source of pleasure to me—if that which has no longer nerves, heart or brain can feel pleasure. But I indulge in the pleasure now by an act of the ante-mortem imagination and so mingle my essence with yours in all the protean transformations of your lives.

Actors and Groundlings.—Imagine! To be present at the tragi-comedy of Life being played in my own soul at morning, matinee and evening performance! I am both actor and spectator, and in a way it is my own tragi-comedy. Each one of us is playwright to the Universal Impresario.

Now, all that I have written—and all that you have written—are just the lines that have been assigned to us to speak. For only we artists—poets, painters, sculptors, composers, essayists. epigrammatists, thinkers, philosophers, etc.—have *parts* in this tragi-comedy. The rest—the billions—are just the mob.

I fertilize the sleeping eggs in the wombs of your brain.

Yogi-Casanova.—I know a man who catches women in his net by expounding to them the Yoga philosophy. The cosmic ruses of King Priapus!

Scenario.—God and Satan are both bored with their jobs. They agree to exchange places for a year—God to go around the earth masked as the Tempter and Satan to mask himself as a messenger of redemption. God becomes the Spirit of Sin, Vice, Joy, Pleasure. Satan becomes an evangelist of the ultra-serious type in our Middle West moron belt. After a year Satan is wild to get back to normalcy; but God is so enamored of Satan's job that he refuses to re-become God.
Call it "The Damnation of God."

Lewis Carroll was the super-metaphysician. Whatever is is nonsense.

My Dream, Again.—My desire is to perform in secret great world-miracles—to humiliate mobs and kings, smash industrial and puritanical America, abolish the churches of the world in a breath, root out of the heart of man all reverence for authority, shatter all instruments of war, but not psychological conflict; make wine the universal rejuvenator, and lift up the Artist to the pinnacle of godhood.
If I controlled all the radios, moving pictures, newspapers and aeroplanes in the world I could bring this about.
Amen!

Joyce.—James Joyce's *Ulysses* grows on me. I return and return to it. It is unique, an astounding picture of the inner life, of the brain, of the soul, of heaven, hell and earth. Is it a new technique, a new form? He caught the mighty ocean of consciousness that rolls through us and imprisoned it in eight hundred pages. It will be done better some day. Any one can imitate. We all do. Imitation and variation are the laws of life. If Blake or Shakespeare had done this about themselves! It is ridiculous to speak of Joyce and Rabelais, to compare them. They have nothing in common, at least very little.

I am tempted to set down my everyday life à la Joyce. But I dare not. Joyce is a great original in that book. What satires can be written in the Joyce manner! The week of a Puritan, a single day in the life of an American businessman, twenty-four hours of the "soul" of a barber!

Midnight.—Tonight I hear again those notes of broken music that produce in me the mood of the fabulous and the forlorn.

Conversational Aviation.—How long can an abstract conversation be sustained in an evening company?

I have succeeded in keeping a discussion based on a generalization among three men for five minutes. This is a record non-stop flight in my experience. Generally, at the end of a minute in these altitude-flights I can see a mental uneasiness begin to glimmer in their eyes and their bodies begin to wiggle-waggle for a landing in the concrete. Then with profound relief begins the series of "that reminds me" and "now, for example." The height frightens them, and as the airplane of pure intelligence gets farther and farther away from the Earth they grow sickish, psychically speaking.

Leonard Van Noppen, the poet, can sustain with me vertiginous non-stop flights into the empyrean of abstraction. We have kept it up for hours. Sometimes we would alight for a minute in the pleasing meadow of a sexual joke or a guffaw at a President or a professor—but zip! the motor would start again with a roar and away we go, winging into the empyrean of Hegelian, Hindu or Platonic abstraction.

Fantasia Impromptu

Some men cannot even rise from the ground. Others stand whirling around on the summit of an aerial weather-vane. They are the wits—and I love them most.

Women cannot mentally aviate at all. I make an exception of Bio. We sustain flights on Spinoza for a whole hour before breakfast, and only come down when the parcel-post man blows his whistle. Bang! We're off again into the sun lit regions of God and his modalities, free will and infinite motion.

All women, I have noted, who take flights are compelled to land almost immediately in the bog of sex—"Mrs. P. —'s first husband had a sweetheart," etc.

Mysteries of the Obvious.—While meditating in the bathroom, my eye wandered to the faucet in the bathtub and I pondered on the mystery of the water running up the pipe. I could see no pump. How does running water get to the top of the skyscrapers? What makes an automobile go? I know there is a battery inside, but how does it keep the car going? Trolley cars are another obvious mystery to me. Building a subway under the river is to me a super-miracle.

The flight of Mahomet on Al Boraak through the Seven Heavens in the thousandth part of a second is comprehensible to my imagination, but not under-river subways.

I cannot grasp the mechanical unless I translate it into imaginative terms.

Christ-Moloch.—The Christ-Golem-Moloch idea of Bio's interests me, works in me, is stewing in the oven of my skull.

Christ as a psychic ghost in the minds of a few mystics. A threadbare basis in fact. Nursed by poets, Jews and pagan reactionaries. The gradual materialization of the emotional need. The Church. Building the Monster through the centuries. Every being has contributed. Takes on diabolistic characteristics. Its destructiveness. Its victims, martyrs. Gets beyond control of its keepers, the churches. Its sadistic tendencies. Its invasion of the Orient—missionaries, consulates, Bible societies and other Christ-fakirs.

It has alter-egos—Christian Science, Mormonism and the thousand and one other slushmushgush beliefs. Then into the realm of the imaginative and future. Christ-Golem-Moloch stalks the earth finally with an independent life, slaying, martyrizing, destroying everything in its path. The degradation of the original poetic idea. "I bring not peace but a sword." Many other texts in New Testament to show how the Idea prophesied its bloody, ruthless future.

Finally, all humanity in the Christ-Golem-Moloch as atoms.

"Forty Immortals."—Yesterday (April 16th) my *Forty Immortals* appeared!

It is a magnificent looking book. I felt it and handled it all afternoon. Piled twelve copies into a taxi and rode home like a god in a chariot.

The Hardy essay is twenty-four years old! Others are of varying dates. The youngest is, I believe, the last one—on Rousseau.

No matter what the critics or the world think of it, 'tis mine own! It's the very spit and spawn of me when I wrote them. There is no longer in me the wild, ecstatic spirit that wrote them, but something else—just as valuable and valid—has taken its place, a colder, more critical, more humorous view of men and things.

Go forth into the world, my children, flower and blossom of my intellectual and emotional loins! Battle for your little place in the sun. Do not apologize for your lives! Soak your opponents on the jaw! Your Lord God is a battle-god.

I regret that James Hunker and Edgar Saltus are not alive to read them—that is my only regret.

The Evening of an Intellectual Faun.—Eddie McDermott's speak-easy bar at five P. M. Old-fashioned cocktails (rye whiskey, orange and lemon peel, ice and water) . Conversation in New York Irish with Eddie. Blows in Tom Geraghty, prancing, dancing, lovable, charming Tom. Some more motion picture re-laxationists. Taxicab to the Hotel Shelton. All happy, transfig-ured countenances. Ready for anything! "Down with the Blue-Snouts!" we sang in the taxi.

At the Shelton. A famous motion-picture actress in her room dressing for dinner. Beautiful blonde, almost nude. She should worry! Scotch. Scotch. More Scotch.

Down to Passerini's, leaving the fair "movie" star at the hotel putting on her stockings. Wine, chicken, sparkling Burgundy, brandy at Passerini's. I led them all singing the old New York airs—the songs we loved before the Southern and Western invasion of the big free city. (The near-beer sadists—may their wombs dry up and their phalluses wither in perpetuity!). I made a speech on prohibition. A poet took me home in a taxi—midnight.

Bio gives me clams and runs an ultra-violet-ray machine up and down my spine. A long, good sleep.

A white-red night!

Vacuums.—In an infinite vacuum (for visible matter compared to endless space is as eternity compared to nihility) we are all, beings and planets, rushing like hell to escape—another in-finite vacuum.

God-Plasma.—Everything has its plasma, its seed. What is the plasma of God? Nothing but the plasma, the seed, of everything else that exists: self-preservation and the will-to power. It is the secret dream, or impulse, of *being God*. It is the final goal of egoism. The idea of God is rooted in the instinct for lawless free-dom.

Tears and Sex.—Subtle meditation this morning on the sex-at-traction of tears. When the heart melts the glands begin to swell.

Anarch-Boobs.—There is a naiveté about anarchists, revolutionaries and Utopian poets which is not found at all among legislators and the Cardinals of the Vatican. No wonder Church and State smile forever and forever with that gay, knowing, Mephistophelian smile!

Five A.M.—What good is five o'clock A.M.? It is a lost hour. Six o'clock is the hour of rising for millions; those who do not rise at six rise at four. Did anybody ever get up at five in the morning? Was anyone ever born at that hour? Did you ever hear (O ladies and gentlemen of posterity!) of any one ever dying at that hour? No! not even a dog. Five o'clock fulfills neither an urban nor a rustic function. (There is a profound mystery about this bogus hour in time. But I'm too mentally lazy to prod further into it; so I leave it to you, O ladies and gentlemen of posterity!)

Don Juan and Saint Theresa.—When I was younger, in my teens and twenties, I desired to spiritualize my instincts. Now I desire to materialize my spiritual qualities. Is that regression or progression (to use the jargon of us finite termites), is it ascension or declension? I feel that it is "ascension," "progress," at least in my case (and I never speak except for myself). The more I follow my instincts the more clearly am I aware of a growing "divinization" (jargon again) of my self. (How did "spirit" and "divinity" ever become so closely associated? Why not "matter" and "divinity"?)
The unspeakable delights of perfect copulation bring me nearer to the sense of Deity than all the sensations of hallucinated fasts, renunciations and concentration. Deity is ecstasy, and instinct is the ecstasy of the body, of the ego, of power. And we intellectuals (more jargon) should ground our thought on instinct, not on "pure thought." When God becomes matter he becomes "divine." When he remains spirit, he may still be God, but he is of little importance to anyone.
I cannot help feel certain that the whole mystery, "divinity" and

Fantasia Impromptu

glory of man lie in sex and its ramifications (intuitive intellect is its highest ramification—Shakespeare, Blake, Beethoven, Whitman, etc.)

"Spiritualization" be damned! It's a form of perversion. Let us have a completer and completer, a more and more daring, a more unashamedly pagan materialization of spirit! Casanova and Don Juan are a "higher" type than Saint Theresa and Saint Francis of Assisi. The Divine Comedy of the Christ had to be written in sexual terms ("filled with the Holy Ghost," "the immaculate conception," the naked man-virgin hanging from a cross with *women* finally laying him away) to catch the crowd. "Spirit" and "matter" are, after all, two words that hold a third term, still unknown to our consciousness and speech. In Walt Whitman there was the completest union of the two qualities of which I have any knowledge. He was Pan in his completest incarnation—as yet.

The Erotic Donkey.—Satire: Adventures of a Sacred Donkey; the Donkey is, of course, Prohibition America. A good title might be "The Erotic Donkey." Or, why not jackass? (We are now the jackass of nations, of course. No one disputes that.) Something Rabelaisian, something vast, something that will cause the whole world to open its seven vent-holes and intakes so wide with convulsive laughter that Prohibition America will be blown to the four winds (flatulently speaking) of the world. I must oil up for this; but no! it will come upon me of a sudden like a vast chuckle in that marvellous region that lies between the top of the brain and the inner lining of the scalp, that blue heaven of laughter born of the clouds, the lightnings, the thunders and the suns in the brain; in that aerial hall of revelry where Gargantua, Momus, Puck and Tyl hold court on affairs human and affairs divine. For humor, too, has its Illuminati, its divine revealers and its preordained moments of incarnation. (It was right here that my wife made me go around the corner to look at an apartment, which I didn't like at all. The Illuminati of Humor have a hell of a time finding silence in this city of Vulcans, Cyclops and sand trucks. How can I go on telling myself about those great halls of laughter, those drunken Belshazzar feasts of un reason that take place between the brain and the lining of the skull when they are pounding and riveting all around me? If we could afford it, we'd rig up a place on top of the Woolworth Tower.)

But about the Donkey, or Jackass, satire—I'll leave that for another day. *"Another day!"*—in that phrase I hear the laughter of Harlequin Eternitatus.

The Palm.—There is a mystery in the palm. Those lines are heralds, manuscripts, tell-tales. Whatever is is expressed. Nothing is without meaning. And the palm is the face of the soul, as the face is the palm of the mind.

Bio has proved to me absolutely the truth of palmistry. "The Moving Finger writes, and having writ—." The Moving Finger writes not only in the palm and on the face but in the nerves, the blood, the flesh and the brain. Prophets and seers read the writing. In the nerves, the blood and the flesh are palimpsest on palimpsest. The cells are archives. We are vast libraries. "It is written," say the Orientals.

We speak of the *Author* of Life. God is a scribbler, too. We are all yellowed and very ancient parchments, sometimes quite undecipherable, sometimes quite readable.

The Daily Liar.—The modern father of lies—the telephone. You can lie over the wire and he or she cannot see your face. You can promise anything, and deny you ever said it. I hate the telephone because every time I use it I know there is a liar and a hypocrite at both ends.

Keep the fire-buckets of reason near the matchboxes of the imagination.

Fantasia Impromptu

"I Think."—"What's your business?" someone, during the war, asked Remy de Gourmont.

"I think," replied Remy.

Could any answer have been more ridiculous to Mr. Some One? Imagine that happening in America! Remy de Gourmont would have been lynched as a German spy for that answer in Los Angeles.

Why Women Read.— I saw a woman looking over "The Wit and Wisdom of Oscar Wilde" in a book-store.

She was neither looking for wit nor wisdom, but for the "forbidden", for smut.

I did not know the woman, but, I think, I generalize safely. Very few women ever read for the purpose of a mental revel, an aesthetic need or to enlarge their consciousness. They read for sexual reasons, with the whole being set for an imaginative debauch, or to read about some woman who has dared the things they have not dared. All of this is true of man also, but in a smaller percentage. The percentage of really intelligent men is probably not much greater than the percentage of really intelligent women, for intelligence is as rare as love and genius. "Brains," wit and smartness are its counterfeits.

Domesticity teaches us the joy of a night's spree.

Portrait.—He never had wronged any one. He gave all his money away to anyone who asked for it. With his ditties and dances he spread sunshine around him perpetually. He asked for nothing for himself but food and shelter. He was what is called "Christ-like." He was buried yesterday and the newspapers were full of the stories told of this great simple heart.

He was Zip, Barnum's famous What-Is-It? He was a congenital idiot. Being as a little child, he probably entered the Kingdom of Heaven immediately—this idiotic and Christ-like soul!

Incontinent Spring.—The incontinent spring has returned with its marvels and memories, and it behooves all poets and seers to introvert their sap. He who retaineth his continence in the springtime may eat his cake and have it, too.

On Fifth Avenue and in the park, the sharp, sweet tantalization of your eyes: the chimerically beautiful promises in your heavy, puckered lips: the stride in impossible gardens of bliss of your feet, O women!

To have and to hold (with an occasional delightful and enchantingly unexpected reverse-gear into Original Sin) in the springtime! The delicious courtship with my eye and my green-and-purple images of ten thousand fleeting faces! The contained pant of the blood, the burgeon of the brain, the swell and surge of desire.

Portrait.—He, a bohemian, married a woman of meticulously cleanly habits. Their apartment shone like a mirror polished with ethereal zephyrs. He was allowed to smoke only in his "den." His cigarette butts must go into silver ash-receivers. He sat on Louis XIV chairs. Drinks were served in individual lily-cups. His trousers were always creased, his collar and shirt were new each day.

Five years of this for our bohemian. He got a divorce, retired to a cellar in the village, took a bath once a month, let his trousers bag, let his shirt run to seed and tobacco juice, threw his cigarette stubs in the dishes and the coffee-pot, burnt holes in the bed and had his apartment cleansed but once a year.

He is now supremely happy. He has reverted to his primitive state. His ego flourishes again.

Wenching Hermits.—I have always admired hermits. I have always desired to become a hermit (with steam heat, bathtub, shower and inside water-closet, for why shouldn't a hermit be up-to-date like the rest of the world? Why should a hermit rough it? There is another dissociation to be made—"hermit" and "hardship").

There is something mysterious, mystical, ultimately egoistic in the hermit. He is hated and feared. Classically, he always has a watchdog at his gate, a Cerberus that guards his hell and his heaven.

The difference between a saint and a hermit is that the first draws people to him, while the second repels people. I suppose all highly individualized men are hermits (a woman hermit is unthinkable).

There are thousands of hermits moving in the millions on the streets of New York. In fact, I have always been one of them. I have seen hermits at balls and parties, and even in barrooms. The latter always drink alone and stare into the mirror on the other side of the bar for hours.

But I am only a modified hermit. My ideal would be to live a secluded life in a hermitage on a mountainside in southern Europe about twenty miles from a valley city, where from time to time I could chuck my Zarathustrian eagle and serpent and come down to the tavern and natives for a day or two, wenching at night.

"Then, Venom to thy work!"—There is a profound double-meaning in this exclamation of Hamlet's. It was not only the venom on his sword that went to the life of Claudius but all the poison in his soul was then launched at the world of mediocrities, arrivists and nunkey-donkeys. It was the final explosion of a throttled and mutilated genius, the ascension of buried superiority to the throne of the world.

I have moments—hours—when venom seethes in me as in a stupendous vat. My impotency before the granite walls of Reality thirsts for vengeance. You smug and successful literary dime-novelist, I could kill you! You triumphant lickspittle sitting on the throne of "thought" (I vomit), I could cut your heart out!

It is thus my weakness foams and rages before those who know the trick. At such times I am a character out of Dostoievsky. But then I douse myself with the fire-hose of reason and the fire-buckets of humor and all is well again, for a while, anyhow.

Ethical Garbage.—There are probably more "ethical" stupidities, more maundering verbal slobber, more Asiatic imbecilities in the New Testament than in all the other books of the world combined.

Crazy Beauty.—I am one of the Lords of Crazy Beauty.
Few are anointed; many imitate. I shall make a Tenth Muse, the Goddess of Beauty, and she shall rule the other nine. Poe and Chopin, Baudelaire and Goya, Coleridge and Francis Thompson, Liszt and Blake, Robinson Jeffers and Odilon Redon, Shakespeare and Joyce, Revelation and Cervantes, De Quincy and Laforgue, Nietzsche and Wagner, Dore and Heine—they are but a few of my twins who have stolen the wild light from the eyes of the Furies and inherited the dreams of Cassandra.
Prometheus stole his fire from heaven but we Lords of Crazy Beauty have filled our fennel-rods with fire from hell. Our beauty is infernal. We are the keepers of a strange and crack-brained music. We rise out of the pyres of dying suns. We are night-magic, and the light in us streams from crazy comets.
We are maniacs who dance our furious bacchanals in the Imagination of God!
We are the black suns of Genius!

The Seasons of Pride.—A woman has written me that the *Chameleon* has "revolutionized her moral life." I know the time when that would have been an intoxicating melody in my soul. Now "I view it with satisfaction," as a man might say in a business letter.
Pride has its seasons. The first touch of autumn has begun to yellow the leaves on that monstrous tree rooted in my sex-ducts and which flowers in my skull.

Did I corrupt the lady or raise the tide of her being by that book?

When perplexed pray to God—the author of your perplexity.

Only the Artist may enjoy his sorrows.

The Miracle Second.—I often have a feeling, lasting but a second, that I am not alive and am not dead. Is this a revelation of Eternity?

Afternoon of an Intellectual Faun.—Up at noon. Very heavy. Too much cheese the night before. Effects of indigestion on the mind, a meditation while bathing. Did a clog of cheese produce "Hamlet"? How is cheese made? Damned if I know.
Why did this meditation on cheese remind me of my round, smooth, flawless, white belly as I rubbed myself down with a Turkish towel? Probably because my belly looked like the Camembert of the night before. To me, the belly is the most beautiful part of the human body. It is seductive, smooth, pillowy, undulating, mysterious. The word belly is beautiful—a belly-sail, a bellying cloud, the bellying sound of a clarionet. The belly is mother—Mother Earth; here is something sacred, healthy, normal about it.
Breakfast. Tragic mood: cheese. I do not think Bernard Shaw eats cheese. "Do you think Calvin Coolidge can be accounted for on the ground of cheese-loving ancestors?" I asked my wife.
Went to the bank. Did some business with the thieves I am a conservative, a Republican, as my bank account grows. As it lessens I become a swaggering physical-force radical. There is no such thing as a "political belief"; there is only *I have* and *you haven't,* or vice versa, I thought as I crossed Lexington Avenue, missing by a hair being flung to Jesus by a garbage-carrying truck.

"Billy" Guard—the warhorse of the Metropolitan Opera House. When will I ever see Europe? I always ask myself this when I see that seasoned cosmopolitan. Motion picture man asked me to

make a speech at a luncheon.

Strolled up Broadway. Marvellous May sunlight. *My* New York in May. Intoxicated, step-springy. Cheese—complex gone. The Columbia Burlesquers. Pictures outside of nearly naked women very attractive. Libidinous dilatation. I went in. Seraphic eroticism on the mugs of the men. Whirling legs. Belly dances. Hip and thigh invitations. Half-negro show. Chocolate-skinned wigglers. One in particular was excessively Tahitan. With jazz band, I got a big erotic kick out of it (Strindberg's phrase came to me—"passed three weeks of erotic blessedness"). Sex is behind everything. From the navel due south the human race takes its way! Southward Ho!—*not* by Charles Kingsley.

Home through the divine evening to Bio, who said my eyes glowed with a Bethlehemic light. I told her the light was from Tahiti. I had been with the eternal secret.

Dinner. Snooze. The shades of night are falling fast, but it's sunlight in Tahiti!

All is Dung!—A dull, dark day in my soul. All veils drop. The agony of disillusion. The Gethsemane of the Stark Vision. The advance of the naked Ego against the ramparts of the Ineluctable. He advances over the bleeding body of Hope the whore and Tomorrow the liar. Dark streamers from the sun. Black stars sparkle in the heavens. Phantom generations curl and break on the sandy wastes of infinite nothingness. The gullet of my soul is dry. The dead cackle in my ear. The unborn are wailing 'gainst the implacable movement of fertilized wombs. My Dæmon urges me to do a miracle. I smoke my pipe, puffing out anarch reveries in smoke. Ennui rams its long, hairy, ashen-grey tongue in the hole in my skull where my brain was. The sidereal system dissolves in black semen. God passes in the whirlwind of my anger and chuckles. Vanity of vanities—all is dung!

All that is written, all that is thought, all that is done under the sun is sublimated eroticism.

Fantasia Impromptu

"Sublimation".—This word has crawled out of the dictionary and is coming into general use. The wand of Freud lured it out. It is a fine word, and I find myself using it constantly in my interior conversations.

There is a Prospero in each of us, and sublimation is the secret of the eternal transformation of forces, of melting down images until they become molten will-power, or the transubstantiation of erotic urge into images of ecstasy, or the eucharistic miracle of transmuting anger into guffaws, venom into irony, hate into indifference, tense inaction into practical containers.

Seated on the internal throne of my self, socketed firmly in my sun, holding the lightnings of emotion, instinct and cerebral fury in my hands, I become a sublime alchemist through the power of sublimation.

Our old friend "self-conquest" is nothing but sublimation, which is again nothing but the transformation of energy by a conscious mind into repeated acts of the will.

Sublimation really means a purifying process, to free the fine from the gross. This occurs, I believe, in every act that is willed, even when the act willed is "evil", for there is a purity in evil, as Robinson Jeffers says. But the word "sublimation" has come to have an extended meaning in the Freudian psychology. The word itself has undergone sublimation, or change of power and meaning.

Elizabeth Browning has a beautiful phrase in *Aurora Leigh*, I believe, "despair sublimed to power." That phrase has haunted me for years, and I have often made it work. This power of sublimation is almost capable of changing our character if the will is strong enough, if the centre of psychic gravity can be found in us and if we can live from it every hour in the day.

What am I? A mass of forces, with a potential God at the centre of them. Find that centre, Benjamin, and you will become a Lord of Life—not rhetorically, but *really!*

"I Say So!".—As the critical sense dominates the mind more and more emotional values lose their hold. The end is bankruptcy in a purely analytical machine.

The critic that retains his emotional values, mixes his sensibility, his fundamental prejudices with his analysis, is the greatest and most devastating of critics: Renan, Nietzsche, Montaigne, Swinburne, Huneker, Symons, Goethe, Sainte-Beuve, Mencken, for instance.

There are no "values" except personal values. The personality, the man, is the all-important thing. American criticism is mostly sterile and valueless because there are so few individuals doing critical work. Our literary critics are standardized formulas, the organized echoes of books and college professors. "I say," not "it is so," should be the motto of every writer, critic or creator. "It is so because I say so" is nearer the truth of the matter than "I say so because it is so."

What is so in a flowing, evanescent, relative universe? Nothing. Not even my own opinion is of any value except to myself, and, personally, my tongue is always in my cheek when I utter anything about anything. The nearest approach to reality that I can find in myself is my emotions, and they change from year to year.

My Insincerity.—I constantly doubt my own sincerity. No matter how emphatic I am, no matter how dogmatic I feel when defending a darling opinion or idea, no matter from what unsoundable depth of conviction my words arise, I am conscious of acting a part, of lying, of not telling the whole truth. "Liar!" some one (Oh, that mysterious Some One!) keeps chuckling in my mental ear.

This is because *only a part of me is here in the flesh, only an arc of me exists on this plane. The missing parts of me exist in another dimension, on another plane. All* of my voice, *all* of my emotions, *all* of my intellect, all of my knowledge is not acting, talking

Fantasia Impromptu

and gesticulating before you. My personality, my soul, my intelligence, my psyche shade off into unseen worlds. And it is those missing parts of me that give the lie to the visible part of me. It is my invisible half, my shadowed part, that whispers "Liar!" into my ear and gives me the uncomfortable feeling of insincerity and hypocrisy. It enables me to take all sides of all questions with equal facility. It is the basis of my satanic humor, for there may even be an interchange of planes, a manoeuvre of transubstantiation, a collapse into another dimension, or, rather, the waxing of those invisible, luminous arcs in my earthly self which sometimes gives me the air of being "possessed." It is then the oceanic guffaw roars through my soul: it is then— rare moments—that my sense of insincerity is cancelled in the cataclysmic laugh-ter of the gods and I am made *whole—and sincere!*

De Profundis.—Hell and all its strumpets, Gehenna and all its gulfs, Inferno and all its Furies have moved into our apartment: we are moving!

Hurry.—Hurry is a kind of atheism. It is disbelief in the slow, solemn rhythm of nature, of time, of events. The slow universal germination and exfoliation of things is in us. Hurry is the Chimera Imagination dragging the slow moving chariot of Life off the road, out of the rut, into the air. Look out for a crash!
Slow, contained, majestic motions are the law. You cannot hurry the big event, you cannot bulldoze the hours and the days. You cannot lash with the thongs of impatience the slow snail Time. We run ahead of ourselves (profound saying!), we jazz the rhythm of Destiny, we are the furious Hotfoot on the placid meadows of eternity. When I hurry I go backward.
So I no longer hurry. "Thy will be done!" (out of the mouth of a sceptic!—but maybe for this day only).

My Daily Dozen.—To keep the soul perpetually young; a mystic-erotic half-hour each day. This keeps me in tune with the Eternal Substance.

Rhythmic Repetition.—In my writings I have repeated myself many times, said the same things over and over. And that's all the universe does.

A Great Book.—To raise reality to the plane of gorgeous fiction has been done many times. To make a myth of reality is the mission of Art. But Sadakichi Hartmann, in *The Last Thirty Days of Christ*, has achieved the unique feat of raising a sublime and gorgeous myth to the level of a tremendous reality! He has transmuted a myth into a plausible fact. He has made, in that beautiful book, a realistic serio-comic drama out of a sombre tragedy. He has taken a "god" and made of him a man, a more difficult feat than making a god of a man. He has humanized and satirized an allegory. He has painted Christ, his disciples and his followers and the whole gallery of New Testament characters with the hand of a great master. They live, they breathe, they move as perfectly describable mysteries—even as you and I. For poetry, irony, plausibility and artistic verity I have seldom read any book that can match this. It is a lightning stroke of divination. I feel that I have been there with the "Master" and his gang of tatterdermalions.

Into Our Beards.—It is an illusion—a convenience of speech—to believe that we can ever talk to any one else or that any one is ever talking to us. We talk to ourselves. We are listening to our own tongues. We use the other person as a sounding-board, just as he uses us as one.
Although beards are no longer worn, the world still "talks into its beard." When we say anything we are the only person who really listens. The other fellow merely hears, if he does. Orators talk to themselves. Many are the ruses that I use to make A or B believe I am talking to him.

Yes and No.—I can say "yes" and "no" to almost everything in the universe. Is this a sign of "release" or senility? Is wisdom in its final form of arataxia, or acatalepsis, a form of idiocy? To see all sides of all questions and laws, moral, cosmical or social, to see the validity of all attitudes weakens my hold on life, but enlarges my consciousness.

What is life, then: consciousness or blind action? Are we most alive when taking sides or when we subside into the smiling Nirvana of indifference? Life is the sum of forces that opposes death, says De Gaultier. But what has death to do with the absence of consciousness? That normal physical action ceases at death is a matter beyond dispute: but that consciousness, or awareness, ceases has not been proven—and probably never will be.

What is life, then? I will tell you what life is, ladies and gentlemen of posterity: life is simultaneous "yes" and "no".

God's in His Heaven!.—Today, another gala day of a pessimist: a whole page in *The Times* about "Forty Immortals." The anonymous writer says things about me that are simply sublime. I am Jove; I am the greatest of all constructive critics: I am unique in the literary world; there is only one DeCasseres: a living wonder, etc.

Then came a three-column review in the *St. Louis Post-Dispatch*—laudatory to a superlative degree. Also, the same day, letters from Havelock Ellis and Jules de Gaultier.

Verily, a gala day in the life of a pessimist. And now I feel like Robert Browning when he entered the presence of God and shouted to Schopenhauer, "Hey, old sourbelly, I told you God was in his Heaven and that all was right with the world!"

Plato and Prohibition.—Does the Idea reside in Experience or Experience in the Idea?

Here is an abstract, philosophical question that the average man would not understand: he could not conceive its relation to him if he did understand it. And yet it is the most important question of the age. It is Plato versus Aristotle, dogma versus scepticism, puritanism versus tolerance, tyranny versus freedom, prohibition versus the right to drink, the divine right of a policeman's club versus my right to protect myself from his club. In a word, if an idea like Goodness, Godliness, Sobriety, Chastity, the True, the Beautiful, Duty, Obedience is eternal, immutable and from On High, then any experience of mine or yours (such as a legitimate desire for your neighbor's wife or the instinct to dodge "duty" or to get drunk or to drown your parents) becomes a sin punishable by this and that. In a word, the individual is nothing and the celestial Moloch becomes more and more. Unless experience is a "pure reflection" of the metaphysical Idea, it's of the Devil (drink, fornication, possession of "Ulysses").

But if the big Ideas reside in the guts, the maw, the bowels of human experience and evolve with it, then we have a life based on epicurean and utilitarian values.

In other words, Plato closed the saloons. Aristotle is for opening them.

Now, I am Aristotelian in the domain of practical life. I want to see the saloons open again. In the realm of pure intelligence I am, however (as, no doubt, you ladies and gentlemen of posterity have noted), somewhat of a Platonist. I am an aristocrat in the abstract, but a democrat when I leave the house and my thirst is on the lookout. You see, nothing is solid in the slipperiest of all slippery worlds. Plato and St. Paul are all right for closet hobnobbing. But when I get out I want to mount my Aristotle and Epicurus and ride them to market.

Now you will see the importance of these abstract questions, my sweethearts and friends of the coming generations: and, above all, the supreme importance to you of deciding early in life (if you are a free-willie) whether the Idea resides in Experience or whether Experience resides in the Idea.

Fantasia Impromptu

To an Exquisite Unknown.—You are reading these my words, and you dream of many things. I may be dead as you dream over this page, or I may not be. As I write these lines I do not know. But you are very beautiful, and tonight I am sentimental à la Heine, à la De Musset, à la Byron. Sweet and strong and inexorable, I possess you à la Walt Whitman. Divine, delicious woman, secret lover of my books, my poems, my ironies, I kiss thee passionately and say adieu forever à la Don Juan.

Pan the Redeemer.—We all need "redeemers." For what is a "redeemer"? A person, a vision, a lever that lifts us up higher and higher, that takes us from routine to novelty, a wing that swings us clear of habit and pain and "evil".
Irony and Art are my redeemers. Jesus is yours, or maybe Alcohol, or Nietzsche, or Socialism, or a new Ford.
Vices have a redemptive quality in a puritanical *milieu.* Love is redemptive because it is tip-to-toe tumescent and causes you to live in a Presence, Eros.
"Redeem" means to "purchase back". From what?
I have a feeling of "divine redemption" when lying on the good earth and looking into the heavens, or when sporting in the sea, or on the body of a beautiful woman, or saturated, nerves and brain, in wine.

Migrate.—If we could see the depths in us as we see the heights! My heights are clear, but my depths are clouded, misted. If I could look down as far as I look up! But may it not be that height and depth are one and the same, that the heights are the depths clarified and the depths are the heights turnd upside down?

Catalepsy?—I had a sudden consciousness today of passing, for an infinitesimal space of time, into the Present Moment. I seemed to congeal in a Now. I seemed to pass through a tiny hole in the swiftly revolving atmosphere of time into Eternity: just a pin-hole in succession and sequence.
What caused this I do not know. My bowels were normal and my

step was gay. It was a perfect day in May: the world was gorgeous. And suddenly Time divided itself like the Red Sea, and I passed into a static arc of No-Time-Land. I seemed to catch the Present Moment and held it moveless for the tenth part of a second. Catalepsy, psychologists would say. Why not? These lame words!

The Fatigued Faun.—My most powerful battle as I grow older is waged against the instinct to return to the commonplace. The race, the herd, the group, the crowd never die. "After forty we return to the tribe," said Huneker to me one day.

I began to feel the tug in the blood after fifty. There creeps up the sluiceways of consciousness subtle murmurs and fears. Maybe I've been all wrong. Common-sense is the eternal wisdom. Why be a freak? Genius is artificial. Back to the bosom of the Eternal Mother!

I must combat these lures. It is a form of fear. They are the tempters. It is the call of the soul for comfort. The tired, lonely, sea-tossed bark veers to a haven. The giant waves of my inspiration seek the Sea. It is a form of death. The planet wants to return to the sun from which it came.

But I know thee! Thou art Fatigue! I need a change. New stimulants, new titillations, new sensations will open in me new depths, new visions, new forms of my differentiation.

A little nearer, a little nearer, the engulfing shadow of race-routine creeps every day. Do as the world does: follow the crowd. But I know I cannot be conquered. Where the tide ebbs it still rises. There may be no more tidal waves in my soul, but I can still flood sterile lands and carry away a town or two while it sleeps.

This is ebb-day. I hanker after the flesh-pots. To hell with the human race! I am one of the Ten Thousand—and though we retreat, we *are* immortal! My Anabasis is not yet completed, for neither the Xenophon nor the Cyrus in me is yet dead!

To My Unborn Child.—I feel sometimes in my blood the cry of

Fantasia Impromptu

a child to be born. No, my dear spirit-cherub, not from me! I love thee too much. I have too much pity in my heart to lift thee from the sweet, soft bed of nonentity and lay thee in the gutters of existence, for this life, my little darling, is a sewer and a gutter, a cesspool. I could tell thee such tales that it were better I had not been born and had remained a subtle desire in my father's veins and a blushing but unfilled dream in my mother's.

There! I will sing thee a lullaby for the unborn that shall put thee to sleep for an aeon.

The Kernel.—The emotion that a thought gives me is more important than the truth it may enclose. In fact, my emotion in its presence is proof that it encloses the truth—and when I say the truth, I mean my truth.

The Demonology of Love.—This theme recurs again to me. I do not recall ever having read anything on the subject. Cruelty, hatred and sadism in love have been treated, but I purpose to write a book (this book, *Fantasia Impromptu*, should be called *A Book of Postponements*) which will trace the demonology of love from its physical and psychical bases.

Desire, the property instinct and egotism being the bases, root-principles of love, its whole structure is demonological. We can never love any one. All love for another is self-love. "Love thy neighbor as thyself"—what profound psychological implications are in that command! The author of that ukase knew that beyond self-love there is nothing conceivable. It was his norm. The more powerful the love-attachment to another the greater the potential fiendishness in the network of emotions.

The demon in love at puberty—ah, those first delicious sighs in the presence of or at the evocation of the image of our first girl-sweetheart!—is so heavily veiled that he is, of course, not perceptible. But with the growth of the sex-instinct and crackling of the amorous fires in the veins he drops one veil after another.

The will-to-power, the war of the sexes, courtship are all expressions of the demon in love. The demon has rare sweets for us, jewel-boxes for his Marguerites and seductive visions for his Fausts.

Sweet Demon, subtle Demon, devastating Demon, languid Demon, sadic Demon, mutilating Demon, immortal Demon, shall we bless thee or curse thee? "Both!" I hear him say as he draws with ironic fingers the veils around another couch.

The Demonology of the Imagination.—An appendix to my *History of the Human Imagination*. Great project for the decomposition of human society through the demon in the imagination: historical, psychological, physical, political. Mussolini, Lenin, Woodrow Wilson, Christ, above all. Paradoxes of faith. Ripping of masks from the faces of "Saviors."

Great imagination is satanic. My own desire to rule the planet by controlling it with miraculous powers springs from my satanic egotism and my inferiority consciousness in the presence of God. But I say to myself I desire this power to liberate man and restore the planet to the ideals of paganism. That's my moral mask. I would make mankind happier very likely but only because I was supremely powerful. Not for thee, but for me! But every "Messiah" has put it that way—"The Great I Am!"

Charles Fort in that tremendous flight of the scientific imagination, *The Book of the Damned*, says this planet has been fought for by titanic beings of another dimension many times, many times won and lost, and is now possessed by "certain parties." They own us body and soul. St. John the Divine, Blake and Charles Fort were on the track of a tremendous truth. Even the stupidities of Swedenborg contain the germ of this truth.

It is only in the demonology of the imagination that I can trace this core-desire, this root-aspiration in me, foreshadowed in *The Shadow-Eater*, that I shall some day control, either alone or with others, this planet. I feel that I am only "passing" through here in my present state for a survey. Only you few will understand. The rest will some day be my property.

The Messianic complex? Why not? Is it not more beautiful, more mirific than your complexes, O race of poor, inconsequential, burden-crushed and mountebank-weighted men and women of Earth?

Prospective Afternoon of an Intellectual Faun.—A double-header today! The Yankees have won sixteen straight and "Babe" Ruth is breaking all records to date (May 28, 1926) in the way of "homers". I'm going to root for 'em! It's a great game, baseball—and I'm strong for Ruth.

My Love.—I foster all the life-fictions that Bio has up to the point where I see they are beginning to harm her—then I smash them with an axe without mercy.

The Decade of the Demi-Nudes.—Higher and higher rises the skirt and lower and lower the cut in the dress in this nineteen-hundred and twenty-sixth year of the advent of our blessed Jesus on earth.

Exquisite legs, with their mystical curves: purple breasts like targets, with their nippled bullseyes seen through the cloth: the copulatory wiggle in back: the boy's bob, suggesting to my fiery imagination androgynous nuptials—on the avenue, in the cafes and theatres every day, ladies and gentlemen of posterity. Delightful world-dance of the demi-nudes. Great out-of-doors bordellos and seraglios.

But I am mid-Victorian: I like a *lot* of clothes to tear off them when I go to it. Treasure chests should be broken open. They cast their pearls before swine today.

Lola.—A curve, a droop of erotic wistfulness at the end of her mouth that fires the blood of men that behold her with love and pity. Wistful, sad curve of a remote pain.

What hidden dream of a Mathos, a Siegfried, a golden-haired

Launcelot has engraved that dream-heavy droop on thy lips! What secret promise of almighty white male arms, what forlorn ideal hath moulded that mouth which causes the love-breath of men to come and go in measured want?

But there is gin upon thy breath, Lola: prohibition gin upon thy breath, Lola, on thy lips that have launched a thousand sighs— and enough gin in thee to fire a world of Ephesian domes!

Christianity.—"You must obey and I shall command!"
"No! — that would be unjust, immoral!"
"Very well, then: I shall obey and you shall command."
"Ah! you have seen the Light! God be with you!"

The Eternal Outlaw.—Every attempt to unify and standardize life results in tremendous explosions and catastrophes. You cannot lock the great god Pan in a bubble.

Life Is Consciousness.—To me, life has very little to do with action. Life is consciousness with its whorls, its circles, its varieties, its depths, its heights. Not what I have done, but how much *awareness* have I?

The Snore of Ego.—I am hard to manage when under the influence of liquor, for then my ego becomes Napoleonic. I trample down everything before me. And my wife has the time of her life staunching the flow of ego and getting me to bed. And even when finally asleep I snore till the walls shake—a snore that is still the challenge of my o'er-swollen ego to the night!

A Portrait.—She is cold, calculating, pale, selfish, unpoetic and dresses virginally plain. She believes in Christ. Locked up in the absurdest dogma of modern times, she has stopped growing, if she ever grew. She will not read Shakespeare's tragedies because they are contrary to her creed. She married for money. She is incapable of love. She is a machine. She is, as you guessed, a Christian Scientist.

Fame and Sex.—"I prefer sensation to fame," writes to me a woman who has no more chance of ever becoming famous than a Methodist minister has of becoming a civilized being.

But fame, my dear lady, *is* a sensation, the sensation of immortality, the sensation of self-propagation and self-reproduction in many forms. But, of course, when a woman speaks of sensation she means only one thing—*amour*. If she has what she calls "an intellectual sensation," it is not for an idea or the dilatation of consciousness that it may breed, but it is always, vaguely or vividly, for the man who has expounded the idea. In a word, she has no "sensation of intellect" conceivable outside of the concrete image of the male who is its progenitor.

Her "aesthetic sensations" have the same base. When she esctasizes over Byron's or Shelley's poetry she is really sex-mad for Byron or Shelley. If she ecstasizes over Rodin's marbles, she wants, really, to sleep with Rodin (if alive). After he died no woman cared a damn about his work any longer.

But there are rare women of real imagination and ecstatic culture who can separate sex from a sunset. Then, again, after all, why should sex be separated from anything? May not woman be profounder in her sex culture and her blending of *amour* with all artistic creation than man?

Suggestion, then, for a brand-new school of criticism and aesthetics: How does a book, a sonata, a picture, a sunset, a statue, a building, a star, a flower, a book review affect me sexually? Croce, Brandes & Co., please take note. You are both as dull as near-beer because you have not seen the seminal basis of all art.

And as to fame, it is certainly an aesthetico-sexual sensation because it gives one a curious feeling of intellectual and emotional copulation with a vast crowd of persons.

The Jews.—When a youth I sometimes denied I was a Jew. Cowardice, fear, shame, the inferiority complex and a born dislike of Jews were some of the elements that drove me to this. I had never met cultured, intellectual Jews, the Cains, the iconoclasts, the deniers, the sappers. I was thrown among commercial Jews, and I loathed them, their broken English, their snouts, their cunning, pig-like eyes. (There is only one thing lower than the commercial Jew, and that is the American Shriner-Rotari-an-Yankee-Security League Protestant.)

As I got into my twenties I began to admit I was a Jew, but weakly and with a blond, small voice. The fear of ridicule was strong upon me. It was not until middle age, when I discovered Spinoza, Heine, Disraeli and others (damn Karl Marx, La Salle and that bunch of sentimental pseudo-thinkers!) that I boldly affirmed I was a Jew when asked—not because I am "proud of it" (the lowest form of the Jew-inferiority complex) but because it was a fact, affirmed in the same colorless way as any other fact, that I was blond, for instance, or that I got drunk for self-defensive reasons.

I belong to the outcast Jews, to the renegades. I am a collateral descendant of Spinoza. I have the irony of Heine and the cunning of Disraeli in my brain: and I would be proud to know that I am a direct descendant of that lewd buccaneer-poet, King David.

For the "age-long martyrdom" of the Jew I do not care a bundle of toilet paper. That is pure racial whine. He has not been butchered and oppressed any more than Christian has butchered and oppressed Christian.

The Jew is, and has always been (read the Old Testament), a creature of venom and hatred. I have intellectualized my venom and hatred, that is all.

Nothing more terrible to conceive (to me) than a world governed by Jews. They are clannish, intolerant, cruel, and believe they are the "Chosen People." The Jews are the fathers of pogrom, the progenitors of the Ten Commandments with their ten *thou shalt nots*. They are naturally propagandists of the ideal (their

Fantasia Impromptu

narrow tribal ideal) and they are the protagonists of all that is rotten in Protestantism. They are the priest-class *par excellence*. The Ten Commandments! An "historical necessity" I hear the chorus of Jewish nunkey-donkeys hurl at my head. Well, then, so am I an "historical necessity", and I break the Ten Commandments over the head of Moses and turn to "my people" and say unto them, "Do as thy wilt!"

A Sublime Drama.—In *Nietzsche*, Jules de Gaultier has written a sublime romance of Instinct in its eternal war against the Ideal: Biology versus herd Morality: the great God Pan flayed alive by the great god Social Necessity: the Individual versus the Religious-Political Moloch. His style is magical, limpid, flawless. The French brain is a polished mirror.

Compare De Gaultier's *Nietzsche* with Spengler's book on the decline of Western civilization (the themes of both books are the same) and you will see why it is necessary for every civilized being to be pro-French and anti-Teuton. It's a matter of style.

My Tree and Erasmus.—We have moved into the Gramercy Park section. My "den" looks out on Irving Place, where I receive vibrations from the grand bohemians that are no more and the wastrels of art and literature and wine. Huneker and O. Henry, Washington Irving and Melba ran around these corners.

I look out on an old beautiful green tree (how I love to watch the movement of the wind in the trees!). The Metropolitan Tower is my clock and its chimes give a cloistral air to the neighborhood, especially at night, when all is silent and red and green and yellow lamps light up the backs of the houses facing Irving Place. These windows with their soft lights are like the cells of monks and nuns shining in the dark. Beautiful, quiet Gramercy Park is in back of me. What lies ahead of me? Hours and years and a stream of time on which I will float (more or less serenely or peevishly) to oblivion.

As twilight falls over the city, I watch my beautiful tree waving in the summer breeze, as trees have done for cycles of time. Meditation at twilight—the highest form of action. And then I pick up Erasmus on *The Praise of Folly* and mount the gray tower of Eternity with that laughing soul.

Plans and purposes: the grotesque pumpkin lanterns of Fatality.

The Literary Gold-Diggers.—They hang on to the skirts of mon-eyed publishers like soft merde. They race up and down theatre lobbies on first nights shaking the hands and booming out the names of celebrities. They are the pick-plates at every cof-fee-house and Algonquin luncheon. They beg, they whine, they flatter, they boost.
Pathetic little knee-scraped worshippers in the Church of Irony and Pity!

The "Huck" Finn of Philosophy.—He hiked it and got "lifts" to New York to see me. He is only eighteen years old. A student of philosophy at the University of Pennsylvania. He spent the evening with us, talking Plotinus, Duns Scotus, Christ, Amiel, Spencer and Saltus.
A bright, romantic boy, to whom the Kingdom of Thought is opening before his hungry mind like the pleasure palaces of a Kubla Khan. I see the old fire, the heat, the breathless pursuit in the eye and brain of this boy that were mine at eighteen. The passion for "truth", the frenzied desire to snare God, the ravenous hunger to consume the "wisdom" of the ages, actually cannibalistic in me at that time: a eucharistic sadism to partake of the brain and vision, if not the body and the blood, of every poet, thinker, philosopher and dreamer from the beginning of recorded time to my date and day—all this confronted me again in this frail, slight boy who looked on me with awe.
But I would not be that boy of eighteen again, for youth is not a good thing for those who are youthful. Youth is never young. It believes itself to be very old. It has the assurance and finality of

dogmatic old men. The real "pleasures of youth" come to men who are youthful but no longer young, the young middle-agers between forty-five and sixty.

"Huck" Finn is an enchanting boy, but I'd rather be Jerome Coignard, and, as a matter of fact, all evening I played Jerome to this Jacques Tournebroche.

"Why Be Serious?"—Tragedy is the raw material of humor. Melancholy is the subtle, airy finger that strokes the first notes of creation on the stretched strings of the psyche. That is the reason I coddle, I exaggerate, I try to hold my tragic, solemn, dejected moods as long as I can and fly into a rage of contempt when anyone says to me, "Why so serious?" Why not serious? Ah, you smug smear in life, you are shaken to your guts at the shadow of Terror and Tragedy in my often laughing and Puck-like face with its slapstick grin? There is something gorgeous, majestic, infinite in my tragic-silent moods.

I am like a colossal inky-black cloud hovering over all of life. But in that cloud, when it bursts, will come forth stars, palaces, planets, singing and dancing houris, maniacally sublime visions and—miracle of psychic transubstantiation!—a laughing, malicious, singing, stinging DeCasseres.

Esoteric.—If you swallow your jewels you will have to recover them in your excrement.

Have Beds Souls?—I possess the bed that Edgar Saltus was born and died in. It is a magnificent old piece of Circassian walnut more than seventy-five years old, and Bio and I sleep in it as though it were the Elysian Fields. But during the night, and at times during the day, the wood in the headboard gives forth terrific and unearthly cracks, sharp as pistol shots. It is sometimes almost like a voice.

This morning while Kreisler was playing the "Chanson Arabe" on the phonograph the bed gave such a terrific and loud report that I nearly jumped. Did the vibration of the music produce a response in the *charged* (charged with the psychic essence of Saltus) atoms of the bed? Could the magnificent mind of Saltus tenant that bed for so many years without leaving its impress? Or does the spot where he was born and died hold in leash his shadow, his shade, his earth-bound envelope (if the verbal pitter-patter of Theosophists be true), and does he try to speak to me, a mental twin, a psychic twin, if ever there were one?

That there is a "soul" in all "dead" (execrable word!) things, I know, as all mystics do. And that being so, what aggregation of atomic matter would come nearer the threshold of sentient life than beds? They are the silent partners and witnesses of the whole human drama from birth to death. We are born in a bed (Christ, of course, being an odd sort of fellow, had his mother make an exception of him), we procreate in a bed, we dream passionate dreams in a bed: we pour ourselves out to our-selves and others in a bed, the profoundest and most vital parts of our silent, unrevealed self lives in a bed during deep sleeps, our sublimest dreams are conceived in beds, we talk with God and Satan in a bed, babies perform their organic functions in a bed. A bed is Gethsemane and Nirvana. It becomes impregnated with every attribute of body and soul. It is the altar of Eros and the Garden of Proserpina. The confessions of a single bed would make Dostoievsky and Rousseau mere babblers of trifles. The confessions of the beds of geniuses and of amorous women would make a tremendous legend of life.

Walls have ears, but beds have eyes. A bed is the Shakespeare, the Balzac of the home. When it "cracks" it opens its mouth to say something, but we have not the organ to apprehend bed-speech.

The Root-Passion.—In some persons I desire to inspire fear, in others I desire to inspire love. The motive is the same in both desires—the conquest of one spirit by another.

Sexual Crucifixion.—The erotic fires still burn with unabated fury in us all after ages of discipline and inhibitions, Christian "morality" and disillusion (all but the last being fuel that feeds the fires, as Mephisto and the subtle Fathers of the Church know). Eros reigns supreme over the twilight of all the gods and the snow-blankets of the saints.

In theatres, on the streets, in the subways I see on human faces either sex-strangulation or sex-satisfaction. The features of the face are etched by red-hot instruments dipped in the roaring furnace of the genitals. On the streets women are looking for It, men are pursuing It. Eros stands behind all these skyscrapers of steel and stone.

Sex-starvation, love-starvation is in back of the restless movements of the human horde, its wars, politics, finance and Utopian dreams. Lingam and Yoni are the fiery stakes to which we are strapped and crucified.

Motto for the Artist.—Whatever is is wrong but beautiful.

The Bombers.—The Artist must reverse all values. He brings not peace, but bomb and faggot. In a rotten world he is a Shelley. In Utopia he will be Satan. If there are no values to reverse, he will invent them in order to squeeze his Beauty out of impact. In Hell he is a saint. In Heaven he is a Demon.

La! La!—I just received a book catalogue from France in which one of the books listed is entitled *The Divinity of Nietzsche: Germ of a European Religion.* So soon! There is material at hand for this—his lonely life, his mountain tramps, his eventual identification with Zarathustra, his insanity. This would delight Nietzsche, I think, for his sensibility was messianic.

Saying and Hearing.—La Bruyere says everything has been said. True enough: but everything has not been heard. There is always a rising generation who know nothing of everything that has been said. Not only an eternal rising generation but millions of old men who have not heard all that has been said. There is always something new under the sun for most people because they have seen and heard very little.

Everything has been said that I have ever written, but I am saying it to ears that have never heard these every-things, especially youth. It is you, O Youth, that I seek to seduce, inflame, fascinate. You are always new, unique, like my sensibility, nay style, and my infinitesimal variation from the psychic group to which I belong.

The first poet was born in the first man who substituted court-ship for rape.

A great many men beget children with the deliberate and sole purpose of diverting the attention of their wives from them-selves and their contemplated *amours*.

Man can fulfill all of woman's needs, but woman cannot fulfill a fiftieth part of man's needs.

The Major Premise.—There is an implacable and remorseless logic in all my books and between my books. You laugh. But, remember, Young Gobbo, you do not know my major premise!

Ladies and Gentlemen of Posterity:—Whatever is taking place in the world as you read this, you will please remember that I, the greatest prophet of all time, predicted it, for did I not say last night right here in my own parlor while eight guests held their mouths and eyes and ears wide open—did I not say, slowly, plat-itudinously and sonorously: All things are possible in the future.

There is a little of the lesbian in every woman and a little of the homosexual in every man.

Exquisite Gemini.—At a private entertainment, a farrago of rot, rubbish and ruttishness, which I attended because of my epicu-rean delight in studying faces, backs, breasts, toilettes, lesbians, arty pimps, Greenwich Village pickplates, German, Russian and Czechoslovakian arteests and collegiate idealists who give ten-minute talks on "The Origins of the Art-Instinct."

My gaze roved restlessly around seeking *the* face, *the* woman, *the* impression to carry away with me as an exquisite and lascivious morsel to turn over on the palate of my mind for a day or two. I found her, a row in front of me. Accompanied by two bare-backed, boyish-bobbed, blown-out, washed-out, sexed-out women of about thirty of the you-know-what class was an exquisite young woman whose attitude was one of adoration and devotion before these two *garconnes à la mode*.

Her face dripped *amour*. Luscious, thick, half-parted lips which curled up and down like tiny waves that will never break, damp with the dew of amorous awakenings. Eyes that were frank and joyous with delights of what they had seen, wide-open eyes stuffed with youthful flesh-wonder. Two nostrils that palpitated when she talked to her androgynous lovers, nostrils that were the tell-tales of an exquisitely tempered amorous nature. A white forehead, a sylph's forehead, a forehead that needed only a mouth to whisper into the ear delicious cerebral perversities. Smooth, rounded, girlish cheeks, cheeks like two virginal breasts, in the centre of which were two delicious dimples, like inverted nipples.

From the ensemble there emanated a light, an intellectual, wide-awake, fully-aware glow that is the divine mystery of some faces: the visible aura of imaginative youth, the halation of the sun of her sex. She had that tantalizing, reticent smile which is like the faint dawn of a laugh that will never be heard.

I call her Gemini—why, I do not know: but somehow I feel that that beautiful creature's name should be Gemini.

"Literary" Success—Write to make women weep. Write to make men guffaw. But don't write to make them think.

Psycho-Erotic Portrait.—Born a Catholic. Then she went over to the High Church, the Episcopalian counterfeit of Rome. Then she became a shouting Methodist. She gave that up for Christian Science. And now she is a Theosophist. But she hasn't found her mate yet, for that is what that pale, underfed, Madonna-faced woman is really looking for.

"Free Association"—A good Freudian term for the rambling style of which Montaigne was king. "Free association" is the great literary adventure. It is the romance of the unexpected idea, image, word. It is writing without will or purpose, obeying only the common-law marriage of sensations, emotions and thoughts. It is the free-love of the brain and heart, and from it there are born the magic, fantastic, often grotesque, but always beautiful, brood of my pen.

Fame is the beauty-parlor of the dead.

Frank Harris—I once called Frank Harris in the Globe "the janitor of the latrines of genius." Today he sends me from Nice his new book, "Joan La Romee," a commonplace, uninspired play about Jeanne d'Arc. Also a letter in which there is a whine about what Sinclair Lewis, Upton Sinclair and others have said about his water-closet epic, his *Life and Letters*. He quotes to me from Heine to bolster up his uninspired filth.
Frank Harris and Heinrich Heine! Why should I comment? Just juxtapose the names, and the irony is implicit.
Harris has never interested me. He has nothing to say. He says it, though, entertainingly. I do not care for his fiction. His "Wilde" is mostly about Harris, who has the colossal egotism of the inferior man, the humorless man, the unimaginative man, the messianic nimcompoop.
Poor, pathetic Harris!—the hanger-on, the pick-plate of fame. I believe half the stuff in his interviews with celebrities is faked. He always has the manner (in his books) of a journalistic doorbell ringer, one of the pitter-patter men who pursue

celebrities, a male Hermione (Don Marquis' Hermione), one of those footmen of the eighteenth century who followed close behind Milord when he walked the streets of London and who were given the name of fart-catchers.

Harris has a sentimental attachment for Christ, Jeanne d'Arc and other paranoiacs of sadistic tendencies. It is uproariously funny the way he patronizes genius, this fussy and pompous cigarette-lighter to Oscar Wilde and boot-cleaner to Renan & Co.

He tells me in his letter that he is glad I am on *his* side against the puritanical element. On *his* side! You see, Frank has elected himself Perpetual Khan of the Imperial Order of Casanovians and Don Juanites of the Ages. And he gives *me* the accolade, decorates me in his private field privy. I am on *his* side! Gloria in Excelsis!

When Harris was the editor of *Pearson's* I sent him my *The Eternal Return*, being the journal of Christ found in a bureau-drawer of the Waldorf. He returned it through Courtenay Lemon, his assistant, with the message, substantially, that he allowed no one but himself to write on Christ. He then and there elected himself janitor of Golgotha.

He has now reached that stage, at 70, where he believes himself "crucified." Why, Frank, we geniuses are all crucified. That's part of our incorrigible will-to-grandeur. But are you sure you have been crucified, or have you just been sticking some moll's hairpins into your hams?

Afternoon of an Intellectual Faun.—Off to the country, four of us, in a car, on a June day in which the sun poured its gold over the earth like a miser suddenly turned Croesus. Through hills and past somnolent gardens to a field, a daisy-carpeted field, buried in a vast hollow that shut out all signs of human beings, their houses and their fences. Threw myself on the earth. Sopped up its mystical strength, letting myself flow out of my self back to the breeding Mother. Grass up to the waist, veritable trousers of divinity. Panharmonic ecstasy of sun, earth, trees, birds: the faint chorus of tiny earth-citizens: the entry of my body and soul into the primal, the eternal temple of man to the fanfare of millions of insects. Greetings! Welcome home! they buzzed in my ear, in my brains. They kissed, they bit my flesh in nympholeptic joy. Panaleptic ecstasy of the God of Creation. My divine shroud, the earth! The nostrils inflated with life, the flesh baked in the sun, the frenzy of Pan the ruthless!

The Stuffed Second.—The sense of eternity stuffed into a second comes at the supreme moment of amorous delight, or at that moment when Hamlet mounts the throne and utters, "The rest is silence," or at certain movements and notes in the music of Chopin and Wagner.

The face of a girl that I passed on a street in Philadelphia during my adolescence, thirty-seven years ago, nearly caused me to swoon in amorous and nostalgic ecstasy, and is still with me, will always be with me.

The sense of the eternal, or, at least, the life-lasting impression, comes on us like a flash of lightning. It is a syncope in time, in which we are face to face with the Immanent Ecstasy or the Immanent Horror.

The Colossi of Boredom, the Colossi of Rhapsody, the Colossi of Paradox.—Here are three books that I should like the leisure to do. If the magic was working in me,

The Colossi of Boredom, the men born without veils what gorgeous books they would be!*

or who have achieved psychic nakedness. Buddha, the author of "Ecclesiastes," à Kempis, Omar Khayyam, Flaubert, Amiel, Schopenhauer, Chopin, De Musset, Gautier, Byron, Leopardi, myself, among others. The creative and lyrical power of *ennui;* the sterile Elysian Fields of boredom, waiting to be sown with dragons' teeth: boredom, a vast blank page waiting for the hand of the master: boredom, an empty three-ring circus awaiting

---

*   This odd line break is found in the original.

                                   Fantasia Impromptu

the fantasies, the *grotesqueries,* the fanfares and parades of the sick men of a star: boredom, the vast stomach-pump of Titans that empties over humanity its ironic bile; boredom, the dark mother of melancholy children and buccaneers.

The Colossi of Rhapsody from Sappho to Victor Hugo and Liszt, wild-swooping eagles that disappear into flaming suns: the "possession" of Swinburne and Blake and Beethoven: the Godolepsis of Plotinus and Spinoza: the frigid-fiery frenzy of Baudelaire; the ego-ecstasy of Walt Whitman: the ethereal copulations of Shelley with heaven, earth, air, wind and the Witch of Atlas: the rhapsodical madness for crazy beauty of Heine and Poe: the Promethean rapture of Zarathustra-Nietzsche as he fertilizes with his colossal phallus a new universe.

The Colossi of Paradox from Heraclitus to Wilde and Saltus; the men who live in the folds of Brahma's brain; the dethroners of the obvious; the *saboteurs* of certainty; the match-makers of Yes and No; the treaders of frightful quicksands; the men who live on the other side of the moon; the mental bigamists who live with and reconcile all opposites; the After-Men, Charles Fort and Remy de Gourmont.

O God of Windfalls, give me the inspiration and the *moneyed leisure* to do this!

Presages of the Air.—As I wrote the above, six battle-planes in battle-formation flew over the roof with their unearthly noise of other-world Titans; visions, heralds of the dreadful things to come, of wrecked and burning cities, of maimed millions, of chants of death-in-life.

Frightful, orgiastic, sadic Man, who will ever write your epic, you miniature of Satan and God! Here they come again!—aweing my soul, putting wings on my heart, inflating my consciousness to inconceivable imaginings—you devils, you gods!

The Magic Pool.—My soul, my consciousness, a clear pool in the morning waiting for the magic of creation: waiting for the first ripple on the surface: waiting for the rise of gods and demons and fairies and visions of hermaphroditic beauty: waiting for the poem, the thought, the image, the paradox, waiting, waiting breathlessly for the magic city buried in my subconscious to rise through the still waters of being into the light of my brain, into the dimensions of my mind.

The Verlaine of New York.—How proud he was of that appellation which we gave him, "the Verlaine of New York." A poet of alcoholic fantasy and passion who does hack-work for the publishing houses between his stays in hospitals and between rotten drunks.

He has slept everywhere, in cellars, barrooms, parks, garbage dumps. He is dressed up once in a while by some person and gets on his feet temporarily. Then he crashes into the depths again. He used to send up to me while I was at work at nights on the *Herald* poems written in the business office on want-ad blanks, on the other side of which were requests for a quarter.

But whether fighting drunk or maudlin drunk, whether hungry or soup-full and brandy-full, his poet-soul always rallied to its full height and he achieved a grotesque but tottering dignity when I saluted him as "the Verlaine of New York."

These gods of the gutter, they move me profoundly: they are my people, although during my respectable and sober periods I avoid them and hate them. There is an arrant coward in my soul—a protecting angel, strange to say.

Dear Boys and Girls.—Nothing gives me more joy than to see a young girl and a young fellow in a park disappear in the depths of a hedge or a wooded clump. Oblivious of the world, of convention, of time and space, they hear only the beating of one another's hearts, these boy and girl lovers obeying the imperious call of amour.

No eye of mine shall ever follow these children, devotees of the primitive call. Were I rich I would create secret love-nests, endow beds in festal houses for the amorous pleasures of our boys and girls, who snatch, right under the noses of the moralic snouts of America, loot, love-loot.

Rain.—A steady vertical summer rain, which always brings my ale-thirst to the surface. Rain and old ale in an old tavern with a couple of ale-hearted, ale-bellied cronies. Waited on by a wench who grows more desirable, more savory as we grow drunker and drunker.

Rain, rain, dream-breeding, sweet rain, how I love to watch it from my window—and keep out of it!

My big tree has been signalling the cloudless heavens for weeks for rain, and now it stands motionless in the vertical rain, drinking in lasciviously the pelting kisses of water. Every once in a while a cluster of leaves at the top moves languidly and cloyingly as if thanking the clouds for the gift of water. What profound *satisfaction* there is in the attitude of my tree at this present moment!

It is the essence of slaked desire, the supreme sighs of mating—the leaves and the rain—finally lulled to a hushed and rapturous fulfillment. And now again there is motion, the leaves gently moving toward one another as if whispering the secrets of their ecstasy.

All life everywhere repeats the primal act. Every atom of matter, organic and inorganic (if there is such a thing as inorganic matter) seeks passionate union with some other atom. Its violent repulsions are qualities of its seeking. The metaphysical idea of *direction* is the *reve d'amour* of all things.

7 A.M.—the Metropolitan chimes are tolling 7 A.M.

Millions of eyes in the city are now slowly opening to the crash of hundreds of thousands of alarm clocks. Titanic forces are being set in motion to be expended in another day of inane energy.

Seven A.M., and the slow tolling of the bell in the tower sounds more like a death-knell than a hosannah to another day, as indeed it is, my confreres and colleagues in misery and stupidity: but it really should be hosannah! Each morning at seven o'clock the chimes in all the towers of the city should ring furiously with joy and our alarm-clocks should crash out hymns of liberation, for, my confreres and colleagues in misery and bitterness, are we not this morning one day nearer eternal rest, have we not gained a day at each seven AM. on life and its nauseous monotonies and agonies?

But now the sun smites the golden dome of my beautiful white Tower, and it seems to say to me, "Thou shalt go this daily round with me until I am no more.

There is no release until I die. You will all open your eyes billions of times at billions of seven A.M.'s to come."

My Tower, which presides over this section of New York like a sentinel in white, is not satisfied with its musical warning every hour that we have gained just sixty minutes more in our travel toward oblivion, reincarnation, immortality or whatever new form of an old swindle awaits us beyond the grave, but it reminds us every fifteen minutes with a blonde-like tinkle of its chimes that time moves forward.

The Holy Ghost.—Lying on the lounge, letting my quiescent spirit run in any direction, flap in any breeze, amble, gambol, bolt or loiter wher'er it list, there finally came to me again that poignant, that profound, that convincing, that overwhelming sense of Mystery that I tried to express in my essay called "Wonder" in *Chameleon* and which I have reiterated over and over in all my writings, and which I shall continue to iterate and reiterate until the end.

I wonder whether any human being that ever lived has had the continuous and vivid sense-of-mystery of life, the universe and being that I have had. I have found it nowhere in literature. It is implicit in Shelley, but not expressed. It is in Carlyle, probably his core-thought, or, rather, core-sense, like mine, but it is not continuous with him, else he would not have bothered with Cromwell and Frederick. Watts-Dunton, I think, wrote something called *The Renaissance of Wonder*. But in me Wonder, Mystery, has no periods: it is a continuous Presence, such as the God-Presence in Spinoza and Bio, the Space-Presence in astronomers, the Beauty-Presence in Keats, the World-Spirit Presence in Goethe, the Nirvana-Presence in the Yogi. In me it is the Mystery-Presence. All these enveloping Presences are probably different names for the same innominate Presence, generally spoken of as the Divine.

The Great Wonder, the Mystery-Presence fell upon me at puberty, and was much more powerful than sex and its lure. The fertilization of the egg in the womb by the male fluid and the gradual agglomeration of a living soul out of the "Nowhere," the sudden and tremendous miracle of leaves on a bare tree each spring rising out of a Nowhere, the mysterious marriage of finger-tips to white keys and the rise out of the Nowhere of music—these things transfixed me with awe and made me conscious of being something miraculous in a universe that is entirely miraculous in its appearances and still more so in its potentialities, in its Nowhere. The hidden becoming visible, returning again to the hidden: the continuous and eternal evocation of dimensional, sentient beings out of an undimensional and non-sentient Nowhere by some Prestidigitateur, who rubs one thing against another and produces a third—it is this Sense that envelopes me spiritually, mentally, emotionally and physically like a Breath.

And if this Mystery-Presence is not the background, the sout, the vivifying power in a book, a piece of music, a painting, a dance, a building, then these products are not Art.

The Mystery-Presence, the Wonder-Sense is the Holy Ghost of this world. And all that is are varieties of the Holy Ghost. That eternal Reality which is that Holy

Ghost is the one thing that is certain. If you have not that Mystery-Presence with You in some degree you, simply, are not alive. The one-hundred per cent materialist, scientist, physicist is not alive: he is just a piece of organic machinery, the very lowest form of the incarnation of the Holy Ghost.

Unearthing Myself.—I sometimes conduct archæological researches into myself. Under the dust and dirt and lava on which is built this magnificent city of gold and ebony and papier maché which is my conscious, every-day literary self, I find vestiges of Buddha, Sappho and Doctor Faust: phallic temples in which I prayed: hermit cells in which I lived: the remains of a supper with Petronius: slivers from the cross of Christ: comic masks that I wore in the plays of Aristophanes: tell-tales of orgiastic high-jinks in Sodom and Gomorrah: the cave in which I hid with my pal King David when he was a free-lance bandit: fragments of the altar at which I slew my brother Abel: an ale-mug which I recognize as the one I smashed over the head of Shakespeare in a drunken brawl in a London tavern: a golden girdle which I gave to Aspasia, or was it Salomé?; a pair of drawers that I saw Jezebel take off one night when the guests were gone and I was elected.

I have excavated from my depths a scroll that I wrote on the crazy kings of Macedonia: a hall of granite in which I dined with the flesh-and-blood superman who afterward became the mythical Apollo: a Chinese (Ming) crystal in which I remembered seeing my reincarnations as Spinoza, Poe and DeCasseres: a hand, well-preserved, that I recognized as my own, being at that time known as Judas Iscariot: a fairy city of some pre-Adamic kalpa in which I lived winged and tiny but with almighty vision: a mighty blonde woman who was my Martian mother, and a tomahawk which I recognized instantly as the one with which I slew, with a heart full of skin-bursting joy, twelve Massachusetts men and women who came over in the Mayflower.

Ladies and Gentlemen of Posterity: I am anxious to know what is the dominant emotion you receive from all the works (including the love-letters) that I left behind. There must be one dominant emotion to be filtered out of my mass of essays, poetry, letters, epigrams, confessions and comic contortions. Will some good, kind disciple take a vote of, say, twenty thousand of my admirers and haters and get a consensus? Was I cerebral, God-intoxicated, Satan-intoxicated, a victim of logomania, an erotic mystic, a nihilist, a Narcissan, a sublime mystic or an ecstatic Aphroditic Dionysian? Or something else? What, my dear friends, is the net emotional "kick" you get out of me in toto? Whisper the result into the air from a mountain-peak or a beer saloon—I'll hear you. I tell you I'll hear you!—I'm not dead.

"Maladie du Siecle"
All day long, said the old Mandarin,
I closed myself in my study to think.
All day long
I was aware of the telephone in the next room
Coiled there like a rattlesnake
Ready to strike.

The above is "a translation from the Chinese" by Christopher Morley. It is the finest thing ever written on the telephone, a device of Satan, but, like all devices of Satan, a blessing and a necessity.

The Redemption of Christ.—The God of the Christians is the Jehovah of the Jews deloused of human attributes. He is already disintegrating very fast, and Jehovah has long been retired. The God-conception will dissolve into its component units, which will restore the glories of Polytheism, as I prophesied years ago in *Broken Images* and the "Coda" to *Chameleon*.
I will not live to see the return of Dionysus and Aphrodite and their son Priapus, and Apollo and Demeter and Persephone

Benjamin DeCasseres   121 and Prometheus, but they already walk the heavens of my imagination and rule my destiny.

Evohé! The earth and the air., the brooks and the oceans, the thunderclouds and death are coming back resurgent and shimmering in the dawn of a millennial tomorrow.

Rooted in life, the gods cannot die. They personify fundamental principles of life, and Jesus himself, no longer a tragic myth of "spiritual redemption," will be *redeemed* by the gods that he denied, for Jesus was the Judas that betrayed Dionysus and Aphrodite and their great son Priapus to the high Priests of Philistia!

Metaphysics.—The gymnastic of the brain in the infinite.

The Witch.—Nothing bewitches me so much as the Heraclitean and Hegelian Eternal Becoming. But what is it that seeks to become, and becomes what? O ironic Witch of the World, I adore thee, dazzling witch of Brahm!

It is possible to invent stenches that do not exist in nature—Christianity inventing sins, for instance.

Democracy.—Although I have pounded the democratic experiment and have said over and over that I do not believe in it, that its premises are ridiculous, I know of nothing better. The aristocratic form of government is just as rotten. There has never been a real aristocracy, just as there has never been a real democracy. There is nothing but a straining after symbols.

All forms of government are makeshifts because the human race at any stage in its political and social evolution is a makeshift. There is nothing to do but to remain one of the inner circle of the Elect, the Artists, the closed corporation of superior men, epicureans and creators—and put money in the purse, for money is the only form of economic freedom that I know.

Shutters.—A house without shutters is like an eye without eyelids. I love to linger in front of the few old houses in New York that still have green shutters. There are a few of them left in Gramercy Park. When I pass them I feel that I am passing the last vestiges of privacy left to us.

Dignity, silence and reticence live in houses with shutters. A house with closed shutters has an air of mystery, breeds a story in my brain and evokes nostalgic, old-fashioned reveries. There is a modesty about these shuttered houses. Houses without shutters have the brazen looks of street-walkers. If I built a house in the city it would have green shutters with perfectly closing slats, so that at high noon on cloudless, sunny days, when the whole world is lighted up like an operating-room, I could produce (as I used to do when I lived on Thirty-ninth street and as Aubrey Beardsley always did) the perfect illusion of living in the night-time for a week if I so wished.

To close all shutters tight for seven days and pull down heavy black curtains within and over them place thick draperies, only emerging at night and returning before dawn, to continue the "huge and thoughtful night" within, with lamp or electric light, that would be one of my *tics* if I were wealthy. Shutters are spiritual things.

Your theme should be a mood, not a principle.

Lease-Breakers.—Christianity brought sin-consciousness into the Western world, just as Christian Science has brought disease-consciousness to full-blown vigor by, paradoxically, denying the existence of disease. To deny the existence of anything starts an inquiry into the existence or non-existence of the thing denied. Atheism—the atheism especially of some of the French Encyclopedists—brought the attention of many minds to God to whom otherwise he was just a work-a-day word.

Christianity pronounces all biological processes sins: as Jules Gaultier says, it made a healthy, sensuous world sick and then invented a lot of quack remedies, out of which Popes, priests, cardinals, ministers, archbishops and Ethical Culturists have made vast fortunes. The tragi-comedy of all this is not individual belief (with which I have no quarrel), but lies in three words— "Be it enacted." The Christian formula is, I live: therefore I sin! The pagan formula is, I sin, therefore I live!

There is no obstacle to you renting a Mansion in the Skies for your vacation in eternity: but while you are alive Mother Earth, our landlady, will not allow you to break the lease on the house you are living in. Just try it!

To My Dæmon:—My guardian angel is a dæmon, a geni, a jinn, a Genius—this familiar, this control, this alter ego has many names. Napoleon saw it as a star. It has walked with me, talked with me, kept my feet in the road it has carved out for me, protected me from suicide by ordaining the baths of alcohol that restore my Dionysian soul to colossal affirmations and has saved me from insanity by its enormous sense of humor and its fertile inventions, for its versatility is astonishing. It has worked miracles for me at moments when financial debacle has threatened me. It calls checks out of the vasty deep, and they flutter in the mail when it calls. It has always been inimical to woman, the external world, the invasion of my soul by other egos and whatever would harm my genius. It is a dazzling being, my guardian dæmon, clothed in green and gold, haughty, ironic, melancholy, orgiastic.

All that I say is out of its mouth. All that I do is done by it. My guardian dæmon is not a giant reflection of myself, an illuminated fiction of my imagination, but, rather, I am a reflection, a flesh-casing, an earth-sack of my dæmon, who is the reality, of which the visible I am the tool: and it may be that after the moment of death he will take me on to other dimensions, other forms of consciousness, other forms of mental and psychic expression.

I am thine, O my greater soul, my protector, my patron, my Light, my Truth, my mundane overseer. And I, thy son, know thy name. But that is our secret, most famous and immortal of beings!

The admiration, salutations and handshakes of two writers or artists who understand one another is the most beautiful blossom on the tree of the masculine emotional life.

"Am I Crazy?"—While in the middle of a book I often begin another book, and while in the middle of that one I begin another one, and sometimes return to the first for a chapter or two while starting a fourth book. Thus I keep my mind fully orchestrated with flutes, drums, oboes, French horns, tubas and violins. It makes crazy music sometimes, but, as you know, ladies and gentlemen of posterity, I am a devotee of the beauty that is crazy, the music that is crazy and the speculations that are crazy, which means, like all genius, I am far ahead of my time; for all that is great and new begins with a doubt even in the brain of the originator. He always asks himself, "Am I crazy?" This question is the life-preservative defense of old habit-structures against the incursion of new habit-forms.

Why is it that there is something ethereal, divine, glamorous, beatified in all forms of insanity, even organic and when the brain is really diseased? It is because the soul of things is a form of ecstatic, irrational demonism, and whatever is new and unusual in the world is born with the glamor of insane ecstasy on its face.

Ethereal Me!—All my life is a hunt for ecstasy, which is the metaphysical basis of all my other desires—money, leisure, art. They all dissolve in the will-to-ecstasy.

I am the muted harp calling perpetually for the sweep of passionate fingers, the silent piano panting for the crash of "apocalyptic thundertones," the quiescent flute waiting for the deep, slow kisses of passionate lips.

Benjamin DeCasseres

Profoundly sleeping at the heart of ecstasy is the desire for ethereality, the dumb aspiration of the soul and body to be alembicized into flame and fire and wind and rain and interplanetary sun-shafts, the frenzy of consciousness to o'erleap the boundaries of the skull and riot in Dionysian heavens and hells.

Awakening the Flame.—Ecstasy cannot be induced by an act of the will; but it can be superinduced by will. Ecstasy is of the blood, wherein all secrets reside. Silence, dreamless sleeps, frugality in eating and keeping a little alcohol in the blood always, the contemplation of beautiful nudes either in pictures or reality and the long retention of the seminal fluid are some of the means that induce ecstasy. The prolonged immersion of the brain in the idea of God, to walk across a lawn in the effulgence of a magnificent sunrise in the cool morning air, the sound of an old barrel-organ after nightfall in summertime, to put my arm around a tree, to contemplate my belly in the bath, to pass a beautiful boy and girl on the street with the glamor of puberty in their faces, to find a colossal paradox in a book or a stupendous line of poetry, to sail over the ocean in a little yacht, to look into the eye of a sweet, laughing baby, to hear Bio's voice and her laugh—a few of the things that are flame and faggot to my heart, my brain, my blood and my nerves.

The ice is on the dumbwaiter, the plumber is in the bathroom and the landlord on the telephone: Ecstasy, whereto art thou flown?

The Evening of an Intellectual Faun.—Leave the house at 8:30 with Bio for a visit to an unknown's house on East Ninth Street to meet Dr. Isaac Goldberg, the biographer of Mencken and Havelock Ellis and also a pretty good appraiser of my own work in the prints. Hostess greets us at door. She is beautiful, a white, intellectual, clearcut beauty. A face on a cameo. Beauty of sex-purity. Beauty of idealism. The beauty that catches my brain with a cold fire. The beauty that is non-sexual, non-cardiac, but that goes through my brain like a glittering dagger of polished diamonds. Beauty that smoothes out my restless nerves. The beauty of the faces of Velasquez's women (opposed to the faces of the women of Dante Gabriel Rossetti, who lure me to nympholeptic death and orgies of erotic madness) . Calm beauty of still waters and moonlit lawns. A face washed clean of passion. Edelweiss. The Seraphita-Seraphitus of Balzac.

Doctor Goldberg, middle-aged, a "regular feller", no tricks, no pose, something of a rustic air about him (Roxbury, Mass.). Enter Paul Eldridge, author of three books that skewer the human race to an Alps of frozen dung. A few miscellaneous nobodies of both sexes that Eldridge, Goldberg, Bio and I use for audience while we tune up for an evening of orchestrated hilarity; mere pieces of sandstone on which we sharpen the knives that we are going to fling at one another; honing strops for our egos.

Orange juice, chocolates, cigars, cigarettes. No matter; orange juice is just as good as wine to me when my bowels are working perfectly. Sizz! the javelin-throwing has started. Goldberg launches a shaft at me in praise of Dreiser. Bang! I fire a bullet about the lumberjack of words. Fast and furious for two hours: Napoleon, Faure, Mencken, Sadakichi Hartmann, Christ, Boston, New York, Goethe, Sinclair Lewis, Frank Harris, France, Huneker, pomp, leisure, Satan, Charlie Chaplin, Emil Jannings, realism, romanticism, Spain. Intermezzos of guffaws, giggles, mental handclasps.

Seventh inning. Stretch! Sing a bit of "The Mikado" and all compare rum-notes. Psychoanalysis: Goldberg tells us what it isn't. Bio tells them about her *The Boy of Bethlehem*. I note the reverence of women for brilliant men. I note courtesy of brilliant men when a woman talks.

Midnight. All leave, feeling better, having yawped out our egos and made a noise. Up Broadway through the night, I pondering on the fact that I am nearly *majullah*.

Damn My Ancestors!—How fascinating to me are the inspired vagabonds, the lives of dissolute genius: Verlaine, Poe, Gerard de Nerval, Baudelaire, Arthur Rimbaud, and so many others. They are so close to me that their lives affect me to tears; but I am so cultured, so civilized, so meticulous that I would probably have shunned even Verlaine and Rimbaud if I had known them, as I shun now the dirty wastrels of literature. Damn my bathtub—and clean-shirt snobbery!

Sublime Paradox.—Gerard de Nerval calls his insanity his *vita nuova!*

Flaming Age.—"The imagination makes us old," says Alfred de Vigny. But not in the sense of years, but in the sense that God and little children are very old

Recessional.—Words and thoughts, images and epigrams used to gush from me like lava and fountains of fire. Now I take a great joy in thinking of a word, a sentence, an idea; walking around it, weighing it and its parts; putting words in their exact places in a sentence like a grammarian; putting the spectroscope on them. This is a sign that the planets in my brain are cooling. There is a recession of flame and fury toward the equator of sex and the polar ice-cap has begun to form at the peak of a star or two!
The soul gets bald, like the body. Volcanoes dwindle to spouting boils. Thoughts that tore through the brain like Mazeppa lashed to the Wild Horse of Tartary become prim and perfumed princelets who amble leisurely astride their ponies in enclosed parks.
My Icarus now rests for hours in a wicker-rocking chair on stars where the landscapes are purely sentimental. My Phaeton, who used to see how close he could come to setting the Earth on fire, has now turned his fiery coursers loose to browse on daisies.
Will I be found dead with a copy of Felicia Hemans clutched to my breast?

Fantasia Impromptu

Hat Unaltered.—While the incense-bearers are marching around me, while women are swooning at my knees, while the trumpets are blowing and while the peplum of genius is being fastened on me by reviewers and friends over my *Forty Immortals* and previous works, it is good in the midst of these ceremonies to have some one throw on my head from a roof a bucket of kidney ozone. It happened this morning. I received in the mail a clipping from the Hartford *Courant*, a review of *Forty Immortals* in which that book is called "windy verbiage," "sheer effrontery," "magniloquently impertinent," "absurd," "froth and fume," "welter of turgid platitudes," "sound and fury," "foolish, pretentious book," "writes like John Cowper Powys," etc.

I am under obligations to the unknown writer in the *Courant*, and although my hair is full of odor (but unbowed) from the bucket of bladder ambrosia, there is a smile of satisfaction curling at the ends of my mouth which is my sense of proportion made visible.

I laugh at my certainties. I laugh at my uncertainties. Therefore I weep.

The Greater Fiction.—The story of Christ is, to me, greater than the religion of Christ. Triumph of Art over morality.

Pipe Dream de Luxe.—If Christ announced (through the new trans-material radio which I am perfecting) that at a certain hour he would walk down Eighth Avenue, and at the same hour on the same day Napoleon announced he would walk down Seventh Avenue, Lincoln down Sixth Avenue, Aphrodite down Fifth Avenue, Mahomet down Park Avenue, Joan of Arc down Third Avenue and the elder Pierpont Morgan down Second Avenue scattering millions of ten-dollar gold pieces, all avenues would be practically deserted except Second Avenue.

Personally, I would be sorely torn between Fifth Avenue (the promenade of Aphrodite) and Second Avenue. At the last moment I would elect Second Avenue, into which street I would go dressed in mail with suitcases and buckets, even if Shakespeare and Shelley were staging an arm-in-arm promenade down First Avenue at the same hour, with Beethoven on a truck in front of them playing on a piano the *Sonata Apassionata*.

Despair the Deliverer.—"It is necessary, above all," says Alfred de Vigny, "to annihilate hope in the heart of man. A peaceable despair, without convulsions of anger and without reproaches to heaven, is the greatest wisdom." I do not know wiser words than these. A serene despair, a radiant fatalism, has been my basic state of mind for twelve years, and always will be. With the abolition of hope, Time loses its teeth. I enter the current of Eternity. I live to loot the present moment. The ideal collapses into a luminous reality. Isis is unveiled. The Sphinx opens its mouth, pried open with the golden wand of the eternal Now.
Losing hope, I submerge myself in the mystical (and mysterious) sea of the subconscious, let myself float in its luminous and ever-changing depths, knowing that nothing is true except that which is fugacious and illusive. A serene despair is philosophical, religious and scientific. It unites Epicurus to Buddha, Spinoza to Hwdey, Omar Khayyam to Havelock Ellis, Marcus Aurelius to Anatole France.
De Vigny wrote his beautiful pensée when he was thirty-five. It was later that I reached it, forty, perhaps, when through the black clouds of my despair there suddenly burst the sun of humor. My thunders dissolved into the star-dancing guffaw of Rabelais and the murderous lightnings of my hate dissolved into soft, ironic moonlight. But, still, I am inundated ever and anon with the old tidal waves of hate and Cimmerian despair. But serenity gains.

A Thousand Ports.—I will never be popular, for I am a chameleon, a changeling, protean, universal, mentally and emotionally "as loose as ashes"; a writer of many masks. To the groundlings and nearly cultured, I am a Houdini, a mountebank, a sleight-of-hand man, a Barnum. Mariners cannot sail by my chart. My compass has a thousand needles and I am going in a thousand directions to a thousand ports simultaneously.

The heart is shame-red because it knows the brain is eternally spying into its secrets.

Thaïs the Eternal.—Man can live without love, but not without sex-gratification. The courtesan is more necessary than the sweetheart or mother type of woman. I can quite conceive of the human race reaching a point where men and women no longer want children; but I cannot conceive of the human race without its courtesans for the male and its Don Juans and Romeos for the female.

The courtesan represents, in a manner, the triumph of Art over Love. The pleasure-woman, with all her arts, her secrets, her inventions, raises the sex-principle to an art. She is the enemy of sex-routine, of the love-illusion, of the thou-shalt-beget dogma, of the broodmare (mother), of the "mystical union" rubbish.

The courtesan, the sex-adept, stems directly from the same root that Shelley, Liszt and Shakespeare stem from—the art-root, the art-ecstasy. The courtesan, and not the mother or sweetheart type, occupies the first place in the consciousness of all men except the clod. The "progress" from polygamous forms of civilization to monogamous forms of civilization finds its law of compensation in either the public or private apotheosis of the courtesan type. She is the artist of physical ecstasy. Thais and Don Juan (the male courtesan) are eternal types of reality, whereas the Madonna type is an ideal invented by the enemies of biological processes.

It has been said by sentimentalists that Don Juan seeks in all his sex adventures an "ideal woman". He is, in reality, seeking the supreme courtesan, a *summum bonum* in sex-pleasure.

The courtesan is necessary to the artist; he can do without love. The middle-class man, the non-artist, takes his courtesan-need out in "chickens", flappers, his second establishment, his secret love-nest, leg-shows, the Follies and revues.

Art and Love are at war always, and the pleasure-woman is eternal because she is as fundamental in human nature as the instinct for joy.

Love in its profoundest forms tends to the de-sexualization of the man and woman affected.

Manhattan Beach.—The Garden of Legs. Woman in all her ugliness. Washed out by sun and water. All lure gone. Just thousands of the ugly human animal, unkissable, unhugable, undesirable. Flat bellies, big bellies, skinny arms, fat arms. No mystery, no romance, no charm. All the defects of their bodies vividly brought out by the sun and water for men to jeer at and sneer at and snicker at. Stench of nudity under the spotlight of the heavens. Woman, thy name is Clothes!

Blood Books.—A book should have blood, brains, guts, brawn, phallus, backside, lungs; in a word, all the attributes and qualities of a living human being. It should be an echo, an incarnation, a psychic mirror of the writer; a palpitant organism. Most books are dead, inorganic, because there are very few living beings that are alive.

I Chortle.—Another kick in my *derriere Americain* this morning. The *Brooklyn Eagle* in an article on Edgar Saltus says, "Mr. Saltus, one fancies, was no more than the Ben DeCasseres of his day." Saltus' bed cracked with laughter. Saltus was the Ben DeCasseres of his day! Fancy that, Hedda! In the same mail two articles were returned from two magazines. But the day is not quite lost. The teller in the savings bank marked $46.99 in interest on our bankbook. I shall call this day pessimo-optimo, splitting it fifty-fifty between Momus and the demnition bow-wows.

How so many billions of married men and women live and have lived together on this planet without killing one another is to me the everlasting psychological puzzle and final proof positive of pre-established stupidity.

Feminine Portraits.—M. is a solid Jewish meal. B. is a harem woman, languid, lazy, sleepy-eyed, serpentine. F. is a cerebral flapper with an old-fashioned amorous aura about her; quite a curio in my collection. V. is a Fury that has been bewitched by a tenor; her serpents are musical eels—till the bans are pronounced. P. is the most voluptuously tired woman I have ever met. D. is idealistic gush with S.O.S. signals in her eye and a waist like a redwood tree. V. recites Paul Verlaine in the original and gets a black eye a month from her lover; legs that would damn the soul of Tommy à. Kempis. E. is hardboiled, cynical, with a lascivious bob and oblong breasts; she is reading the life and letters of Walter Hines Page. W. is Juno-high, wears flat heels, has a pug-nose, almond-eyed, and travels between Chicago and Nice with two dogs and a pimp. H. has starved herself to 108 pounds while waiting for Annie Besant to litter a brace of Christs. L. is Swedo-Parisian; grotesque courtesan out of Paul de Kock; drinks brandy and lies on the floor invitingly and bawls a nude *chanson de lit*.

Why I Write.—Why do I continue to write, write, write in spite of the fact that no one will publish my works? To see the face of my dreams and the eyes of my thoughts and the trembling lips of my melancholy. All writing is photography, positives made from negatives in the dark-rooms of the soul.

For Life.—With both hands at the bars, I stick my face through the interstices as far as I can and howl for the Turnkey, beg him to come; swear at him, plead with him to show up. While I howl and bawl and swear, faces appear at other cells, laughing at me, jeering at me, sneering at me. From still other cells there issue long peals of derisive laughter, jokes, sobs, curses, ribald songs, screams. But the corridor remains empty. The Turnkey never appears. C'est la vie!

A Grotesque.—If Europe had remained in its early fifteenth century state of mind, America would still be an undiscovered country. I would at the present time be a European going up in smoke in the grand square in Toledo for being a heretic; or, maybe, celebrating high mass to save my bacon; or playing with the rats in some Italian donjon for suggesting that the earth was round and the Pope's head was flat.

Oddities of Ma Vie Amoureuse.—Curious and subtle sex-attractions in me for beautiful pebbles, Oriental rugs, seascapes, yellow walls and polished dishpans. Copulation with color and form.

Grandeur-Madness.—We all have our dreams of grandeur—grandeur-madness, the French call it. But why madness? And if so, why not?

The fictional apparatus in us is the one thing that separates us from the animal world. When our dreams of grandeur overlap into our real life we are called mad.

I have always had my dreams of grandeur since a boy. I have seen myself rescuing people from a fire (there is always a huge crowd watching and cheering me): I have visualized myself to the point of hallucination in seeing myself man the boats at a fire at sea, holding back cowardly men (of which I probably would be one in a real disaster) at the point of a pistol. My triumphal entry into port; loud acclaim of the populace. I have seen myself riding (I am always in the cavalry) into battles, the bravest of the brave, slaughtering in the name of Anglo-French-Latin civilization. I have seen myself as a miracle-worker like Christ, bringing peace and happiness to the earth at last to the acclaim and incense of vast crowds (grandeur-dreams must always have an audience; the ego must plash in multitudes).

The grandeur-dream has always changed with the periods of my life. *The Shadow-Eater* conceives myself as the judge of God. Just now it is to assume intellectual and moral dominion over the planet on which I live.

Physically, like the rest of the race (there are no exceptions), I am a coward. Morally and mentally, I believe I am rather brave. I fear harm to my body. I welcome anything that happens to my mind, soul, psyche or what-you-will. Like Heine, I prefer a bad conscience to a toothache. Remorse is velvety. A physical pain is a cold steel. I used to have, when in my teens and early twenties, the martyr complex. I saw myself mounting the barricades and dying sword in hand (I always died in front of vast crowds and retreating followers) à la Dmitri Roudine, à la the barricades in *Les Miserables*. I saw myself being burnt for a great idea (weeping women on hills in the distance). I have died like Bazaroff, like Sebastian Van Storck. I have fasted and flogged myself like Saint Anthony (chorus of pilgrims in the distance coming to worship and picnic at my hut).

And so on until Irony was born unto me, and I saw my little life was rounded by a leer. Which has not, and never will, kill my grandeur-madness, but tempers it to artistic forms. Irony and grandeur-madness are both health-forms; both are legitimate. My will-to-grandeur is a promise of my profoundest being that someday, somewhere——.

But mounted on this enormous Chimera of nay being is Irony, with piercing eyes and sure bridle-grip. He guides my Chimera past consuming suns. He is Reason, Proportion. He is my Guardian Demon who drives the mystical car of my Imagination through grandiose and inimical heavens.

The above was inspired by a book by Henri de Régnier that I am reading, *The Heroic Illusion of Tito Bassi*. This is one of the finest books I have ever read. Here are the comedy of tragedy, the irony of illusion, the pathos, the humor, the bovarystic depths of life. It is a perfect work of art, a human allegory on a level with Don Quixote. Dear, wonderful, pathetic, ridiculous Tito Bassi! I am thee; thou art I.

Tito Bassi is the human race.

My Translation.—In moments of profound despair, when my brain becomes rolls of involuted crape and my heart is a crypt and my very life-breath has turned to thick black smoke, I inflate, idealize, etherealize my black hour with the music of pathos—Chopin, Liszt, Tschaikovsky. I rival my hell with the music of black stars, the heat of black constellations.

Deepen, enhance your melancholy with music. Make your grief world-grief, cosmic-grief. The mournful music of the masters identifies your soul with the sadness of Lucifer.

Never shall I kill my despair with joy again. It is too precious. I pile black on black, Cimmeria on Cimmeria.

My Mystical Bathtub.—Music produces in me a feeling of mental, spiritual and corporeal cleanness. The first notes of great music disperse all the dirt that I have gathered to me during kalpas of time. The pores of my brain and body and the corpuscles of my blood are rinsed by an ethereal bath-spray. I am bathing in the bathtub of the primeval universe. A sudden duster made of rainbow strands, in the hands of Zephyr, takes all the dust out of my cells with the magical quickness of the advent of Eternity. My phonograph is a great wash-rag, a shower, a fountain, a bar of magical soap. The lice in all the beards of all the Russians have no power against music.

An amusing satire may make one weep—Life, for instance.

Only the obscene can arouse us from profound fatigue.

An artist who has not venom in his nature is like Prometheus without his curses.

Hour of an I. F.—Here sits the intellectual faun in his B.V.D.'s writing because he has nothing else to do at this time. It is ten o'clock in the morning, a torrid July morning. The sun has a sickly yellow tone. The chimes in the Metropolitan Tower peel out wearily. The usual New York noises are slow in coming to life. My tree is deadly rigid. Not a breath... Why do people blush when they admit they "have written some poetry—just little things?" Do they confuse poetry with confessions of self-abuse?... The plumbers have arrived to fix the toilet... Yesterday was a red-letter day, for I discovered this in a book of Charles Morice's, which I glanced through in Brentano's: "Poetry is a bouquet laid on a Tomb." That is what I call a pistol-shot epigram; and I am going to put it in Walter's book of poems, which are to be published in a few weeks... My tree has begun to stir. I hear the bell of a scissors-grinder somewhere... The franc has fallen to two cents. Poor France! I would like to see her breed another Napoleon and exterminate her hypocritical friends; she needs her enemies. I am always pro-French. Right or wrong, France forever! She has never been wrong because her gesture is always dramatic and aesthetic . . .There's the damned 'phone!

A strong woman is generally an unhappy woman.

Je t'Adore!—I who analyze all things do not want to analyze music. I never read books about music (a book about music is like examining the digestive processes of your passionately adored sweetheart) except for the style of the writer: Huneker, Symons, Rosenfeld. I do not want to know how music is pro-duced or the values of the instruments. I don't care a damn whether what I hear is a scherzo or a rondo. About music I desire to remain in a state of total and abysmal ignorance. It is my form of Roman Catholicism. I accept it in dumb, mute, plenary faith.

Music is my eucharist: it is literally the body and blood and soul of My Lord. To study music (as a layman and non-instrtunen-talist)—what a blasphemy!

The World Is Still Healthy.—While there are no armies in the field at the present time, every country is at war. Mexico wars on the Catholic Church; Ireland wars against the De Valerist republicans; America wars against rum (this is purely a paper war): France wars on American tourists; England wars on the right of her working-people to live decenḍly; Italy wars on the individual; Russia wars on capitalism (la! la! —also bull! bull!); China wars on China; Japan wars on progressist activities, movies and cigarettes; Germany wars on herself openly and secretly on France; Sweden wars on rum (la! la!—also bull! bull! : Science wars on the coy germ; the coy germ wars on the scientist; Catholics war on Protestants; Protestants war on Catholics; the Jew wars on the rest of the world; Christian Science wars on mortal mind; mortal mind wars on Augusta Stetson; and so on and so on.

The only country, the only people, completely at peace, where there is no war of anybody against anything or anything against anybody, is Switzerland, a country that has produced in a thousand years hardly anything except a vast crowd of yodlers and waiters. Chere Switzers, *requiescat in pace!* For where there is not war there is nothing.

War is the natural state of man; peace is the laboratory wherein Mars invents new modes of war. When this healthy instinct for mutual destruction is no longer with man, then, dear Woodrow of the crocodile tears, the heart of the world will no longer break, and Little Lord Fauntleroy will ascend the throne of the world with his consort, Little Eva.

Theme.—The evolution of the erotic imagination from the caveman to Paul Verlaine. Refinement of images and symbols. Final union ("union sacrée") of the Holy Ghost with Venus. Ballet of the great Ecstatics on the Field of the Cloth of Stars.

Theme.—Evolution of Laughter. Belly-laughter, larynx-laughter, mind-laughter, cosmic-laughter. The grunt, the smile, the guffaw, the brain-tickle, the diabolical chuckle. The social grin. The philosophic smile. The chortle of God.

Rondo Capriccioso.—My wife sent me out on Third Avenue to

buy Heinz's cider vinegar and Rajah sandwich-spread. I brought home Atlantic and Pacific cider vinegar and Smitkins' sandwich spread. Boob! dub! Silence. Then: "Ain't cider vinegar cider vinegar? Ain't sandwich-spread sandwich-spread?" Boob! dub! "But what difference—" Boob! dub! Then she dressed her prettiest, I lit my cigar, and we both sat down to read D. H. Lawrence. Night fell, the moon came up; we lit the lamp. Helen's lips are drifting dust, but remember Heinz and Rajah for vinegar and sandwiches, my laddie boys!

Bleeding to Death.—My God!—time oozes out of my belly, my back, my skull. and my feet, and still fourteen of my books are not published. I hear the hurrying feet and beat of Time behind me, before me, over me, under me, and still I have not flowered. Drop, drop, drop, drip, drip, drip go the minutes into the bucket of oblivion—those minutes, my life-blood, my essence, never, never to return unto me! To die without hearing the shouts, the acclaim, the ridicule, the curses, the mockery, the fanfare! *That* is death before corruption!

"The Song Divine."—The religious silence of a midsummer Sunday afternoon. I am alone in the apartment. The Abyss of Despair, like the "gulfs" of Pascal, open in me and around me. I open the music-box. Caruso sings for me "The Song Divine," the "Stabat Mater" of Rossini, "Triste Ritorno" and "Ingemisso". I am transported to God. All my pride, hatreds are dissolved.
I understand why the faith of the emotions is mighty and will always prevail over the intellect. I understand the mighty need that gives birth to this music and these songs of spiritual translation. I respect the illusions of the millions, for I had the same sublime illusions while the marvellous voice of Caruso ripped up the flooring of my conscious self and poured cataracts of tears and religious emotion into the very foundations of my being.
How little I am when the deeps of my being open, when the bitter cry of the ages thunders at the dammed-up emotions and

carries them away like paper! How petty my judgments, my likes and dislikes, my attitudes, my egotism, my rotten arrogance, my silly individualism before the almighty scream for help that goes up from my soul, in choral union with all who have lived and died, to the throne of God! We are a nothing in the tempests of His will. He can only be reached through the emotional life, through the humility of music, through the dethronement of the ego.

There are only two forms of atheism: dislike of music and dislike of poetry.

Mother-Earth has just one ideal: the phallus.

With me, to take off my clothes—even my overcoat—is an erotic gesture.

Books à la Cart.—I have friends who buy and read every current book about which the publishers and the reviewers make a noise. It is just as if I bought the whole cart of vegetables from our Billy the Huckster every time I heard his bawling under the window.

America will not be free until it rubs out the national motto, *E Pluribus Unum,* and puts in its place the annunciation of its greatest son, *"Great God! I see no sin in fornication!"*

Popular Bunk.—Idealism, idealist—something spiritual, good, clean. Remember, Nero was an idealist; so was Torquemada. So is Mussolini. An idealist is either a thug or a soggy sniveller.

Smash It All!—D. H. Lawrence is right. Let us get back to the dugs of things. Let us smash up everything except the elementals, which cannot be smashed. Come on, let us smash up everything material we've made—our machinery, our civilization, our moralities, our ideals, our sciences. Afraid? Well, that's just why it all ought to be smashed—because "we are afraid." That's why I'd smash it all—just because it has made you and me afraid to part with it!

The Seraphic Mephisto.—George Bernard Shaw was seventy yesterday. Vegetarian, puritan, non-drinker, non-smoker, non-girly, he is the freak of the world of letters. He has a witty, paradoxical brain screwed on a pious Christian-Socialist soul. His artificial intellect saved him from being an evangelical Red or one of the stinking breed of Moody and Sankey. He has given me hours of the most unalloyed pleasure. But when I read his Socialistic, humanitarian, international, workingman's slop, the only thing that prevents me from vomiting is the amusing paradoxes he employs in his arguments and rantings.

Morning of an Intellectual Faun.—Bath at seven-thirty. Meditation: Has a man with hair on his chest more sex-vigor than one who has none? Why is hair a revealer of sex? The Greek Gods always look as hairless as the tip of Pike's Peak. And they were notorious at sexual leapfrog. Hairy saints. Cold but hairy women. Was Casanova hairy? Well, so was Christ. Tub running over—just in time! Shave. A wild hair. Sudden pause —why not a series of love-letters between Mary Magdalen and Jesus? I let out a bawl. That's a great idea! What an exposé! What a study of psychoanalysis! With my many-sided genius, I could play it from any angle—romantic, confessional, erotic, humorous, reverent, messianic. Colossal thought! Damn that wild hair! A little blood flows. I *must* do those letters! Private subscription. Twenty dollars a copy. Leisure—when will I have it? Mental leisure. Must make household expenses. Shall I go back to motion-picture titling? Ugh! But I need money and leisure! Choice of three talcum powders. "Dance of the Goblins" while I dress. Gerard de Nerval was a great genius. Hanged himself in the street. Tears on my heart. Breakfast. Wife: "What do you think of Mexico?" Me: "Hope they clean out all the churches. Good Job! Hurrah for Plutarcho Calles! Turn the hose on the priests—they can't stand water. Wife laughs out loud. Bell. Janitor with plumbers.

A leak below. Well, if they rip up the bathroom, where do we go? Tree looks fine. It says "good morning" to me. The same to you, my fine fellow. Letters. One from George Jean Nathan, the only man with courage and brains writing about the drama. I wrap up a presentation copy of "Forty Immortals" for him. Wife begins to type my story of Hollywood for the Tribune. Fifty bucks, if it doesn't come back. 'Phoned Tom Geraghty to find out whether a certain scenario editor was male or female. "Co-educational", came back the answer. Good old Tom! A profound answer, if you get what I mean. "Psalms of King Booze" back from Vanity Fair. Another week gone. It seems like a day. Soon a week will be like an hour, a month like a week and a year like a month. And at the end my whole life will be like a minute of consciousness in an eternal night. Bite my pencil and scratch my leg. Heigh-ho!—it's noon. I'll read "Othello."

If you have no ideas, beware of your tenses and your grammar.

Meditations of an Intellectual Faun.—Twilight—Sunday evening—Silence like a seduction in a church—Puff, puff at my cigar—Necromancy, for on the sill of my window stand, suddenly, Columbine, Ariel, Pierrot and Caliban; they smile at me and vanish; but their eyes said to me, "Kick the bucket, Ben, and join us for a radiant year in the ethereal interstices of Time with Prospero"—Paul Bourget on the Goncourt brothers; superb essay—Balzac looks as though he never took exercise—Don Quixote was a great walker—I see Blake sitting stark naked under my tree; he is talking to himself. Himself? No. He parleys with God. I hope no one calls. I was drunk last night, and feel sleepy now. Yes, my dear, D. H. Lawrence must have gone through hell with women. He looks as if they had gnawed him to a shadow—Met John Russell last night at the Players. Great short-story writer; looks prosperous—It's midnight in Paris—Will I ever get there? —Yawn, yawn, yawn—"Drill ye tarriers, drill!"—darkness—Cigar is out.

Vox Dei, Vox Populi.—Literature is just this: to say something in print that everyone else has thought of and in a manner that every one else wishes he could say it. There is no such thing as a unique experience. Men who are the slaves of the remotest and most unusual moods (Poe, Baudelaire, Joyce, Blake) find instantly their mood re-echoed in thousands of beings. The extreme individualist is only a brain and a tongue or a pen that dares. There is the seed of universality in every "original" genius. There is in the foreground of his consciousness what is in the background of every one—or at least thousands, maybe millions, of others.

There is nothing "original" in me. I am merely one of your potencies, one of your latencies. I am tombed in you, and you are expressed in me.

Enchant Me!—All knowledge should be a form of white magic. I do not want to know; I want to be enchanted. Unless Science carries the wand of Prospero or the lamp of Aladdin in its hand, it is of no interest to me.

After Reading My "Black Suns".—My books—my poems, my prose, my satires, my epigrams, my fiction, my pensées, my fables, my essays—are a gigantic melting-pot of all ideas, of all systems, of all dreams, of all ideals. Black arrows soaked in vitriol aimed at optimist and pessimist alike. A torrential spew of ideas from my burst belly-brain. I am not the "malady of the age," but the malady of the ages. I am a dirk in the veil of Time. I am the Crazy Beauty of Lucifer and Israfel.

August 12, 1926, 4 A.M.—At this hour forty-five years ago there was born into the world Walter DeCasseres, poet, seer, nihilist and one of Nature's terrible apparitions. My father awakened us (my sister and myself) and brought us down to the second floor, the bedroom of my mother, at about four thirty o'clock. I heard a squalling in the sheets, saw something very tiny and saw my mother smile wanly at us in the dim gaslight. "You have a little brother, children," my father said to us.

It was all very awe-inspiring and mysterious to me. After all these years the whole scene remains vividly in my mind. And now, Walter, on your forty-fifth birthday and twenty-six years after your death, Fame comes to lay a bouquet on your bosom. You are to be "The Sublime Boy." Your poems, fragile mementos of your life in this pit of hell, are about to be published and sent broadcast.

It may have been, Walter, that you have urged this thing through me, for you are Essence now and would naturally gravitate toward me for expression. The irony of it, Walter! Consciously you know nothing of the fame (ephemeral or not, I do not know) that comes to you long after your death. But irony and paradox are the law of life, Walter.

Something awoke me from sleep at three A. M. this morning and compelled me to get up and write this. There are impulses and memories in the soul which seem to be incarnations. Did you awake me, Walter? Do you preserve a life, a consciousness through me? Strange and tremendous things are at work in me. We are two, Walter. I am two, thee and me. I carry you with me to the end of my earthly career—and you, Sublime Boy, are not "dead" until I breathe my last.

To-day you enter your forty-fifth year, the year of your fame. You would have desired what I have done for you in the publication of your poems, although at the depth of the tears of your joyous surprise I see the sparkle of the ironic smile that comes only to the lips of God and genius.

The Big Boys.—Spinoza is the only thinker that I accept one hundred per cent. I take over eighty per cent of Nietzsche (this varies—sometimes I accept him one hundred per cent. His exaggerations about "cruelty" and "evil" are not to be taken literally, but as excess emotional baggage). Schopenhauer I accept in the same degree as Nietzsche. One supplements the other. Buddha I accept one hundred per cent. Buddha, Epicurus, Spinoza, Emerson, Nietzsche, Schopenhauer, De Gaultier and Walt Whitman (whom I accept as a poet one hundred per cent and as a seer and prophet about eighty per cent) are all ye need to know in the realms of thought. They are the great liberators.

Spinoza was mathematical illumination. He reached the Nth dimension of tolerance. His sun is in the meridian after nearly three hundred years. A great work is to be done by some one who will get his work before the world in popular form. But pure thought, "philosophy", has very little influence on human history. The great thinkers are for the cultured few, the aristocracy of the race. It might, on second thought, be a good thing to keep the books of the Intellectual Kings from the public as the Catholic Church forbade the reading of the Bible. The people twist, deform and vulgarize all sublimities. My instinct is snobbish in this regard. I stand for my spiritual class, for my esoteric and hereditary privileges.

The Sleeping Prospero.—Sleep, its nature, depth or lightness, determines the quality of my mornings. Sometimes my mor-ings are clear, quiescent, limpid mentally and physically, like a flawless, cloudless sky on a winter's day. Sometimes they are nervous, crabbed morose, venomous, as though the night had tossed a nest of tarantulas out of the depths into my brain, veins and heart-ventricles. Sometimes they are erotic, lascivious, evocative of the nudes of Rubens, the obscenities of Rops, the delicious tease of a ballet of hips and hams. Sometimes they are suicidal, carrying with them, until I get out of doors, the desire to extinguish myself immediately. Sometimes these mornings are playful, dancing, mischievous; Puck and Tyl are in my brain, my heart laughs a wanton, pizzicato laugh at all things, and I desire to do what Gargantua gayly did from a roof—all over the world. Sometimes my mornings are full of will and audacity; sometimes they are will-less and flabby; sometimes I could conquer the world in an hour; sometimes I roar and rant because I have lost my collar-button.

Sleep, digestive processes and the bank-account are the causes of these variant mornings. I half believe, though, that the psyche in deep sleeps goes elsewhere and participates in ethereal romances of pure thought, or joins the bacchantes in wild vinous and erotic revels—sometimes linking itself with Pure Spirit, sometimes visiting the hells of lost dreams, where it participates in the revels of erotic and intellectual ecstasy, of which our *amours* and philosophical speculations here on earth are merely the preludes—or memories.

The child is an artist. He descends to a species of death when he begins to reason.

"World-Strangeness".—The difference between the public and the genius, between the crowd and the individual, between the philistine and the artist is the difference between the familiar and the unfamiliar. In plays, books, motion pictures, paintings and ideas the crowd will show interest only in what is familiar, what they can instantly recognize. Recognition is their touch-stone. Opposed to them is genius, the artist, the individual, who pursues the unfamiliar, whose craving is for the thing not yet seen, not yet felt, not yet apprehended, not yet experienced.

What I do not recognize sets up great throes of joy in my soul. When I come across the unfamiliar, the new, the novel—especially if it destroys something familiar and iterant in my mind—I experience the lover's thrill. I want to be thrown off of my feet of certainties all the time. Hence I wait perpetually on the borderlands of the brain for the hourly rendezvous with the Goddess of the Unfamiliar.

Between me and the world around me is the impassable abyss of the division of the race into those who seek recognition and those who seek the strange. To me, even the familiar is unfamiliar, for I have lived in this world for fifty-three years, and it is all strange, all unrecognizable, a house wherein I feel *persona non grata*, a place *where I have never been before.* *"World-strangeness"* William Watson calls it in one of his most beautifully and least-known poems. *Least known* of course! Because "world-strangeness" is the least popular and least known of experiences.

The Craig Gesture.—Last night at the theatre all we men applauded when Craig smashed a rare ornament to a thousand bits on the floor of his wife's sacred drawing-room to show that a man is greater than a thing. We husbands all applauded the Craig gesture, but would any of us, in a declaration of freedom, dare to do the same? Still, that was the great moment in the play and a highly symbolic moment historically, psychologically and socially. It is a good thing for peoples, races and individuals to grab, every little while, a sacred or "priceless" ornament from the place where it is worshipped and dusted and petted and hurl it to the floor. It makes us all feel better, as it did Craig when he opened fire on his wife by smashing her pet ornament.

I've got more stones in my pocket at the present time than there are glass-houses in the world. When anything gets a heavy hold on you, your God, your wife, your mother, your business, your pet idea—smash it! Make the Craig gesture! Once a year, walk to some sacred place in your skull, your heart, your house—or the bar-room—and hurl some sacred ornament to the floor. It is good blood-letting.

Make the Craig gesture—and make it often!

The "Aesthetics" of an Intellectual Faun.—Has an intellectual faun, like myself, an "aesthetic"? What is an "aesthetic", anyhow? Benedetto Croce would say it is a theory of beauty". What a detestable Germanic term—"theory of beauty"! Still, there are moments when I step out of my magic world of dreams and ideas and images, stand aside on the ice-cap of my brain and try to dissect the Beauty miracle. With the result that after some pondering I have no theory, unless it be: the one I borrowed from Plato and built on—that Beauty is an immanent evolving, eternal Idea of the Essence.

My theory, as a faun, is implicit in my work, as Rodin's "theory of beauty" is implicit in his marbles and bronzes. Beauty is not composed of images; images are a quality of Beauty. It is not wholly color; color is a quality of Beauty. It is not "expression" (as Croce says), but expression is a quality of Beauty.

Beauty is to a faun like myself any manifestation of the immanent and eternal Ecstasy. Where there is Beauty there must be Ecstasy. Its individual form is determined by the sensibility of the instrument that it floods. Beauty is Ecstasy and Ecstasy is Beauty, and in a faun like me it takes prankish forms, deadly forms, Apollonian forms, Dionysian forms, erotic forms, mathematical forms, intellectual forms, sadistic forms, childlike forms. But it is all Ecstasy. And my soul is one prolonged flood of ecstasy that pounds the keyboard of the stars and carouses with the succubae in hell.

I am Narcissus, and I have never beheld anything more startlingly gorgeous than my own soul in the mirror of my consciousness. It is true of all humans in varying degrees; each one is in love with his own soul. Each one of you, ladies and gentlemen, is a Narcissus. But you admit it only privately and blushingly and whisperingly to yourselves. I say it out loud, which, after all, may be the only difference between us: I am a Voice and you are a blushing hypocrite. You are afraid of the word "Narcissus". I use it and affirm it boldly. It is the profoundest myth of the ancients. We reject everything except that which reflects our own image. It is the philosophy of the eternal Ego.

So my aesthetic is, finally, Narcissan Ecstasy. And it is yours also, you crimson-mantling hypocrites!

It was Nietzsche who "killed God" and then closed his eyelids with the golden pennies of his epigrams.

The Housebroken Faun.—I am now developing my finer household instincts. I was a bohemian before marriage, and it has taken seven years to housebreak me. I sweep the crumbs off of the table. I dry the dishes. I pick up papers from the floor. I empty my own ashtrays. I am refining myself into the Thoughtful Husband. These things do not come naturally to a genius, one like myself especially, whose whole life is psychical and cerebral. But I find quite a new joy in helping to keep house. I can think and meditate while I'm washing a saucer. The action of the arms stirs up the blood in the brain.

Besides, these thoughful niceties of mine pave the way beautifully for a night out with the rowdies (how I love them!— Evohé! you midnight rascals and taxi-burning souses!), which is necessary for my health once a week, although I cannot make my dear wife believe it. So I ease myself out by helping to keep house.

Woman!—but Down with the Female!—I am the most bitter and militant anti-feminist it is possible to conceive. I am pro-woman, but anti-feminist. A woman is one thing, a female is another. A woman is the part of the female I love; a female is the part of a woman I hate. I bring no judgment. The female is a natural product, like boa-constrictors, vampires (if any) and insane devils. I bring no judgment, because I do not approach a serpent or a destroyer of my life of any kind with reason. I bring no judgment—I bring a sword, or a deadly vermin exterminator. Now, the tragedy that all real men most confront, and, above all, the artist, is this: Woman is disappearing and the Female advances. Not in the sense in which Huneker exclaimed, "Lo! the lesbians, their sterile sex advancing!" No. More power to the lesbians! They will kill off one another, and as to their sterility, more power to their barrenness! I would like to see reproduction cease for fifty years, if not forever. Not the lesbian as the lesbian, but the lesbian as female concerns me. The lesbian is only a small detail in the tragedy of the conquering Female. Woman is disappearing, and the Female—the enemy of man, the tarantulas of the Medusæ—advances!

This world is a man's world, and rather than see man abdicate to the female I would lead a general slaughter of females even if it necessitated men becoming homosexual until we could replenish the earth with real women again—women of whom we are the masters, women who love to be mastered, women who will develop their womanhood along biological lines, women who will stick to their own domains as men must do to theirs.

But maybe I exaggerate the menace. It is a passing phenomenon, maybe, this attempt of the female to supplant men, to dominate us, to upset and transvalue all biological values (like the lunacy of Lenin in the economic sphere). Nature knows her work. She will send forth a strong race of men to clean house. Her Generics and Attilas will never die.

I kiss the heart of Woman while I plant a *dagger* in the breast of the Female!

Exposed Roots.—Patriotism—the real thing—is sane and healthy because it is egotistic. "Internationalism" is stupid, anti-biological and unhealthy because it is altruistic, hence hypocritical and sentimental. Whatever is egotistic is anti-sentimental. Whatever is egotistic is right, even when it is "ethically" wrong.

I am a Latin patriot, although born in America. I am Mediterranean. I am a patriotic Frenchman, although there is no French blood in me. There is such a thing as psychic patriotism. You *must* belong to some country, some race, some region. You will know where you belong—where your patriotism belongs—when a war breaks out. And it is impossible to hide your sympathies. You cannot hide your country.

It Was My War!—I am not a product of the war. The war was a product of me. I needed verification for my cosmic pessimism and my proclamation of universal evil, and his Satanic Majesty, God, answered my need with the deviltries and inutility of the World War. My most pessimistic books were written before the war (with the exception of "The Litanies of Negation"), and I naturally took a certain amount of cynical pride in that event. But every pessimist and nihilist can prove his case with facts if he waits long enough, while the optimist whether he waits for a day or forever has merely the pleasure (or pain) of watching his ears grow.

Mirrors and Bobsleds.—There is about as much "local color" or "human interest" in my greatest writings as there is in an earthquake or a comet hitting the Earth. Two or three of my books are understandable by the crowd. If any one looks in a mirror long enough he will see a jackass. Those two or three of my books are mirrors. The others are for bobsledding over the polecaps of the universe.

Romance and Realism.—Everything I do is romantic, for romance is my reality; and all forms of reality are to me romantic. And that's all there is to "romance" and "realism", the Romantic School and the Realistic School. They are one and the same thing. Zola was a romantic; Cabell is a realist.
Reality is my special reaction to anything. A botanist who minutely describes a plant is romancing about it. Science is all romance; fiction is all reality. At bottom all is romance—and that is the Great Reality. They blend at every point. Shakespeare is the greatest artist that ever lived because he, more than any other artist, made Romance and Reality one thing.

Early Mass of an Intellectual Faun.—I can, again, divide the human race into two classes: the Illuminati and the Illiterati. The only point of contact of both divisions is their common eroticism. The eroticism of the Illiterati takes its highest flight in the sex magazines. The highest erotic flights of the Illuminati are co-equal with the highest flights of the imagination and pure intellect. Those lines from Shakespeare, one of the Erotic Illuminati, have always stuck in my head:
"So Lust unto a radiant angel linked

Will sate itself on a celestial bed
And prey on garbage."
I may not have the quotation exact (damn looking things up!—the spirit's the thing), but it is an example of a tremen-dous flight of the imagination of one of the Erotic Illuminati.

The erotic imagination of the Illiterati always has something of the water-closet and the sex organs about it: Frank Harris is an example, although Harris is not one of the Illiterati but is vulgarly erotic. The Erotic Illuminati may indulge in vulgar images at will (all things are permitted the imaginative gods), but the Illiterati have no wings—only at best a flying mattress or a flying hayrick.

I think that all the motions of suns and planets in the cosmos are caused by the measured love-embraces of super-beings. As the intellect evolved on other and higher planes these embraces would tend to become more and more conscious, measured and prolonged.

The ether may be a colossal, measureless bed.

Noli Me Tangere!—I have the feeling that when I am in the presence of or in the same house or room with another human being I am only half of myself. Something is missing in me phys-ically and psychically. I am being absorbed by another soul. I am not co-ordinated, completely integrated, whole. The minute I am alone, completely and wholly alone, some-thing flows back into me that belongs to me and was other-where. I become gay, buoyant, productive, creative. Even when in despair I feel it is *my* despair when alone. When anyone else is present, I must di-vide my sadness, which is ridiculous, humiliating.

Liberty and solitude are synonyms. Slavery and crowds are synonyms. The artist should have no family, no children; only places and persons to visit at will when the gregarious and social instinct floods him. He should be a hermit king who selects his hours when he will give audience, selects whom he will receive or visit, and be perfect master of his hours and days of amorous and vinous recreation.

Ah! If we artists only had the courage—and the power—of Big Business thugs, diplomatists, military commanders and other species of garbage to insist insolently, snobbishly, sublimely, brutally on the sacredness of our ego and our time.

We *are* "holier than thou", you tenders of the stink-pots of the world! And our motto should be *Noli me Tangere!*

Temperament and insolence; vice, perversity and excess—the soil of genius.

A Portrait of a Lady.—She had been away for four days in the country. Husband left behind to grind out something. A good hubby. She stepped out of the taxi laden with flowers, radiant, overflowing with laughter and gayety. Her dimples were deeper than usual. There was amor in her eye, her step, in the "Hello! Hello!" in her voice. Madame had had a "moral holiday". She had slept well and wisely.

Hubby hatless, solemn, carried her grips up the stairs. She burbled, gurgled all the way up. I followed. Youth, new youth; in her rear prodigious horns on hubby.

Ah! Madame, thou hast thy secret, but not hidden from the eye of me peeping and ironical intellectual faun.

Huneker Anecdote.—One night "Jim" Huneker and I were sitting in "Jack's" trying to break the seidel-drinking record (how we could lap up the beer in those ambrosial days!). I told Jim that the night before Murray Schloss (a bore of a Socialist and an arty culture hound of the Los Angeles type) had said that Kipling was a far greater poet than Swinburne.

Jim's gray eyes flashed as he said to me:
"Didn't you smash him in the jaw?"

Ladies and Gentlemen of Posterity: I'd really like to get a peep at some of my biographies. Those of you who are reading this forty years from now (1926) know of course that there are three or four of them.

Are they still doing biographies á la Lytton Strachey or have they gone back to the classic style of Brandes? I suppose my biographies would rather amuse me. Various styles, various points of view, various "explanations", psychoanalyses and all the other stupidities.

Then, the hundreds of articles that must have been written after my death—DeCasseres the cynic, DeCasseres the mystic, DeCasseres the poet, DeCasseres the nihilist, DeCasseres the erotic Narcissan (the Stuart Shermans, Paul Elmer Mores and the other critical nunkey-donkeys let themselves loose on the "erotic Narcissan", I'll wager my urn-full of ashes to your Aunt Tillie's womb-shield!)—DeCasseres the *prosateur,* DeCasseres the "God-intoxicated", DeCasseres the "Satan-intoxicated", DeCasseres the "word-drunkard", DeCasseres the egoist (or egotist—now, I'll bet they did themselves proud on that score!), DeCasseres the lover, DeCasseres the souse, DeCasseres the-the-the-the-the—

Is there a statue or a bust of me somewhere? (I hope you haven't forgotten Walt Whitman, ladies and gentlemen of posterity. Thirty-seven years after his death there is no statue to the grand old man.) I have noticed that dogs make a specialty of statues, so you will please put me at a height no dog, however ambitious, can reach.

I am really not "kidding" (does that word still live in 1975? I like slang) fame or posterity, for I desire that the best of my work shall live and influence you. But I am curious about post-mortem things, and you, you know, are my coroner's jury.

Be soft and live humbly if you want to learn something about the human race.

The Amours of the Eye.—One of the greatest pleasures to the dilettantes of love is the amour of the eye. In the street, in the subways, in the theatres, in evening companies there is perpetual and thrilling eye-suction between the sexes.

I have delighted in this for years. What delightful messages flit from brown eyes to brown eyes, from blue eyes to blue eyes! Sudden glances that interlock at corner turnings in the street. Sudden secrets flashed from soul to soul. The quick parry and thrust of images and dreams. the *amours* of the eye! Intoxicating game—exquisite sport!

Le Jour de l'Amour.— I read today that in the next war subtle, rather sweet-smelling gases will flow over whole cities from radio-directed airplanes that will put, to death millions very gently. So seize your women quickly, my buckos! It is not far away, this Age of Satan. You know what you'll want above all things for the sweet, quiet voyage into No-Man's Land. Pick 'em out now!

Nirvana is simply the mentalization of the sex-climax.

Everything points to the incarnation of a new God. Let him look to it that his doctrines fit in with Big Business.

The Drink Sublime.—How well I understand the youth of Coleridge—his swooning in abstractions, his ascension and abiding in Eternal Ideas, his transmutation from the real to the ethereal!

When a boy, I used to collapse suddenly, without warning, into the abstract and remain there for five and ten minutes, then take up again what I was doing. It was a form of catalepsy, a profound, objectless revery. I held my breath in the Infinite. It was the ecstasy of total equilibration. Sweet seizure, divine immersion! Rarely comest thou now! My soul lies open to too many influences. I am split into a million bits. I need the insulation of the Infinite, the aegis of the hypostatic union, more than ever.

I have a demon in me; but I do not want to suppress it. I want to express it. That's the difference between me and a Christian.

The Family Photograph.—When you are entirely "different" from the rest of your family, there begins a contest as to whom you look like. He (or she) *must* look like some one—like uncle, like aunt, like papa, like mama, like cousin Lightstonesn or Aunt Roundbottom. It is simply inconceivable that you should look like yourself. "He's one of us, by God!—and he's going to look like one of us if we have to fake the resemblance!" It begins with the baby. See how much he resembles his uncle Flathead! The comedy of the tribe, of the family trying to hog-tie you to them!

Morning of an Intellectual Faun.—Paid the gas-bill. Began my article on Spinoza. Killed a mosquito on my hand. Second paragraph of Spinoza. Mind drifting. God! how exquisite her ankles were! Did I pay for the papers for last month? Should write a letter to Don Marquis. Spinoza the God-cataleptic. What about Blake and Arthur B. Davies? Dog barks in neighboring yard. Gorgeous day—the Yankees still winning. But I really ought to be writing that sketch of Cabell for Mencken. Put Spinoza aside. Read a bit of De Musset. Noon. Eddy McDermott has a new grade of beer. What is the favorite drink of Mephisto? I'll go to the club. My article on the French debt created a hell of an uproar. I am abused. Ha! Ha! also Ho! Ho! Got their goats! No, I'll drowse and dream of dryads and fauns and the gunmen of Chicago. The vegetable man. Another manuscript back. Now, I lay me down to sleep, and if I should die before I wake—but I won't! Too damn healthy. Racca on everything!

I may die just in time to salute my dawn.

The Prospero of Anarchs.—Perfect liberty can only be attained by one man on an uninhabited island, and even there his privacy will soon be invaded. He will begin to hear "voices" in a few months—voices from the sea, the hills, the ground, the air. For the ear, the brain, the mouth are gregarious. So unless he is very strong, he will become mad.

Now, the lone madman on an uninhabited island attains the very highest degree of liberty conceivable. He is king of "a realm fantastic". His movement his speech, his habits are absolutely free. He is the perfect autonomous Anarch of the extreme individualist's dream. He is the Prospero of Anarchs.

The "voices" that he will hear, the "beings" that he will talk to are out of his subconscious worlds. He thus multiplies himself, and his egos expand till they fill heaven and air and his island universe. Being of his own making, they are more delightful companions than those he meets in cities, and the "voices" are non-adenoidal. He is the hermit of the universe—the perfect "free soul".

To All Deserters.—To the "slacker", the man or woman who plays "hookey" in the brutal "School of Life", the sullen being who stands aside and "won't play", or who laughs and goes fishing while the world sweats, wars, loves, steals and sinks in the cesspools of business: *Prosit!*

The cowards are those who are afraid to run away. The brave are those who have the courage to dodge the social draft. That's the secret wish in your hearts, O uncourageous and pitiful millions—to jump the job, make a getaway, assassinate the Big Boss, Social Necessity.

When I was a young man I used to slip out the back door and run down the alley to Berks street when people came to the house for a "party" or a social gathering. I found my freedom in Billy Ziegler's saloon or a wild hike through Fairmount Park, all alone.

The gospels of Work and Social Necessity be good and goddamned! And you are always dreaming of that back alley to a Billy Ziegler's saloon where you may dine and wine and break the fetters of the social gods.

Prosit to the Judases and Benedict Arnolds, the Huck Finns and the Tyl Eulenspiegels of life!

Great Is Brahma!—Down to the depths where Life peels off all its clothes and I see the vermin-covered skeletons of Brahma's infernal workshop. But he is merciful is our great god Brahma! For at the point where the last shred of color and light dissolve, where the ghastly machinery and the infernal truths of the universe are revealed in all their grinning terror—when I am about to dissolve in a star-shattering scream—there crawl out of the light of this unexpungeable hell the solacers, women, naked and alluring, and dancing wine-vats immersed in the mirages and auras of creational dreams and fantastic adventures. Then my dying soul incarnates as Tantalus, and I fling myself on the breasts of Maya, and we chant hosannahs to the stuffed and glittering illusions of Earth. Great is Brahma, the consoler, the Paraclete, the Father of Lies!

Two Presences.—Bio has her super-double. It is a divinized, glorified, beatified Bio, her guardian angel who comes to her in her life-crises. My double is satanic, an impassioned world-egoist, a marauder, a titanic Mephistopheles. They fuse in the higher synthesis. The Devil and Mary copulate in the dimension where parallel natures meet.

The Faun Sentimentalizes.—September winds rack my tree and it waves in the air like a demon chained to buggy roots and soggy soil. It hears the call of October-death. Its leaves yellow. Its little branches talk to me in wild algebraic terms which I cannot translate. A leaf floats up on my sill. The mystery of that leaf! You were not last March; you have been all summer, and soon you will be not again, and so this world and all it contains—but there! I'm going into quotation, sentiment and platitudes. More important—will Tunney lick Dempsey?

The Under-Superman.—The Jew survives because he refuses to live up to his conscience. He obeys life, not an ideal. The "Christian conscience" is envious of the implacable realism of the Jew and hates him. But the Jew is the superior being because he is both lower and higher than his conscience.

The Day of an Intellectual Faun.—Week began with the rejection of my "Psalms of King Booze", first mail Monday morning. Three cusses, a perfect evac. and a cold shower put me right with the world. Second mail; a letter from Maurice Maeterlinck, a wow of a letter, in which he praises my *Forty Immortals* as one of the greatest books of criticism he knows and says I sometimes put into a page more than a man can learn in a lifetime. Laved my soul for an hour in the bath of his praises. How I enjoy praises from men who really comprehend me!

My fall hats come back from the cleaners. While trying them on to see whether they have shrunk I think about my essay on Cabell for *The Times.* Sat down and wrote my article on Coleridge. Ah! opium, landanum if I dared! What peace, what visions, what veils to put on over these tired inner eyes!

Poisons, opiates and brandies should be had for the asking. Life is not important enough to bother about the way you die. The main thing is to escape pain. But I will never take drugs—I'm too cowardly, too cautious, too mirror-conscious of changes in my face. They who keep the solaces of drink and drugs from us are all rich drug-addicts, sexual perverts, giant profit-whores and preachers of "efficiency."

"Ice!" I always lift it off the dumbwaiter. A long hike up Broadway, where the stench of humanity soils my very bowels. The library. I'm cleansed the minute I enter. The empire of brains, the pleasure-palace of the soul. I love the men and women sitting there soaked in thought and eucharistic communion with their intellectual loves. I read a bit here, a bit there from the open shelves. Everything has been said. Why do I write? I open the drawer DE and see all my own works listed. This flushes me with pride, and while the flush still suffuses me I catch the eye of a beautiful dark girl with her large amorous eyes fixed on me. For just the dart of a split second we fuse on the couch of the air. She's gone forever. Our inhibitions are the Caesars of the blood. Damn civilization!

At night a jackass musical show (I'm a dramatic critic now, ladies and gentlemen of posterity), an orangeade, crackers and camembert, and the bed, where I hear a long, muffled laugh up the heights of my brain to Satan's throne.

Portrait.—When B. talks why is it that I form the image that his brain is a roll of toilet paper that runs out of his mouth?

Evening and Morning of Your Pan.—Canned up, we start in a car for a birthday supper at a good old tavern at Bensonhurst. Cocktails, a shore dinner, flowers, oceans of real beer (here's to the death in boiling oil of all the enemies of Bacchus and Gambrinus!), song, music. I dance the dance of Pan with a stranger, a young fellow flooded to the crow's nest. My suspenders are used for a harness.

The bar. Alfonso de la Passione, grand mixer *de luxe* of cocktails which I pour down between beers as Chris and Sam and Al and I sing "The Life of a Jolly Commodore". Furious jazz, "My Old Kentucky Home". The ladies in great glee at our antics. The patrons applaud. Taxied back.

Profound and dreamless sleep. The next morning hot lemonade and cream of tartar. Perfect! Blood sings in my veins. I write with tremendous power and gusto the introduction to Bio's book, *The Boy of Bethlehem*, in which I demand that Jesus—(but you know what I wrote, ladies and gentlemen of posterity, for you value the masterpiece at a great price, do you not?). Receive news that Walter's book, *The Sublime Boy*, will be out in a week. Beloved child, fame comes to you, and you know it not!

Rome and Hot Lemonade.—Jean Cocteau and Giovanni Papini

have gone over to Catholicism. Cocteau nearly died on opium. He wanted another sensation, and so is going to play with Jesus. Papini went over to Rome for publicity purposes. His "movie" Christ is being filmed. Cables, congratulations, orders for articles.

Here are two cases of bad bowels. Both Cocteau and Papini have complained of their agony on awakening each day. "Another day in the filthy stew of the world!" A quart of hot lemonade and cream of tartar, my pair of transparent mountebanks, would have set you right with the world and saved you from the opiates of Rome. It cured me, and God knows I'm pessimistic enough to be in Buddha's Nirvana.

Bad bowels, boys! Bad bowels! Look to't!

To hurt the feelings of one another impulsively and without malice every two days or so often deepens and doubles the love of two persons closely attached.

Opening the Cage.—It is 4 A.M. I rose because thoughts, memories and ideas roved restlessly in my skull like caged beasts. My mother, the tragedy of her romantic, novel-fed imagination when it came into contact with the facts of life—that it is sordid, vulgar, mean and filthy—this and many things, rose out of the dark silence that was in me and the silence that engulfs the city. The martyrdom of my parents to four children, the monotony of their lives, they who entered marriage so gayly and with what sparkle!—to see each year locking them up tighter and tighter in routine and slavery and poverty. The bitterness of having produced two poets! The weekly hell of having to count down to each nickel. A great pity came to me in bed. For their history is the history of the vast majority of the human race.

There seems to be no law that governs the sudden incursion in the brain of a certain series of thoughts to the exclusion of others. There seems to be an Imperial Wizard in back of it all. I sense a reason for every sudden feeling and thought, but I cannot put my hand on it. It may all be a matter of chemical goings-on in the stomach or blood—these sudden knocks on the doors of our sleep by Memory and Death. A thousand other things rose and fell in my brain in the space of ten minutes—an unconnected (?) stream of thought, profound and trivial, that is now lost as I sit writing this.

But I am conscious of a gnawing in the stomach. I am hungry. Is that all that thought is—hunger? Can genius be produced by starvation? Are all the whimper, joy, bitterness and hope of the isolated and pathetic soul nothing but belly-gas?

Every satirist tends to become the thing he ridicules.

The Black Eagle.—That troubled look on my face which falls like a gradual shadow from the top of my forehead to my chin, engulfing eyes and features in a night of thought—it is the passage, slow and measured, of the great Black Eagle as it passes through the firmament of my consciousness, eclipsing the sun of life. Some day it will stop above me, immovable, implacable, and when it goes on its way again it will carry in its talons my soul.

Marriage is a career of unearthing and covering up.

The Lust Dimension.—My bitterest thoughts strike nearer the core of some central reality than my sweet, human thoughts. I wonder whether on the "higher planes" of existence there is such a thing as love. It may disappear in the course of astral and karmic evolution. Terror, Beauty, War and Intelligence may be the attributes of life in other dimensions, with romantic lust taking the place of what we "down here" call "love."

The Unimportance of Being Earnest.—How shallow all things are may be seen in the case of a person in profound grief, despair or "the dumps". Crack him a good joke or point out a humorous angle of his trouble and he will smile or laugh.

October Ecstasy.—An afternoon in the country by car. The trees preparing for their gorgeous love-death and reunion with the Invisible, amorous of all life. Twilight: the sun turns to marvellous dyes on the hills; a purple mist creeps through the trees; the crickets and the frogs deepen the silence in my soul with their eerie noises; a solitary bird wings its way west to the setting sun. I am suffused with a delirious enthanasia. I flood, flow and fuse again with the secretive God of Nature as I did when a youth. The pantheistic ecstasy is not dead in me! Living, I slumber in God. Conscious, I drowse into earth and sky and tree and sunset. Self disappears and I become incorporated in the eternal life of things.

No! I am not dead! It is thirty minutes of the resurrection and the life, discarnate re-embodiment with the All. Blessed, sweet moment, when all earthly things, all earthly loves dissolve in the shadows that creep up the hills and only timelessness reigns in my soul! Almighty Pan, the healer, the redeemer, the consoler! Delicious reversion to youth, amorous, panaleptic recessional!

Death and the Bull.—Is death a city-fear? When I am in the country, in close communion with the earth, the fear of death diminishes. The idea causes me to swoon with pleasure as I lay on the grass. And then a bull starts for me—and I race in terror to a place of safety. But was that fear of death? No—it was fear of torture, of mutilation. We do not fear death, but *modes* of death.

The No-Dimensional World.—Little "Bobby" Miller, age 5, climbed up to the telephone while her parents were away and telephoned to Bio, twenty miles away, reminding her that yesterday we had promised to buy her a real baby at a police station—a new-born baby with golden curls—and take it to her. Blessed kingdom of the children! Which I can no longer enter. It is another dimension—or a world of no dimension whatsoever, but we never know it until we have fallen into this cesspool of three dimensions, where we look back and weep.

The Magic Flute.—Bio and I strolled into a church and listened to a girl evangelist preach. Two hundred pathetic beings looked at her agape. I looked around at the faces of the males, and as we left I remarked to Bio what this girl *really* wanted was not to be had of any man in that church. She will be cured of God-sickness when Pan comes with phallus and flute.

Sullen stoicism is the only resistance that conquers without loss.

Morning of an Intellectual Faun.—Up at eight. Hot bath. As I lie in the water dreams of ecstatic death—a flowing out, time sinking to its bottomless sockets in the skull—dissolution in the elemental—sensuous hypostatic union with God. Cold shower. Notice there is no toilet paper.
To the doctor's for boils and to find out what is in my urine. On the way I think of Emerson, the World Series, a colossal satire on Presidents, the drama of "The Captive" last night. Lesbianism. Is there anything "unnatural"? No, nothing that can be done is "unnatural". Some people like haddock and some like bluefish. Pah! You sweet and happy hypocrites—turn around till I sanctify your backsides with my boot.
Injection of something. Diet, strict diet; no alcohol. Farewell, farewell, to all my sprees! What a tragedy! Life without a periodical jag! God damn! But it may be only temporary. "Yes, Doc, I want to live—fifteen years yet. I've got things to squirt out of my cerebral syringes." Doc doesn't know what I am talking about. All doctors are illiterate.
Slow walk down Fifth Avenue in the sunshine admiring the semi-nude women. I possess all of them mentally. Thank God the bitches have little power over me physically! My dæmon protects me.
Home. Write an essay on Wyndham Lewis, the bore. Yawn. It's noon. I read Aldous Huxley (fine), Will Durant's essay on

Herbert Spencer (fine), Havelock Ellis' "The Soul of Spain" (fine), the newspapers (slop) .

To Walter.—Walter's book is out!—My dream of twenty-six years. "The Sublime Boy" is between covers.
Sublimity is that which transcends circumstance by an act of beauty or sacrifice. Walter DeCasseres was the Sublime Boy. He walked in the few years of his life with the Crazy Beauty which hallucinated the souls of Shelley, Keats, Poe, Blake and Heine. He walked out of life with a gesture of sublime disdain that raised him to the shining summits of the Morning Star, where the souls of all child-gods go.
The fury of a Titan foiled of his heaven, the frenzied paroxysms of an eagle trying to gnaw its way out of its cage of flesh and bone, the rage of Ixion as he picks up the stone that he is doomed to roll forever and hurls it with imprecations against the ramparts of the gods—that was Walter DeCasseres, who, in his eighteenth year, went with the same passionate hurry and joy to the everlasting sleep as Youth hurries to the breasts of Venus. He was a boy who spurned his manhood before he had lived it. He abridged the agony of years; he curtailed his drama to a curtain-raiser; he compressed life to a song and a curse.
He came, he saw, he yawned. He was the mystery of precocious and elemental genius. There was a colossal mirror in his brain that reflected the hells of the Past and the grinning disillusions of the Future. On the exquisite keyboard of his nerves Satan and Medusa executed in thunder-tones the Ninth Symphony of Pain. His heart was the Mystical Rose stuck in a dung-heap.

One Process.—Reading and writing are the same thing. When I am reading I am writing mentally a running series of commentaries on the book before me. When I am writing I am reading off the things that an impalpable finger is writing on the pads and folds of my brain and which I merely copy off.

I have loved, enjoyed fame and wine, but I have not committed murder or betrayed a friend. Have I *quite* lived?

The Guilt of the Quick.—That obscure feeling of birth-guilt, something wrong in bringing a child into life. That curious feeling about awakening one out of a deep sleep ("it is a crime to wake him up"). Is death more sacred than life? "Macbeth bath murdered sleep." Curious, remote vestige in the soul chat all consciousness is guilt. "Life is an error." Romantic admiration for murderers, national and individual. Is death more sacred than life? The solemnity in the presence of death; the frivolousness about the birth of a child (which frivolousness and gayety are anodynes for a vague disquiet and uncomfortable feeling that a wrong has been done).

Yes, yes, I believe it—death is sacred; Nonentity is the perfect religious state of the soul.

Elimination.—"Faulty or improper elimination is the basic cause of physical disease," a man said to me last night. Faulty, improper or lack of elimination is, I think, the cause of all troubles, physical, psychical or social.

I cannot eliminate; hence I suffer. Society, the State, cork up all our outlets—amorous, egoistic, natural. All our escapes are clogged by laws, inhibitions, fears, opinions, spinelessness. All my ills arise because I cannot excrete when I want to and in the fullness that is necessary to psychial harmony and buoyancy.

Nearly all of us should go through the streets with the skull and crossbones of the druggist on our faces and the word "Poison" branded on our foreheads.

Shadow-Boxing.—How I secretly brag to myself always. I repeat "I never whine", "I'm not afraid" "My head is bloody but unbowed," and a hundred other phrases which prove I do whine, I am afraid and my head is bloody and bowed so God-damn low that the subways are above me. And just to get even with myself for this shameful confession, I'm going to accuse you—you are the world—of the same auto-lying and weaknesses.

A Nude.—She blew in last night. A golden-gawdy thing of forty. She gave me her lips. They were spiced with rare promises. She twirled my satanic prong which projects at a right-angle triangle from my Olympian skull. She nuzzled deep into the couch. Skirts up to the knees, leaving on view the two solid columns to the Temple of Abysmal Sin. She must have "love" night and day, she cooed, her eyes receding to the Cave of First Knowledge. I took the veil of philosophy and discussed Bacon's *Novum Organum* with her. But I could see she was not interested in new organs. And so the night flowed on until she disappeared through the door, taking home the Bacon, her crinkled spouse.

The Isle of Tears.—This morning there came to me a great desire to weep, weep, weep—to weep for a year, a kalpa, on a deserted island. My brain, my heart, my blood bulged with bags of tears ("faulty elimination" of the emotions). There were bags of tears for God, for Satan, for humanity, for Bio, for myself, for crippled and blind children, for those who succeed and for those who fail; tears for Christ and Caesar Borgia and Francis Thompson. Mother of Sighs and the Island of Tears, why? Buried pearls of my own impotence before practical life. I have no magazine into which I can toss my lightnings and thunders. Publishers reject me. I behold the great march of mediocrities and nonentities in the pages of the book sections of the newspapers of the world, and I am not there. But am I not beyond "processions"? Ah! I am on the reviewing stand with the distinguished citizens of the Cosmos!

I desired a desert isle, where I could weep bagfuls of tears for kalpas, with only the invisible Mother of Sighs smoothing my brow. My tears dissolved in the sunlight and rain. They ate into stone. My soul plashed in tears. Tears, the salt spray of oceans of venom. Tears, idle tears, I know exactly what you mean; tears from the depths of my divine despair at my hopeless impotence before the granite walls of business that rise to my eyes when looking on the autumn had severe temperamental prejudices against this member of the Birch-Rod School of literature. I had formed from those bits of his writings that I had gleaned and glummed over in the reviews of his books the image of a completely fossilized professor of literature, a standardized college dummy of purest rhinestone serene. But I met one of the livest, most humorous, entertaining, goddamning old fellows (he's in his seventies) that I ever shook hands with. He told one story after another, some on himself, some on Dumas, some on Salvini and some on the world at large.

I saw before me one of the tragedies of the literary life—a man who had got a reputation as a college professor, as a moralist, as a highbrow Pope of the nunkey-dunkey school of criticism which he had to continue, for purely financial reasons, after he had started to evolve toward emotional and mental radicalism. He is a human being forced to write like a schoolmaster. He dips his sword in milk. Why not give 'em one blast, Brander, before you pass? Or maybe it's ready—post-mortem recantation of your ethical attitude on earth. A lie is peace. Truth is war.

The Descent to Intellect.—I come down from cerebral emotion to pure intellect. There is a descent in me from enthusiasm to calm knowledge. My irony is not intellectual; it is a red flame, a devastating fire locked in the glass tubes of an idea.

The bases of stupidity: temperamental sanity and sobriety.

Ladies and Gentlemen of Posterity:—I am watching—and those among you who are surgeons of style will no doubt note—what changes will take place in my style (and my style is *always* the mirror of myself, of my foods, my temper and my continuous evolution-devolution-involution) now that I have been ordered by the doctor on a strict diet in which I cannot eat foods with starch or sugar in them and in which alcohol is absolutely taboo.

Chemical changes beget mental, emotional and sexual changes. Can you diet a man into a saint or a devil? Would the absence of starch, sugar and alcohol in the daily fare of Shakespeare have made him a Tupper or a Nero? If Bernard Shaw had been a beef-eater and a whiskey drinker would he have been shot in the Tower during the war?

All my life I have had sugar, starch and alcohol in my blood. Now it is suddenly withdrawn. I feel better and am clearer in the head. I do my daily dozen in the morning to a jazz record. I am lighter in thought than I was two weeks ago.

Put a lily in my hands, boys, and crown me with pansies.

The Boy Is Liar to the Man.—A curious "spiritual" perversion of mine often recurs to me. When I was eighteen I saw a gorgeous, hallucinating October sunset as I looked west through a cross-street. At this apparition of cosmic beauty I averted my gaze and murmured to myself, "That sunset is sensuous. It awakens my flesh. It is a sin." I hurried on like one running away from a bad thought. Every east-and-west street I crossed thereafter I turned my eyes resolutely to the east, whose sky was turning leaden with night. And when darkness came I was relieved. The sun, the tempter, had gone into its black hole.

How different I am from that boy now! Whatever is not sensuous is not true. I long to be trapped in flesh every minute. My most abstract thought is based on my blood, ecstasy, sex-longing, flesh titillation. I was then Saint Anthony, and I saw Satan in all things. Now I am Dionysus, and unless Satan is present in the eucharist of my daily experience, I feel "lost", without grace.

"True" and "False" Thoughts.—I know when I have a "true" thought and when I have a "false" thought. The true thought comes up from my emotional vats dripping with feeling, prejudices, passions. The false thought is one manufactured by the intellect. I reject the latter. It is often very "clever," but is not true because it does not inhere in my innate character. Every

thought in this book, or books, is a true thought, even those that seem merely "smart." That smartness, when it occurs, is a part of me. I choose. I eliminate. I throw away in the wastebasket of oblivion all that I *feel* is false.

The Undying Psychic Worm.—A man talked to me the other night for one hour on God, music and mathematics in an absolutely abstract manner. He didn't know that he was only talking of one thing—himself.

Happiness is an abstract idea. Gayety is its fleeting incarnation.

My Tear-dikes.—They are bitterness, fantasy, will, walking, Bierce, Swift, archaic curses against God, and other things. Arteriosclerosis of the tear-ducts should be treated early. Keep all starches and sugar out of your brain-food. Strict diet on the world satirists. Beer weakens the tear-dikes. Whiskey fortifies them.

Right above the heart a solid wall about three inches high should be built that will prevent the heart from washing into the brain. But leave the spine open. The spinal-marrow should have free flow from the bottom to the heart, to the brain. Tears that come up the spine from the lairs of the heart reach the brain transfigured to shapes of tragic terror or colossal guffaws. Examine your tear-dikes every month or so with the literature and plays that used to make you weep, at the time when cardiac micturation into the pisspot of the brain took place easily.

I find many breaches in my dike that need patching. Some times whole bits of it melt away, especially when reading of the struggles and humiliations of geniuses. Music—certain sad songs of religious longing by Caruso or Gorgoza—wash away the whole structure. Chopin melts it down to a giant, sweet tear. Under his sway I enter such a realm of pure sweetness, sadness, pathos and trans-earthly sentimental ecstasy that I swear I shall never build the dike again.

Fantasia Impromptu

I confess a great pleasure in certain kinds of weeping. All women revel in it. Men are ashamed of tears. Why? It is a confession that their strength has broken down. Hence dikes. You can measure the strength of the dikes in any man by the quality of his satire. The more bitter and terrible the satire, either verbal or written, the tenderer his heart. No one has fought against tears like cynics and ironists.

The Voice-Bibber.—I take a great epicurean delight in sampling the voices of people I have met for the first time. Delightful surprises for the ear. The voice is the heart and the brain dramatized. There are blond voices, brunette voices, hennaed voices, amorous voices, cowardly voices, courageous voices, wheedling voices, voices that are whole symphonies in a fifteen minutes' conversation; exquisite etudes, waltzes, mazurkas; satanic voices, sparkling champagne voices, piggish voices, steel-trap voices. When I meet a person I have never met before I await the opening of his or her mouth with the same palpitating breathlessness that I have before the rise of a curtain on some tragedy, fantasy, farce or melodrama.

Death-Illusions.—Each one must have his death-illusion, his lullaby as he goes to sleep in the cradle of his cadaver. Yours is Catholicism, yours is Elohim, yours is Theosophy, yours is Nirvana, yours is annihilation. The atheist as well as the devotee must have his final cradle-song while Prosperina slowly rocks the cradle. What will be my special soothing-syrup at the final moment? A resumption of life in latency?—refusing in the Universal Spirit? A smug belief that my books will prolong my name for many years after my disappearance in the flesh? A brittle immortality!

When they go to the chair murderers are given an injection of morphine. Prepare your "dope" early, children. If you do not, you may not find Prosperina crooning you into a soft oblivion, but the famous Medusa sisters. I have always comforted myself that at that moment I will go where all genius has gone. I am quite content to accept their oblivion or their transmutation. Resumption in the Eternal and the Formless fills me with ecstasy—now. But will it then? What a bother about nothing, after all? Ego! Ego!

Age.—A sure sign of the coming of absent-minded age is to discover off and on that you are walking the streets with your trousers unbuttoned in front.

The Suds of the Jest.—Today I was in closeted conference for one hour with a wealthy manufacturer of soap. Yet this soap manufacturer read to me a letter, which he highly prized, from Mencken. It was in Mencken's characteristic whimsical strain. The soap king put it carefully back in the drawer and asked me whether I had any letters from Mencken. "Barrels of 'em," I replied. "Keep them all," he said solemnly, "they'll be worth a great deal some day." "Some day" means when Mencken is dead. That's about what the soap king saw in literature—so many tons of soap in storage waiting for a rise in the market.

The love of man for God is a form of homosexuality. The love of woman for Mary is a form of lesbianism.

Ennui is Death conscious of itself.

Martians, Please Take Notice.—Science and satanism have always been closely associated in the philosophy of Catholicism. The Church has laid hold of a profound psychological truth. Science today is both satanic and sadistic. There is something cruel, demoniacal in the scientific experimental mind. It is primarily destructive and only incidentally humanitarian and "healing". I read today that a professor had "disintegrated" a living mouse by a half a second's exposure to the Cathode ray.
Science will soon discover a force that will cause whole peoples to evaporate in a war. I would that the Martians or the Jupitereans

had knowledge of this force and could apply it to the planet Earth, causing it to evaporate in a second's exposure. I should call the Martians or the Jupitereans great humanists, however, if this should occur.

Idea No. 4602. — The evolution and incarnation of the Satanic spirit. Satanism in sex, in religion, in art, in science, in sentiment, in love, in metaphysics, in poetry, in friendship.

It is curious the thrill I get out of the word "Satan" and its variations. To look at the advertisement each day in big type in the newspapers of *The Sorrows of Satan* gives me a thrill. The word always causes to rise in me a whole panorama of complex and inter-related emotions, ideas and super-normal abstractions. I still believe Satan is a vast Thing, not an abstraction of moods, prenatal experiences and beliefs. We are the miniatures of abstractions, and abstractions are made up of an infinite number of miniatures. Thus do I reconcile Plato and Aristotle, Science and Religion.

That Thou Art!—I have been ridiculing and satirizing mentally for days the obsequiousness, the grovelling of the American public before the Queen of Roumania, who has just arrived in the country. When, presto! out of the mail today there tumbled an invitation to meet her at the Hotel Plaza next Sunday. I accepted, felt flattered, flushed and honored. I felt the same tug and haul at my knees and head that the rest of the groundlings feel. A merry imp laughed in my ear and threw dung all over my superior attitude.

"My Hero!"—I went to a party last night where the liquor flowed like water. I did not take a drink and for two hours watched them all getting mellow, then stewed. Will-power? Not a bit of it. Fear, caution, self-defence. But I made them all believe it was will-power and was looked upon as a hero. That's about what nearly all "will-power" and "heroism" come to.

Prometheus and Jesus.—Prometheus stole the fire from Heaven and gave it to man. Jesus stole it from man and put it back in Heaven. Prometheus was a utilitarian and Jesus was an idealist. Prometheus attempted to topple God off his throne. Jesus caught him before he fell and put him back. Prometheus was sublimely foolish. Jesus was foolishly sublime. This game between the two of them, under various names, will probably go on forever.

The Truthful Liar.—All my thoughts are hermaphroditic. "Each thing is double one against the other," says Emerson. For me, merely to think positively is to think negatively also; to think affirmatively is at the same time to call up a precise negative. The persistent union of these opposites in my nature gives birth to my paradoxes. My "yes" implies "no"; my "no" is a mask for "yes." I can will to go in two opposite directions at once. My left hand not only knows what my right hand is doing, but does the opposite with an equally sustained force and certainty.

The Dumb Hermit.—I had a gorgeous hour with my Deity in bed this morning between eight and nine o'clock—so gorgeous that no tongue or pen could tell. Had I had a writing-pad in bed at the time I might have attempted it on paper. But, no! my Deity would have left me at the first physical movement. My Deity guards its privacy with inviolable and ineluctable barriers.

Two.—I know two beings—a man and a woman—who have beautiful, delicate, profoundly private feelings, revelations and confidences to exchange—so beautiful, so lovely, so aged and heady in the vats of their hearts for thirty years that they could only be made in the amorous hours of first union, which has never taken place. Each has told me his and her need. Each has revealed to me the profound attachment which binds them physically, mentally, morally. Each has revealed to me part of their quivering souls—quivering to gush into each other. I have not told either that I am the mutual confidant of both. And so they stand aloof, the merest commonplaces passing between them—both proud, cowardly, timid—while the years pass away and the shadow of the Eternal Silence looms across their lives. It is the most tragic thing I have ever witnessed.

The Laughter of the Ego.—When I am tolerant, understanding and forgiving of all human acts, faults and crimes it is because I desire absolution for myself. Universal tolerance is the confessional of non-religious beings. Humor was born of forgiveness. "Pardon's the word for all" means may God forgive me. Understanding is the laughter of the ego.

The Blessedness of Giving.—The universal law of the will-to-power is the desire to have slaves. Each one desires to enslave someone. It is a hieratical scale. There was a profound metaphysical basis in the saying of the anti-Abolitionists that "slavery is of divine origin." It is for this reason that we hate those who constantly do us favors. It is for this reason that we expand when we put some one under obligation to us. "It is more blessed to give than to receive"—subtle Jesus! Every act, all conversation, every smile is an attempt to capture something other than ourselves, or an attempt to get out of the shackles another has imposed on us. We are all slave-owners and we are all slaves awaiting a messianic Emancipation Proclamation from a Lincoln who will never exist.

Ecstatic Atonement.—When I was nineteen I used to say to myself: "As long as there is one suffering human being on the planet I have no right to laugh." That consciousness of world-responsibility has never left me. I have used alcohol, sleep and books to drive it out. But it pursues me, wraps me up at times in a shadowy, impalpable despair. I have always understood the doctrine of vicarious suffering and atonement. Understood it!—I am the very thing itself. There is an element of ecstasy in this cosmic despair. The power of universal pity and sympathy lift me to the vibrations of Buddha, Prometheus and Jesus.

Debacle!—The mark of Cain on my forehead, of which I have so long been proud, as you know, ladies and gentlemen of posterity, has this day (October 22, 1926) become a boil. Heels.—I can get anything from M. if I ask his opinion about something confidentially. I can get anything from P. if I tell him he's a perfect craftsman. I can get anything from N. if I tell him he's publishing the best magazine in New York. And so on. My Achilles heel? I have none when sober; but when drinking I'm heel from head to foot. Certainly I love praise and admiration and can be flattered. But no one can get anything out of me that way. Besides, what have I to give?

In a Cafeteria.—When I enter a cheap restaurant—an automat or a cafeteria—to get a bite I mutter to myself when looking at the poor and the middle-class feeding, "The swine!" Then I look in the mirror at myself when I am eating, and behold! I, too, am one of the swine! Eating and stooling abolish all differences.

The Alcoholic Laugh.—There is a certain period in drinking when the alcoholic laugh takes possession of us. A series—a continuous series, sometimes, that has lasted with me for hours— of tremendous bawls, guffaws, belly-shaking, eye-watering, pants-wetting (almost) earthquakes of mirth. The hilarious souls of all the comedians, jolly good-fellows and devil-may-care rogues and rakes of the past awake in us, overwhelming Fate, Death, Gabriel's trumpet and the Coolidge-Hoover souls of the world in showers, tornadoes, hurricanes and simoons of unleashed and boundless gayety. The room becomes charged with festal howls. The Wandering Jew, God, Jesus, Lucifer, Macbeth, Hamlet, the Medusa Sisters and Orestes are caught in its fold and take it up. Ha! Ha! Ho! Ho! Oh, my God! Stop! I'll die! O! my belly is bursting! Do you know it?—the wild, care-free soul in the belly of the grape?—the Emancipation Proclamation of body and soul that breaks your ribs and makes your nose water? I hear this alcoholic mirth sometimes in the dead of night from neighboring houses, breaking the dark like an exploding sun nine months gone with a race of Pucks and Falstaffs. And then I am sad, for since prohibition and my dieting this great release has been denied me. I used to rock for hours with gayety when in my mellow stews, my soul the buffoon to God, my face twisted to grins or convulsed as if a bomb filled with the Devil's laughing-powder had gone off in my brain. Now, I snicker, smile, emit a wispy Ha! ha!—often hypocritically, insincerely.

In America the crashing alcoholic laughter is taboo. It must be done in private. Where can I go to laugh as I used to in Mouquin's, Jack's, Joel's and the Brevoort—those Mansions of Momus, those Cathedrals of Unreason?

A pogrom, a pogrom on Seriousness, for our masters, for the moralists, for smugmugs and the stinking, tobacco-chewing jaws of the dried-up testicles and withered-bellies that rule us!

To the Imp of the Perverse.—My dear Imp: you play tricks on me, lay snares for my temper and mock me with your Tantalian tricks; yet do I love thee, for thou art my genius, my blessing and my blight, my crimson Morning Star.

You urge me to do the things I should not do; you whisper the forbidden in my ear and take from me the power of willing it; you turn my black into white and my white into blue; you force me to dance on the crazy ecliptic of your orbit; you lead me to the Palace of Success and then topple the walls on me; you put a tongue of yes in my every no; you inflate my brain in the morning with glowing plans and blow them out in the afternoon when I begin to execute them; you hide books from me when I go to find them; you steal the papers from the closet when I look for them; you whisper to me the names of publishers who will print my books and then whisper to them to reject me; you twist my mind to agonized veins of torture with your contradictions; you show me the kingdoms of fame and fortune, but abolish all the highways that lead to them.

You, my dear Imp, are my torturer, my Torquemada, my Caiaphas — and my Intercessor at times. And though you strangle me, laugh at me and slay me, yet do I believe in thee!—until it is time, either here or elsewhere, to wring your God-damn neck and make you my slave, my dear Imp of the Perverse!

A Portrait.—She is a fantasia of the times—the cerebrally secretive type. Tragic coquetry with perversive ideas which dance before her in the red-hot coals of her images. A woman out of Manet. Large nose, large mouth, large eyes that fall before my gaze in a second; bangs to her eyebrows, giving her the air of a Parisian decadent. Brilliant mind for a girl, but afraid to show it before men (self-defense of woman, who must always archly and coyly play the baby before the lords of the world). Talks electrons, atoms, the transmutation of metals. Her body a corkscrew that is forever trying to straighten itself out. Wrings my hand from her heart and brain—a man's clasp. A voice that dies away wearily almost before it begins to speak. Behind her long, pale face there roars a flame and a Fury—and also an abasing woman in the arms of her man, whom she will never find, for she is looking for a man who will be both Don Juan and Darwin.

La Ville d'Alcool.—One month on the water-wagon! But the shining City of Intoxication lies ahead, gleaming and glowing in my starchless, sugarless, alcohol-less imagination. I'll stay a night—only one night—with you soon, oh, delect able city of spilled inhibitions and guffaws like the eructations of the Colossi.

George Sterling wrote me today that this was his seventy-eighth day on the wagon. But he, too, says he is getting ready for the Great Spill, for Mencken is heading west and so is Edgar Lee Masters, and the three have planned a grand guzzle in San Francisco in November. Fall well, my boys! Fill your bellies and brain with the crazy stuff till you turn the universe into a realm fantastic and fill with rage the smug soul of the mathematical, reiterative, platitudinous God.

Ramblings of an Intellectual Faun.—Books, thoughts, writing, theatre; my ears droop, my pipe is cracked, my wild bacchic shouts are cackles. I want the Witches' Sabbath, a night or two on the Brocken, lewd and amorous hours, to regain the sap and vigor of my purely animal nature. Peace, health, routine: the three crosses on my present Golgotha.

But my urine is clear again, my bad tooth is out. My buddy, Old Nick, beckons. By God! I'll slip up on my bottom some night soon until the white bellies of two dawns bulge in the east!

I went in to see a woman at noon—in her office at the very gizzards of Broadway and the White Lights. She sat with her dress rolled up darning her stocking above the knee. Quite unconcerned and matter-of-fact was she. She discussed plays and books with me (the door closed) while she widened her legs subtly and invitingly. I kept my eyes on her horn-rims while she played Penelope-Circe. She finished darning and closed up her thigh shop. I departed, my business unfinished.

I went into the booth today and voted for Al Smith and the wet referendum. When I think of Lenin, Trotsky, Mussolini and Primo de Rivera, I kind of thank God for Calvin Coolidge, as much as I despise him. Yes, I always vote—its a form of socialized erection out of which I get a kick.

The Naked Jest.—Our lives are perpetually dual. The universe is perpetually dual. We do not do a thing, say a thing. We do things; we say things. Our existence is plural, simultaneously multiform. We create and destroy simultaneously, we love and we hate simultaneously, we live and we die simultaneously. For this reason all judgment, all logic, all theories of cause and effect are false. Well, then, why do I do anything, say anything, if I am undoing and doing in the same act, the same speech? It is just because of the delight that my Imp of the Perverse takes in looking perpetually in the comic mirror of its own contradictions. To know, to feel that I love and hate, create and destroy, live and die in the same act produces in me supra-human transports and unites me with the Great Jester. I am then the Naked Jest.

Damn the Heart!—Throw away your heart! Brain and sensation are enough. The intellectual sensationalist is a free man.

On a Car.—I got on a Madison Avenue car. Terribly depressed. My face was set like a Chinese Buddha's. The rest of the men and women on the car also had faces set like Chinese Buddhas. Each in his private hell, inviolate, completely isolated from one another. This man, maybe, was riding to escape the idea of murder; this woman had a huge tumor under her dress; that man was going to commit suicide; this girl had just found a baby moving inside of her; that man was going to be dispossessed tomorrow. And so we rocked, jolted, swayed along the avenue, each with his face like a Chinese Buddha, each one of us flayed, skinned and rotting in his private hell. A great truck should have come smash! into the car and killed us all. But it didn't. They got on and off, those silent Christs and Cains and Jobs—those slop-jars of God.

Show Him, Harry!—Harry Houdini is dead. When he enters Heaven his first duty will be to show Christ how to "trick out" of the second crucifixion that awaits him if he should ever return to this world.

When I get up in the morning in a tragic mood, I know I am going to write something comic, satiric.

How to Be Your Own Tantalus.—Keep willing for things out of your reach, invent impossible women to sharpen your desire, conceive yourself in terms of Shakespeare, Christ or Napoleon. Gayly, satanically tantalize yourself. Do not do the thing that gives you most pleasure. Postpone—deliberately, by act of will — all the things that will make you happy for an hour, for a night. Fondle, smooth, caress the surface of your desires and dreams; but do not close the fingers on them. You will thus always be on edge and never disillusioned. Live this way all your life, and when you come to die you will curse yourself for an ass, just as you will if you do not live that way.

Ladies and Gentlemen of Posterity:—From my ashes (which may be at the bottom of the sea, heaped up in the eyes of the Statue of Liberty—how is the old trollop?—or reposing in an urn in some black-eyed Sappho's drawing-room) I am asking you whether polygamy has yet been legalized?; has "free love" become bullet-proof?; have our Presidents (if any) reached Nietzsche?; did the Cabellians or the Dreiserians win out?; who is president of the Chamber of Commerce?; is Tammany still a "menace", is France still "decaying", is England still "tottering"?; has my *Litanies of Negation* become a college textbook?; has Mars been entered?; have the women put on their clothes yet?; have the men taken theirs off?; has Arthur B. Davies survived?; has Philadelphia become human?; what has happened to God?; did Christ come back, and what was the manner of his butchery?; has the parlor electron been invented?; has New York seceded from the Union?; is H. G. Wells still a-babble?; are there any public, licensed palaces of amour?; has the kitchen cockroach finally been exterminated?; has the puritan finally lost his trousers?

Theodore Dreiser and Sherwood Anderson.—Two alchemists who can turn sewer gas into ink. Aldous Huxley.— Gargantua laughing with clenched teeth. H. G. Veils.— Cyrano de Bergerac puking Utopias. George Bernard Shaw. — Karl Marx engraving epigrams on the rump of John Bull.

The American confounds size with exaggeration. Size implies reality. Exaggeration implies imagination.

A person who can pose in the face of certain death is a born artist.

George Sterling.—George committed suicide at fifty-seven. The perfect age for poets to pass. He took a quick curtain instead of a slow one.

A charming man, a "regular" fellow, a bohemian of the old school. I received a letter two weeks before he died which was full of hopes and projects—one was an article on Bierce, another was his intention to visit New York. But the Imp of the Perverse suddenly reversed gear on him. He had not received his copy of *The Sublime Boy* up until two weeks before his death. But he had got it, unquestion ably, before he committed suicide. A thought has come to me that the story of Walter's death may have influenced him.

My New Version.—Ask me no questions and I'll tell you no truths.

Bouquet for Myself:—For a man who never received any financial help from any one and who has been compelled to work for his living since his thirteenth year, I have probably written less that I am ashamed of, less that I would repudiate, than any living writer who has fought against such odds. Even when compelled to do a pot-boiler, I always contrive to redeem it with a touch of irony, malice or venom somewhere.

The Cannibals.—If I have three or four ideas in my brain, I let them compete with one another for days, and the one that survives their communal cannibalism is mine. The lost ones were mere fatteners.

The Tucked-In.—They race into your house, the type of oozy, sentimental man that you know—throw their arms around your wife, hug her on the sofa every ten minutes and snuffle about "finding the real woman", "a home like this," etc. They are harmless, preposterous, tucked-in souls who are still a-dangle from their mamma's umbilicus.

Essay.—Sexual sufferings of a chivalrous gentleman.

We live two lives; the one we live and the one we missed.

Suicide.—The one single proof of the beneficence of God is that he has left us one exit. It is a cure for insomnia; as Nietzsche says, many a spirit-tortured man has slept soundly on that thought. There is always a last boat hanging to a foundering ship.

Am I a Spirit?—It is hard to think of myself concretely. I am always a giant abstraction. I am an Idea, not a Thing.

"The Boy of Bethlehem".—Bio's book is out! A beautiful book, a unique book, a daring book, written by the loveliest, the sweetest, the strongest, the greatest woman in the world. She is heart of my heart, soul of my soul. Any one who can live with me for seven years and love me is super. Bio is super.

Sterling Again.—George's suicide was like his poetry—classical, artistic, finished, conscious, deliberate.

A Portrait.—She has a head like some strange polar bird. Pale. Large semi-circle for a mouth. Hardly any body. Lesbian inclinations. At twenty-five she stands at pause between a man and a woman. Follow your nature, girl! Which ever you choose, your life will be tragic. And to hell with *On dit!*

A Fireman Shall Lead Him.—"Mussolini's life is guarded by Destiny. He walks among his enemies fearlessly. He has escaped death miraculously six times. He is as brave as a god". This is the stuff we are listening to now, ladies and gentlemen of posterity; but it applies equally to any fireman in the New York Fire Department, any one of whom faces death oftener in a year—a terrible death, deliberately faced—than Mussolini will for the rest of his life.

Procreation: the triumph of the bedbug over reason.

A Good Little Soldier.—I was a fool to drink myself stupid in the old days to kill despair and the suicidal impulse. Now that I am on the water-chariot and still suffer frightful psychic crises, I begin to see what enchanting tortures and exquisite agonies I missed by pulling the curtain of alcohol over my hells. Now I stand them, and indeed go through them with something of a perverted epicurean joy.

Dear Madam Destiny.—I am a suckling in your arms. From your right breast I draw the golden honey of fame. From your left breast I draw the black milk of death. But my hand is crawling up toward the crown of diamonds on your head, which I desire to grab, scamper away and pawn. It means ease, security and Power.

Health is a liar.

The Perpetual Moulder—I doubt whether there is such a thing as environment. Whatever happens to me is caused by my character. We shape and reshape the external universe every minute. That which surrounds me is an extension of myself. My environment? My "environment" is part of my character. The Earth creates its atmosphere, not vice versa. Character projects shadows — we call it "environment". It will disappear with the disappearance of the special character that created it.

Lazarus and Another.—Whenever I think of Lazarus rising from the dead I am moved to uproarious laughter. He must have looked ridiculous. Did they bury him in a night shirt? What a figure—grotesque, Chaplinesque! Something like a man whom you know who has tried to commit suicide and who failed—another ridiculous figure. To be both a failure at life and a failure at death—isn't that the essence of the absurd? To be the mock of *two* kings of terrors, Life and Death! To funk in life and to funk in your try at eternity—Lazarus and the suicide-muff.

Constipation and Grief.—The classic look on the faces of figures in painting and sculpture that represent Grief, Melancholy, Despair and Pain is the look of a constipated being. Now, this is true, for grief, melancholy, despair and pain are caused by a constipated will, the checking of the free flow of desire, the thwarting of the wish. Close up the out lets of our natural activity, constrict the canalization of our will and there is produced the same look on the face that appears when one has difficulty in excreting. Tragedy is constipation. Comedy is perfect mental and spiritual bowel movement.

Psalm of Life.—Perfect sincerity means that the whole soul believes—head and heart, emotions and intellect, instinct and apperception. This is ridiculous. There is always war in us. The brain and heart hate one another. I am never wholly sincere. You are never wholly sincere. I am partly sincere and partly a hypocrite—and so are you all.

Genius feeds itself on serpents.

Sobriety.—The dangers of sobriety: sadistic impulses, continence, chastity, venom, retained anger, staling health, growing sense of my importance, decay of humor, dullness, work, unification of personality, moroseness, taciturnity. In fact, a perfect hell-broth of stinking mediocrity. I envy the man with *delirium tremens.*

Civilization tends toward the ant: mechanical organization. Then will come the giant heel of Anarchy to smear it in the dust.

This planet is my carrousel—I ride with donkeys, lions, lambs, eagles. Sometimes I grab a golden ring of Beauty as I go round.

Publicity is the Heaven of the American.

The Circle.—When intolerant, when critical, sarcastic or satirical, I look into myself and I see a mocking face. It is the face of the person I have attacked, condemned or satirized. He mocks, he laughs because I am he and he is I. That is the tragedy that leads to indifference. For if pessimistic invective leads to bitter irony, and irony leads to self-mockery, why, the circle is soon closed, for self-mockery will soon lead to auto-invective and self-pity. And the rest is equilibration—silence.

Genius and ignorance may be careless with impunity, but carelessness is fatal to mediocrity. Hence perfection is the aspiration and heaven of mediocre minds.

Prose and Poetry.—Great poetry contains all the prose that may be uttered on the chosen theme; but great prose does not contain all the poetry that may be uttered on the prose theme. *The Hound of Heaven* condenses all the prose of a hundred volumes on God and Man. "Ecclesiastes" condenses a thousand volumes of pessimistic philosophy; it says more in fewer and more comprehensible words than the combined works of Schopenhauer and Leopardi. Poetry is the ultimate utterance.

Verily.—Read those things that antagonize your sensibility and temperament. Read what you dislike. It is the beginning of creation and destruction at once. It is the beginning of dissociation—the law of mental and spiritual progress (by "progress" I mean the widening of individual consciousness, the deepening of insight; the excavation of the unknown).

Pilgrim's Progress.—I am still dieting. Resumption of power and energy. The brain freed of poisons. Now I know why those who seek earthly power and dominion are abstemious: alchemy, sublimation of forces. Sobriety, continence and abstemiousness breed a natural biological intoxication. All power comes from elimination, concentration. Yea is born of nay.

"Jack's" Salute.—I had seen her, met her on and off for years. She was rather boyish—in fact, every one called her "Jack." One day she saluted me in mock-military fashion in a theatre lobby. The salute was the sword of instant desire. It went straight to *the* place. Did she know the trick? What was occult in that salute?

Why had she never kindled a fire in me (I have seen her low-necked, half-dressed) until, fully dressed, with her fur coat over her and her hat on, she saluted me with a peculiar motion of the right hand to her cap and a heel-click? The subtle ways of *amour*! Probably Balzac, Stendhal or Havelock Ellis are advised on this matter.

The Friendly Liar.—I went to bank this morning. I had been there a hundred times and had always nodded to the uniformed attendant. He asked me on this trip to have a calendar for the new year. I thanked him and said spontaneously, "Well, this time a year ago—just this day—they said I would not outlive the night—double pneumonia. Shows what the doctors know! Here I am!" And I drew myself up and puffed out.

Of course, there was not a word of truth in this. I was not ill a year ago and never had double or single pneumonia. Why had I lied? What antic disposition had seized me?

But it was a beneficent lie, for the old cock poured out for fifteen minutes all his family troubles to me, how his daughter lay at death's door last winter from double pneumonia, etc., etc., etc. Having lighted the match, I had to listen politely, cursing myself for a liar and the old man for a bore. What was I to this Hecuba or Hecuba to me?

Now, why had I uttered this utterly absurd lie? I sought to repay him, I suppose, for his calendar and thought to entertain him with a supposititious case of double pneumonia. Sickness is what preoccupies the mind of the poor, and I suppose my subconscious nature wanted to be friendly with him by showing a common bond between a bank depositor and a flunkey. If so, the intuition was genuine. It struck fire, and I got an earful of his Iliad. Hereafter he will get *only* a nod.

The Good Pal.—You can accomplish anything if you carry the thought of suicide with you when you are going to dicker with a man, demand the body of a woman or have to face a dispossess.

It is the secret get-away door that the other party does not see. All audacities are yours if you march along with Death.

If you haven't the will-to-grandeur in some degree you must be a vacuous nonentity.

Chance is the unknown element in fatality—some call it free will.

New Year's Eve of an Intellectual Faun.—Six of us in a limousine down to Larsen's at the Narrows—quarts and quarts of rye—all tables filled with gorgeously gowned nullifiers of the Eighteenth Amendment—I wear a crazy hat—superb supper—at midnight I stand on the table and raise hell—why? Because I'm a year nearer oblivion?—Three hours of play, foolishness, wine, whiskey, laughter, clowning—Back to New York soaked to the skin and happy—Bio reads in our hands that 1927 is positively our lucky year!—Masseltuft!—1926 was a year of disappointments; serves me right for living with the whore Hope.

January 1, 1927.—Fantasia Impromptu: The Adventures of an Intellectual Faun. In going over it I have made few changes and have no regrets as to what I have herein put down.
It is a mirror of my moods—of my tears, lubricities, fantasies, laughter, defiances, humilities; of my paradoxical, unearthly nature; of my whimsical, human nature; of my spontaneities, my effervescences, my profundities, my superficial-ties; my introversions, my extraversions; my fatalities, my aspirations. It is a mirror of my dull moments, my inspired lyrical moments; of my Godolepsies, my satanic moods; my hatred of life, my love of life; of my realism, mysticism, scepticism; of my gayeties, of my melancholies.
It is not my whole self. There are things in each of us that the heart dare not whisper to the brain. There are instincts and impulses in us that are so shameful that even the Devil would recoil from recording in his diary. They are common to us all; hence are not mine, not individual. But I have put down here

whatever has marched boldly into my consciousness.

If I have lied to you, then I have lied to myself. But I say that in confessions *there is no such thing as a lie.* Merely to think a thing is a fact. All images are facts. All dreams are facts. The universe is a metaphysical lie; but I am—and you are—a physical and psychial truth, with a double manifestation: action and dream. So all in this volume is truth—my truth, *my* truths. All that is in this volume *happened* to me, happened to me physically, psychically and mentally as here written. Take it or leave it; that is your business. My business is with myself.

If I died tonight, I go out with this core-thought: some where in some cycle, in some unimaginable guise, I shall appear before the Author of Life and plead the cause of suffering sentiency in all spheres. I shall ascend, or descend, through multiple incarnations with an unappeased *why?* on the lips of my mind. And if there is no answer, there will always remain the question— why?—which is a final judgment until it is answered.

First Epigram of the New Year.—He who lives in the house of the whore Hope will go forth with the syphilis of despair in his blood.

The Biological Imagination.—The whole conflict in the human soul is a war between biological facts and the imagination. Reality and the Ideal are figments, and the conflict be tween them is fictional. But biological processes and the imagination are both facts, and not hypotheses, like the Real and the Ideal.

Now, the conflict between Biology and the Imagination is not necessarily a conflict between two antagonistic forces. They often blend. In fact, the imagination is the mental form of a biological need. The imagination expands in inverse ratio to the suppression of biological needs. The conflict is born when the sinless and roving imagination is conceived in terms of the ideal, of morality, when the free-flowing imagination takes an ethical form of bias. It is the poison of inherited ideals that deforms the image and causes the panic in us before "bad thoughts".

My biological imagination tells me I have a right to possess everything I desire without any regard for "laws," state-made or church-made. But there are centuries of inherited fear to be overcome, and in all of us, with few exceptions, they are never overcome; hence the imagination and biological processes are made enemies.

Exceptions: Napoleon, Mussolini, Casanova, Jesse James, Jesus, Goethe, Petronius, Nero, Spinoza, Oscar Wilde, Francois Villon, etc.

Deformations: Nietzsche, Verlaine, Shakespeare, St. Augustine, Tolstoy, etc.

I desire to be in the first class of names, but remain in the second. The biological imagination in conflict produces literature, painting, music, oratory, propaganda, venom, satire.

"Take Care of Your Health" says a good friend to me. But just what does it mean, "take care of your health"? How does one take care of his health? Suppose his health demands periodical excesses? Suppose he declines psychically under a regime of prudence, moderation and watchful surveillance? Suppose carelessness, imprudence and violent sensations are laws of his nature?

Health?—what is it but the harmonious adjustment of outer and inner? Suppose the inner is abnormal and irrational? Suppose poisons are my meat and bread? Suppose there is no outlet for my *unhealthy* instincts? Well, then health becomes a form of routine, death.

Shall I add years to my life or add life to my years? That is the only question. Health is a negative joy. Is it preferable to a positive pain? Is health a form of cowardice, fear of penalties, remorse, tomorrow?

As in all things, I stand at pause. My good friend, I do not know what you mean by "health". Like virtue and goodness and "safety first", there is no drama in it.

Continued in My Next.—Suppose I die. Leaving my body behind, I take with me—a disembodied consciousness seeking a supra-terrestrial body—my knowledge and experience accumulated on the earth, say, in my sixty-fifth year. Now, what would I take, exactly, into that other world? What have I gained here? What is the net result of my having lived?

These things:

> An enormous curiosity.
>
> An ecstatic sense of Mystery.
>
> Pitiless irony.
>
> Profound cynicism.
>
> Worship of Beauty and Power.
>
> Insatiable craving for novel sensations without regard to their perversity.
>
> Monstrous egoistic pride.
>
> Absolute belief in a Devil-God or a God-Devil.
>
> Sex-ecstasy in all forms.
>
> Understanding and sympathy as higher spiritual developments than love.
>
> Hatred and antagonism as the motor forces of life (it has been well said that the ultimate of love is extinction—life is war; death is love).
>
> Love of little children.
>
> Music as the divine, mysterious, ultimate intoxicant.
>
> Admiration for superiority of any kind.
>
> Liberty at any price—even to the point of murdering all I love if it block my path.
>
> Solitude.

These are the elements with which I would begin my life on the next plane. But it is highly probable that Maya, Goddess of Illusion, is too wise and powerful to permit any such manoeuvre against her being. She might, permitting this, finally raise up against herself a mighty Demiurge of anti-illusion, an extinctionist, a god of nihilism, such as I had premonitions of in regard to my own ego in *The Shadow-Eater* and *Litanies of Negation*.

Or she might permit it by keeping me baited with my illusion throughout an eternal series of spiritual evolutions, the colossal jest of it at last being that I should fade into her essence, become Maya herself—and play the game that I came to destroy!

Dear Imp of the Perverse: The days pass and still you tease me to "the top of my bent," as my Lord Hamlet says. You are in the pay, my dear Imp, of our common owner, Saint Tantalus, and his two brothers, Ixion and Sisyphus. You contrive every means to drive me to insanity, to suicide, to fatal outbursts of demoniacal rage. You have crowned me with red-hot nails and use the ventricles of my heart as corridors of laughter. You surround me with swords and ram needles in my skin. There never was such a beautiful green as your venom.

But I dare not war on you, my dear Imp. You are my genius. Give me gold, gold, gold and I will sign a pact with you—à la Faust. Give me gold, and I will promulgate your glory and diabolical greatness to the world.

Come, Imp, let's go the whole hog! To hell with Gethsemane and the Temptation in the Wilderness. I will fall down and worship your forked feet for unlimited money and twenty-five years more of virile, creative life. You know my reasons for this request—they are sublime (*we* define *our* own terms—*sublime*, I said!). Come, a pact! I am no welcher, like Faust.

Chained to Routine.—When I have blocked all alleys of release— alcohol, Venusian carnivals and travel—how shall I get rid of the madman in me? (There is, of course, a madman in me, as there is in every genius and in millions who are not geniuses but have the complex and multiple nature of geniuses.)

This madman in me is a gorgeous creature who requires wild sports, vivid sensations and experiences frenetic and thunder-toned. Sometimes he is satisfied with monstrous dreams and sometimes he runs riot at the end of my pencil; but he has a body, too, and his congested blood seeks relief. For weeks he has been caged. There is nothing more dangerous to the brain. He cannot be slain. I have no desire to get rid of him. He is too gorgeous a being. He is part of my Self. What to do?

Pattern-Images.—If the law of cause and effect is eternal and unbreakable, it must produce images of future events on the psychic waves. The future has not yet happened, but there are patterns of every event to come. It is these images, these patterns, that those rare minds called "prophets" see. They predict what they see on the psychic screen of another being. A seer is one who sees, and what he sees is a patterned image that will materialize in future time.

Benjamina.—Benjamina I call her. She is the feminine counterpart of my soul. She lives in me. She is the twin soul, the eternal sister-lover of Benjamin. She is jealous of all women in the flesh. She has kept me from them, using her weapon of intellectual analysis.
Every genius is psychically hermaphroditic. Every genius has this twin sister-soul locked up in his soul. Narcissus Narcissa.

A Death-Struggle?—I am in dispute. The positive and negative demons wrestle for control of my destiny. Each one now demands full personal materialization. That which was merely literary and psychological now demands its earth- frolic. They battle on the threshold of Reality. Faust and Job—how well I understand your epics!

History!—We overcome one evil with another evil. The newer evil being a novel experience, we derive pleasure from it. "Progress" is just that. It is the illusion of "good" produced by a brandnew experience.

God is Good!—If one could *smell* what goes on in the world in one minute, universal death would take place in that minute.

Engrave on Your Brain.—In re-reading that masterpiece of irony, *Murder Considered as a Fine Art,* by De Quincey, I came across this quotation from Marcus Aurelius:
"It is one of the noblest functions of the reason to know whether it is time to walk out of the world or not."
Engrave that on your brains at puberty, young men and women!

Ladies and Gentlemen of Posterity: I have never been an atheist. So many persons say to me, "I know of course you are an atheist." I quietly reply, always, "I am not an atheist." But it is useless to explain to such groundlings who confuse my criticism of life, the universe and the non-ethical attitude of the Creator with denial of the existence of a Creator. They cannot dissociate "belief in a God" from "reverence for God".
I "believe" in war, but I do not advocate it or reverence it. I "believe" in disease, but I do not advocate it or reverence it. I believe in their existence. What are we going to do about it?
So with God. He is, to me, like Shakespeare, Napoleon or Beethoven, beyond concepts of "good" and "evil". He is Power, Force, Beauty, Ugliness, which are purely relative terms. I do not like his universe, ethically considered; but what draws me to him is that he doesn't care a damn whether I like it or not. His method is evidently mine in writing this book and all my others: I do not care a damn whether you, men of my own generation and ladies and gentlemen of posterity, like what I have written or not.
Like Lucifer and Prometheus, I have hurled colossal thunderbolts of hate at the Creator. Now, what I admire more and more about the Great Spirit is that for answer he immures me in a deeper hell or sends a fresh brigade of vultures to nibble at my liver. His remorseless irony is admirable.
My evolution as Pantheist is toward a completer dishumanization of myself—and I get nearer to the secret of the Universal Spirit in my intellectual withdrawal from life than I do in my hypocritical humanism.

If He reads at all, I believe he gets more satisfaction out of my *The Shadow-Eater* than from any book yet written on this planet. His companion-volume to *The Shadow-Eater* is the *Ethics* of Spinoza or, maybe, "Ecclesiastes". We three are his triune incarnation. The Preacher, Spinoza and myself are no doubt multiplied many fold on many stars and in many dimensions.

So you see, ladies and gentlemen of posterity, I am not an atheist, for of all mental morons the atheists are the lowest. Please set me aright.

"We Are Adapted to Infinity."—Between midnight and one A. M. this morning I sat under the lamp alone (Bio having gone to bed) re-reading Emerson's "Swedenborg". One of those rare silences prevailed in which everything in earth and heaven seemed to die. Not an automobile horn nor the sound of a slamming taxi door. On the floor above absolute stillness. I heard the hum of Silence in my ear, it was so profound at that hour. It is like the hum in a sea-shell. The very breath of Silence, the subtle aura of Negation, the rustle of the shroud of eternal death in the dying breath of the last God.

And again I came across that marvelous sentence of Emerson's, "We are adapted to infinity." It fell into the great pool of silence within me and spread its ripples into the night outside of me and unto endless circles of meditation on the silent sea within me. The soul is "adapted to infinity"; but the will, the body is finite. This is the comedy and tragedy of man. In that hour I was a god of infinite proportions groping through millennial pasts in the Unconscious up to the present incarnate consciousness and exfoliating into the infinite and the eternal.

That hour this morning, pondering over the great aphorism of Emerson, confirmed me once again in my life-belief that what I do, what I think, what I see are only a very small part of me. I am a colossus of immeasurable dimensions. A part of my special being lives a life wholly in the Unconscious. Bits—only bits—of that stupendous existence in my pasts float up into the world of my consciousness, which is, again, only a very small part of my complete Self. I am at this minute thinking, acting, walking and talking above consciousness in a transcendental, supra-material world. The margin of my identity below my consciousness is hidden in shadow, eclipsed in the deep shadows of time. I cannot see my identity above me because my mind's eyes are not made yet for the blasting light from that sphere. My normal conscious life is lost in it like a flake of fire in a sun.

This law of triple being—of three in one and one in three—applies to every living and "inanimate" thing. It applies to the planet we live on, the stars we see, to this pencil I am using, to an idiot and to Shakespeare. In genius the triple life—extensionless, dimensionless—is nearer realization than on the lower strata of humans. In Shakespeare, Plotinus, Spinoza. Beethoven, Chopin, Blake, Shelley, Swedenborg (with all his comic descriptions of the angels and the prolongation of himself which he called Heaven) and myself the Mystery becomes almost a visible shape. I am not adapted to the finite at all. I am adapted to infinity. The atmosphere of my daily consciousness does not contain sufficient oxygen to sustain my colossal proportions.

The Black Beatitudes.—Grief is a form of ecstasy. So is profound sadness. Great physical pain if illuminated by stoical pride may also be a form of ecstasy. I know so well the Black Beatitudes!

Morning of an Intellectual Faun.—The riveters have invaded Gramercy Park; no sleep after eight o'clock; I dream of quiet country lanes and the silence of the woods; New York is the final form of the insanity of Doing.—In the mail invitation to hear Padraic Colum, Ernest Boyd and Dudley Digges debate on Ireland; into the waste basket; to hell with Ireland!—I ponder on that saying of Fourier, "The attractions of man are proportioned to his destinies." Profound and beautiful, and true of man in the mass; but for the individual it is another form of the legend of

Tantalus. I have heroic attractions, but my destiny here on earth is shabby. Elsewhere? We'll see when the time comes, and when the time comes there will be newer attractions and newer destinies; and so the game will go on for eternity unless by a prolonged act of my will stretching over cycles of time I can abolish both attractions and destinies and repose in static beatitude.—Dog yowling next door. I'll poison that damn mutt yet!

In my ferreting around in the human heart one of the choice little morsels I have discovered is the satisfaction with which we go down into our own pockets to help bury some one else.

Saint Damocles.—All my life there has been hanging over my head a Great Catastrophe—Alcohol, Suicide, Poverty, Insanity, Dispossess, Fire, Doubt—what else? The many faces of the Great Comedian as he watches me contort my soul and face in anguish! But he has kept me healthy and agile—yea, agile, dear Saint Damocles!

My Dear Ben:
It is true that in creating you I did some thing which I sometimes have regretted. I knew of course all that you would have to go through, and on few of my geniuses have I ever put such burden of suffering over such a long period of years. Others I have caused to suffer more excruciatingly than I have you, but I ended it much earlier, having achieved what I intended to achieve through them.
I will veil the future from you, as it is not well that any of my creatures should see his destiny or fate. You no doubt agree that I am wise in *that* at least, my dear boy.
Now, also, you must admit that I am foreseeing, for while I have decreed that there shall only be one way of coming into the world and I bring you all in against your will, I have left a score of gates open to get out. There are water, pistol, poison, war, the knife—you may commit suicide in any way; and here, too, I

think I have been beneficent, for I have given you the illusion of free will in doing it—a slight sop to your pride.

My dear Ben, I have listened all these years to your prayers, curses, blasphemies and threats against me, and, really, from your point of view, you are justified in all your plaints as well as your from time-to-time admiration for my aesthetic aloofness and sheer Spinozism. Indeed, I may count myself a Spinozist, and, in a certain sense, a DeCasserian.

I want to say, my dear boy, that for what you have gone through in the last thirty-seven years almost unremittingly (and which alone is only known to you and me) places you very high in my regard. That you remain sane, alive and in fairly good health after these tortures is due entirely to my foresight, for I saw very early in the incarnating of your soul that I would have to put a drop of the miraculous in your nature to keep you alive until the thing is done for which I brought you forth.

In the tempests of time and sidereal changes, what you are and what you have written are of no importance, for they shall be scattered in oblivion in a laughingly brief time; but you are of importance to me, and what I have done to you and what I shall further do to you, as well as to your beloved Bio, remains my secret alone.

Be brave, be stoical, be miraculous always, my beloved boy.

God.

My Dear Ben:

I looked over your shoulder this after noon and read the letter that God (whose aesthetic beneficence I cannot subscribe to on the ground of its utter immorality. As I embody the principle of active evil, I believe I am really the moralist of the two; but that is, and has been for an eternal number of aeons, a moot question between us two)—as I say, I read the letter that God wrote you, and I hope you'll pardon the impoliteness, for although I am known as the "First Gentleman", I am also the Spirit of Curiosity.

Now, my dear boy, it is not just precisely true what God told you. As a matter of fact, it was I who prevailed on Him to leave the gates to death open to man by way of suicide. He was for eternal life à la the Wandering Jew. That, I explained to Him, would spoil my plans, as the lethal bath of death, taken in the natural ways of accident, disease or age, or suicidally, kept our children open for the same experiments over and over. If each one were to live indefinitely and were denied all means of "natural" or auto-exit, my inventions would soon be at an end and I'd die of *ennui,* which must not be.

We have compromised that way from the beginning, and I feel peeved that He did not give me credit for my work in his letter. We, my dear Ben, had a hell of a time (as my friends say) over you. I have my plans about your future, too; but what they are must also remain a mystery to you for obvious reasons. That "dash of the miraculous" in your nature is a little of His blarney. What He calls such is just my love and care and watchfulness. There isn't any real conflict between God and myself, as you will know some day.

And as for your suffering—why, my dear boy, you do not know the meaning of the word. I, being eucharistic, have gone through all human and divine hells, and my brain is baked to a cake of ice, if you see what I mean.

Accept my salutations and profound admiration for your unique and curious soul, which you did not fashion, but which you carry with so much *aplomb* and so beautifully masked.

Satan.

My Dear Ben:
Nothing so relieves my infinite boredom as the discussion among some of you about "a personal God," "an anthropomorphic God," "an unknowable God," "an impersonal, extensionless, eternal God." Especially am I amused at those who deny disdainfully the existence of a personal, anthropomorphic God. There is, as

you know, my dear boy, *only* a personal, anthropomorphic God. Nothing else is conceivable in your brains. I so arranged it in your making that nothing else should be conceivable. On Earth, I am—must be—related to a brain, a sensibility, a network of emotions; and whether you conceive me as a cow or as the Eternal Substance I am only a reflection, a creation of some one's personal need—therefore always a "personal God." I am always as "personal," as "anthropomorphic," as the statues of Rodin are to Rodin, the nocturnes of Chopin to Chopin, or the creatures of Shakespeare are to Shakespeare.

When Plotinus, Spinoza and Emerson—three of my most exquisite bits of joinery on Earth (ah, Ben, you should see some of my automatic marvels in some of the constellations!)—when these three assert they have "attained me," that they have "lapsed in me," they are merely performing feats of transcendental Narcism, like yourself, my boy, in your rather sublimely silly frenzy to attain my power for a decade or so. In their God-intoxication they have created highly burnished mirrors of themselves of a texture so fine that they cannot reflect any material object of Earth, but *do* reflect the most exquisite and most highly purified essence of their own psyches, which they call "God."

By "personal" and "impersonal" God of course you mean, on the one hand, a Being (the capital B is yours) who is specifically related to the fate of an individual, and by "impersonal" you mean a Being who is absolutely oblivious to your prayers, blasphemies and the whole tragi-comedy of your individual existence. You among a very few, Ben, know what pure word-jugglery all that is. For "personal" and "impersonal" are two of my illusions. Other than me nothing exists, although I am like nothing you know, dream, think or see.

With profound admiration, and even love, tempered by a satiric smile, I am...

God.

My Dear Ben:

Peeped over your shoulder again.

What he says about Himself (capital H is mine) and you earthlings is true in every particular, line for line, of Me (capital M is mine).

With profound admiration, and even love, tempered by a tear, I am...

Satan.

Evening of an Intellectual Faun.—Dinner—Bio and my self—at home. Deep in our couch, under the big lamp, I plunge into Emil Ludwig's *Napoleon*. Here is great stuff, dramatic, tense, ecstatic, and by a German! So few of them are readable; their grey matter travels like molasses. I put this life alongside of Elie Faure's *Napoleon* and Taine's great study of this unique apparition on the planet. I must not forget Hardy's Napoleon in *The Dynasts*; but that is "supernatural" and cosmic. Napoleon would have been an astounding product if he had only been a writer. The clarity of the man's style, his cynical philosophy, his sure appraisal of men and their motives, his lyrical flights, his historical and psychological clairvoyance! I would not have been Napoleon for all the dazzling grandeur of the man. Why? Simply because I have not his courage. But he feeds my egotistic pride. He was a super man in every sense of the word. He was a demi-god. Anatole France calls him "a sublime buffoon." That applies to all mankind. We are all sublime buffoons. Why pick out Napoleon?

Richard Jefferies' *The Story of My Heart*, which I reread after some years. Here was another Napoleon, another kind of "sublime buffoon," a man who dreamed of being a spiritual superman, who *was* a spiritual superman. His book is one of the finest and profoundest confessions ever written, bold, dazzling, beautiful, sane. Here is the utter ecstasy of Man before Life—and his appraisal of practical life as useless. A pessimist with titanic wings. Napoleon only dreamed of conquering the world. Jefferies dreamed of conquering God and Immortality, abolishing them in the fury of his aspiration and mounting to higher concepts! Jefferies' Saint Helena was Matter. Have you of posterity, ladies and gentlemen, forgotten Jefferies' book? Maybe so—for the most exquisite things decay first.

Nine o'clock! I leap from the couch. I had almost for gotten! This is the night of the Delaney-Maloney fight at the Garden to decide which one of them is to challenge Tunney for the heavyweight championship of the world. Into the subway, up to the Newspaper Club. Squat at the radio, we listen to the roars of the crowd and get the fight punch for punch. I howl over at Don Marquis that Maloney will win. The crowd gives me the razz. Maloney wins on points. "I told you so!" Don and I talk for an hour—Napoleon, Maloney, plays, the suicide epidemic among students, the chastity of husbands, "The Captive" (a lesbian play, ladies and gentlemen of posterity, that the hypocrites and the Pharisees have just closed—a great play), and is conscience disappearing?

Oysters on the half-shell in a restaurant that used to he "Jack's" white-room. Memories of those bacchic nights in that very room before the decline and fall of American freedom. Near-beer, bellywash—pah! Stinking Methodists! stinking Volstead! Calm walk at midnight down Fifth Avenue under the stars. They always wash me clean. One long look up at them and a silver glow inundates my spirit. I rise to them as on wings, spitting on the Earth as I disappear in their depths.

Home, bed, a restless night and a parade of the ironic furies in my skull.

Native, natural honesty is so rare that when I encounter a case of it, I open my La Rochefoucauld to find out the sinister motive behind it.

Conscience-Decay.—One of the fascinating studies that I have undertaken lately is the current decay and slow disappearance of conscience. Being of purely artificial and anti-biological origin, this self-defensive mask is always the first to disappear in the heat of war or great social and sexual changes.

If I believed in "progress," I should say that the disappearance of conscience would be a gain. Conscience hog-ties us to honesty and fair-dealing. It has been the cause of my failure in life.

Conscience is fear.—"makes cowards of us all." This remark of Hamlet's has never been taken at its full value. No one has dared to. Break down mass-conscience and we should have a great planetary blood-letting. It would cleanse and prepare the way for a super-race of cynical beings whose motto would be "Do one another," hammered in granite in the Cathedrals of Mephisto.

Thin Ice.—To assume the attitude of thought or meditation in a public place is the height of impoliteness. It is an immodest unveiling of your superiority. It is a form of mockery. It assumes that the people around you are of no importance. It gives you the air of a conspirator. Then some one will utter rudely, "A penny for your thoughts," fearing you have found him out.

Spiritual Metabolism.—I write as if everything I wrote was of profound and vital importance to the human race now and for an eternity. That is the only way to write, whether one writes tragically or humorously. Artists and thinkers should have the seriousness of children, who when they build their sand-houses and castles of blocks have no conception of fugacity or oblivion. Children and artists who can concentrate in Yogi-fashion have achieved eternality, for eternality is the very opposite of the temporal or diurnity. Eternality is not sequential or spatial; it is simultaneity, achieved in moments of total inclusiveness.

There is no sense of time when one is totally "absorbed" in one's work. Ponder that word "absorbed". That is eternity. And as that absorption is not of time, I, thus absorbed, speak and write against oblivion, for "oblivion" is as great an illusion as existence itself. What I write, what I create lasts forever. Burn all the printed matter in the world, destroy all the paintings in the world, annihilate all the musical scores in the world— Shakespeare, Rubens and Chopin will be reborn with all the other artists who created in absorptive simultaneity.

Psychic heredity is the law of the universe as well as physical heredity, and one has simply nothing to do with the other. And after the planet goes hulking and crashing through space as a cinder, all that we have done will exist in chemic processes in a finer essence, in the brain, stomach and bowels of the ether. Spiritual metabolism is also a fact.

If all this isn't so, it makes little difference to me, for I think it so, and so it is so to me. There is nothing but belief. Others have handed their thoughts and intuitions on to me from distant spaces and times, and I hand my accretions on to others in distant spaces and distant times through my power of absorption and eternality. *We may be doing it at one and the same time—eternal simultaneity!*

There are two ways of enslaving a being and making an enemy of him: to take away all that is necessary to him or to bestow on him all that is necessary to him.

Brahma in Embryo.—My Imagination in an entity. When it leaves me I am a walking corpse. When it returns inflamed and molten with ideas, alcohol, sex or intellectual flights into the vast domains beyond the conceptual and knowable, then my soul has returned to my body. It is then I attain "happiness," which would be nothing short of godhood could I externalize it or sublimate it to earthly or super-earthly power.

The imaginative life is a universe within a universe. Poetry is its sun. Irony is its North Star. When I am "lost" in imaginative thought, I have found myself. When I find myself in practical life, I am "lost."

Caesar and His Scavenger.—The greatness of Jules de Gaultier lies in the fact that he has made the imagination the foundation of all psychic life. Without imagination life could not persist. There is no being of whom it can be said, "He is totally without imagination." Such a being is inconceivable. He may have no poetry, no music, no mysticism, no love of the arts in his make-up, but he has imagination so long as he plans, if it is only how to make two pennies earn four. He lives in images.

Wish, desire, which are the essences of earth-life, manufacture and project *images* of the thing desired. An expert accountant—to instance a very low form of animal intelligence—lives in an imaginary world of numbers and figures. His imagination is organic, unconscious. His fiction is the infallibility and eternality of Number. The man who believes in "facts"—only "facts"—is living an imaginative life, a fictional life, although he would spurn the accusation.

"Cold reason" is all imagination. It is the skeleton of image. Its ends are purely imaginative and evanescent—utility and stability. Reason can be dissolved in the imagination, but the imagination cannot be dissolved in reason. The imagination destroys reason when it lies in the way of its imperial march. Reason is always a coward and fears the poet, the ironist, the mystic and the prophet. It knows it exists only on sufferance. In the boulevards of the soul it is the scavenger and street-sweeper before the imperial chariot of this all-conquering Caesar, the Imagination.

The Uses of the Good Man.—Faith, honesty, modesty, justice, decency are survivals in us like their opposites. They are obstacles, ghosts, handicaps. They feed our pride. They are ideal, artificial, but of immense value in keeping the herd in order so that the great man can rise on the mob's cowardly inhibitions which it calls "virtues" and air his ego, beneficent or otherwise.

Sex-Sheen.—This is one of the rarest things to be seen on the faces of young women. It used to be almost universal when I was a boy. Its mysterious and poetic quality made us breathless and set haunting dreams in our brains. The roses and wine of sex-glamour in the faces of those girls! I see it rarely now; but when I do glimpse it—on a street, in a car—it revives in me the wonder-days of the blood, the romance and the roses of a time that is gone forever. Today—strumpet faces, and instead of virginal sex-sheen we have whore-sheen. The young girl and the young boy are sex-free at last!—and suicides among them are as common as their embraces!

The quality of our laughter is determined by the quantity of our hells.

At Eddie Bernays'.—A psycho-analytical evening. Chaim Weiszmann, the inventor of TNT and the Zang of Zion, related some curious waking-dream experience in Palestine, and Sandor Ferenzci, the Hungarian pupil of Freud, "explained" them psycho-analytically to the laughter of every body. General discussion—mostly academic piffle and copy book stuff. But the only thing that remains to me of the evening was a beautiful young woman in a thin sky-blue dress with whom my eyes and blood made a perpetuate rendezvous in the gardens of our desires.

Adieu, Time!—By mechanical means time is being short ened more and more on the physical plane. We may go to Paris some day in an hour by radio tube. I am shortening time on the psychical plane. The older I get the more I become conscious of the artificiality of sequence. Time is ideal, merely a part of the machinery of thought, as Kant discovered and Einstein re-announces. It has no objective existence.
Time, I believe, moves with the rapidity of light. It seems to move slowly through an illusion caused by material and objective actions. That man lives for seventy years, for instance, is purely an illusion of relations. As a matter of fact, I believe our lives are

but a flash, occupying probably the billionth part of a second. All that I do is crowded into that flash—all that has been done on this planet since its beginnings has probably taken place in less than the billionth part of a second. The centuries, the years, the hours, the days are merely divisions of this flash in Eternity. There are insects that live for a minute and believe they live for years—or would believe it if they had a time-organ.

I am on the track of discovering the nothingness of man and his final non-existence in time and space (what here holds true of time is equally true of space).

I sense, imaginatively, a profounder and different life than our life in time and space. I believe we are living in a timeless and spaceless universe of spiritual consciousness, of which nothing can be affirmed except that it is.

Dear Ben:

We both peeped over your shoulder as you wrote the above paragraphs on time, space and existence. You are not quite right, but to tell you the truth would cause an explosion in your brain and kill you, and we do not wish that as yet, for reasons best known to us both. But, my dear boy, you are so nearly right, you are so clearly on the right track, that we are both somewhat admiringly fearful.

God & Satan.

A Psychic Einstein.—As the heart and the brain continue the work of dissociation the mind acquires the power of making the near seem distant. It lengthens the space between myself and the outer world. The sensational and emotional become spectacular. My brain begins to manufacture space. By the magical power bestowed on us of contracting or lengthening space at will, I can bring distant ages, events and persons so close to me as to see them almost microscopically; and presto! by waving the wand of my will I can cause them to recede to a speck or to vanish in the abysmal spaces of consciousness.

We can dilate and shrivel the time-sense by the same power. I can see my past life contracted to a point or expand it to a weary succession of never-ending hours. I can contract the future—my days to come—or expand it, with all its content, by the same power. Hope is given to those who dilate the future; despair to those who contract it to one dreary day in which the disillusions of the past are repeated. These boys and girls who are new committing suicide at such a great rate are time and space contractors. They have not the gift of dissociating head from heart. Space and time dilation are laughter-creating. Space and time contraction are tragic.

There is a third secret of dissociation—to live in what Emerson calls "the Eternal Now;" give no thought of the morrow or yesterday. Act and think without regard to consequences or fears. This abolition of both Prometheus and Epimetheus is the most difficult feat of all, and is rarely attained or sustained. It is quite common to fake it, but as a natural, continuous product of willing it is almost impossible—if not quite impossible—of fulfillment.

It is only by space and time dilation (which I cal now handle like an adept) in great spiritual and imaginative crises in my life that I have saved myself from suicide or insanity hundreds of times. (And I wonder whether it was worth while.)

Ladies and Gentlemen of Posterity: You naturally lave some curiosity about my little habits, those peccadilloes and personal characteristics that sometimes index a genius in his mere human guise more than his work does. My work can give you no conception whatsoever of my every-day self. My work is not related to living; it is related to Life. So if you wish to reconstruct me out of my ashes here are some of my little characteristics set down helter-skelter (helter-skelter is, by the way, characteristic of my whole mental life, as you no doubt know).

I have a horror of lying in a barber's chair. I feel he ought to cut my throat, or wants to, and sometimes I have tried to put the idea subconsciously in his mind. This obsession became so strong that I now shave myself and am even nervous when I have to go into a barber-shop for a haircut.

I am excessively irritable in the morning—my best mental hours. A voice goes through my brain like a knife unless fortified by drink the night before, which generally puts me in hie humor the next day. I can stand breakfast talk only uncle: those circumstances. To be disturbed by a voice, or any noise, when I am thinking or meditating produces a violent brain-storm. I become murderous and suicidal. I can, however, cure the spell by laughing at myself.

Before small talk of any kind I turn pale and begin to collapse physically and mentally unless curtained and fortified by drink. My expression by turns is infinitely sad or diabolically impish. Puck and Hamlet possess me by turns in ceaseless alterration.

I am lazy physically, but almost supernaturally active psychically. I think and feel from head to foot, like Shelley. My body is a nuisance.

I smoke cigars and a pipe almost incessantly. I never use cigarettes—no kick.

Bio says I have the most perfect ear and foot of any human being she has ever known. I never get tired of admiring the perfection of my feet. I am no judge of my ears. I have fine brown eyes which can burn holes in a soul or turn as soft as a dove's. I can veil their fires at will. I can plunge them to the pit of a person's secret at will. Fine, weak chin. A mouth both sensuous and cynical by turns. My forehead is famous. The hair over my temples grows naturally like the horns of Satan. A good nose, but one betraying a weak will.

Contradiction inflames me to almost physical pugnacity. My pride and egotism make enemies. I can't hide my feelings easily before stupidity or mediocrity. But I mask my soul perfectly.

Most persons think I am a born comedian, that I never worry. After seeing me howling at a ball game they simply cannot, or will not, believe that I wrote *The Shadow-Eater* and *Forty Immortals*.

I pass persons I know on the street because I do not want to go through the stupidity of commonplace greetings and the hypocrisy of "Well, take care of yourself," etc.

Women embarrass me. I seldom know what to say to them, as, if they are beautiful, I only wish to ask them the primal favor. All other conversation between a woman and myself is rubbish.

I blush very easily, which always causes women to kiss me and pat my cheek. I never blush at praise or compliments about my work. My blush is always sexual.

I never cry except when drunk. When sober I can weep easily at anything that hurts a child. Crippled babies or boys and girls melt me to an ocean of tears, which I have great difficulty in repressing.

I am sometimes effusively polite and again can be very insulting and cold.

I am a neat dresser and despise anyone who looks like a bum. I will not meet geniuses who look like bums. I have a horror of ever looking seedy or shabby-genteel.

I dislike "visitors," new acquaintances, curiosity-seekers and can murder persons who "run in on you to say how de-do."

I am only completely happy when reading a great writer, listening to great music, creating without regard to the public or anybody, or sitting in some lonely spot near a mountain or the sea.

I am uneasy in the presence of a rich man or woman. I feel inferior, venomous, envious. Wealth cannot help showing its insolence even before genius. But it is legitimate, for money is the greatest thing in the world. It can corrupt genius, and it knows it. My uneasiness in the presence of the rich is a compound of fear that they will buy me and the manifestation of the inferiority complex of fragile spirit before brutal matter.

These are mere fragments, ladies and gentlemen of posterity. More anon.

Infidelity.—There is a rare, an exotic charm in unfaithfulness—to your wife, yourself, your ideals, your real nature, to life itself by suicide, for instance. There is perpetual adventure in being "untrue" to something. Perpetual humor, too. There is what "William Butler Yeats calls "the Anti-Self." Conceived tragically, this Anti-Self may result in insanity; but conceived with intellectual humor, he is a gay, blithe, careless I, a Pierrot-of-the-Minute.

In the Empyry of Humor all things are permissible—all treasons, all infidelities, all anti-self acts. But beware of ever repenting of your gay apostasies! That way lies insanity or suicide.

What is commonly called "insincerity" is a conflict be tween the brain and the instincts, between conscious knowledge and unconscious knowledge.

Just as the individual moves steadily and inexorably toward the grave from the moment of his birth, so the cosmos and all that it contains—astronomically, morally, socially and geologically—is *always* moving toward a catastrophe regardless of all prayers, aspirations, hopes or temporary "happiness."

Flattery is ridicule with mush in its mouth.

My Dear Heraclitus: In re-reading your Fragments I find this, written apparently apropos of Dionysus, "Souls delight to get wet." Then further on you say, "A dry soul is the wisest and the best."

Well, my old Ephesian friend, if it is a *delightful* thing to get intoxicated, why is sobriety wise and good? You were the original Puritan, I fear, my dear Heraclitus. As profoundly as I admire you for your identification of opposites and your sublime paradoxes, I must put the blue-snoot on you.

Souls delight to get wet (as you so quaintly put it); therefore, it is a sin to drink. I transpose it, you see, into modern puritanical, theological terms; but it comes to the same thing.

Now, Epicurus would never have said what you said. He would have put it this way:

Souls delight to get wet—but don't drown yourself.

But your division of the human race into Wets and Drys is so modern! A wet soul, a dry soul; on this division there can be built a theory of civilization, a theory of human evolution, a theory of culture. The wet soul is the dynamic, tolerant, riant being. The dry soul is the conservative, unimaginative, Henry Ford-Coolidge thing.

Honor Be Damned!—Honor, pride, honesty, conscientiousness, scrupulousness, fidelity, friendship, truth-telling all those qualities which I have held in esteem within my self—of what use are they, of what use have they been to me in the struggle for existence, in the aspiration for recognition? They have hampered me, almost killed me. They are all forms of fear. Without them I would have had money, place and power.

From walking up and down this earth and going to and fro I have gathered that the simpletons and the sap-heads are full of pride, honor, honesty and faithfulness, and that to the crooked of mind and the audacious and the foxy belong the spoils.

Why "delicacy", "modesty", "character", "charm" unless they put money in my purse? Why have I not pimped it on women and men like other artists? Why have I not swindled, lied, blackmailed to achieve my great end, which is the intellectual (not *moral*) domination of the world by my pen?

Success is all ye need to know on Earth. Personal honesty and "being true to one's self" (Shakespeare put that into the mouth of *stupid* Polonius) may be a means to *success*; but if that doesn't work (and generally it doesn't), *go crooked*—but keep out of jail and try not to be found out.

On a Faun's Birthday.—Only the beast can say "I am." Only the animal or insect lives in eternity. Having no ideals, no sense of past and present, no intellectual or ethical inhibitions, it alone can claim to be "happy."

The "ascension" of the species to man is an ascension to hell. The decline of a race or a species, the degeneration of mankind, is an ascent to "heaven", to happiness, to primal biological principles, any variation from which is an increment of pain. The beast lives in the eternal present of its immediate needs. It is nearest the divine.

Among humans those who are limited to sex-needs, food-needs and the will-to-power founded on money are the darlings of the gods. The pursuit and pleasures of women and money are the only two legitimate needs of man. Everything else is pain and piffle. The pleasures of the senses, the pleasures that money brings are alone real. Let ideals like honesty, fidelity, principle or honor interfere with the pursuit of women and power and you are lost. These ideals are tumors. Cut them out of your spirit early before they destroy you, unfit you for the pursuit and the sensuous pleasures of the libertine and the heavens of the dollar. The brutal materialist is right. All hail to you! All hail to Women and Money! I have lived in vain. I have forsaken the real world for a world of ghosts—for intellect, culture, ideals, meditation. God-damn, and thrice God-damn, my genius, my pride, my conscience, my humanity! God-damn, and thrice God damn, my civilized soul!

It is through the power of the imagination that I comprehend reality.

The Prisoner.—Both the inner and the outer worlds conspire against me. The outer world is inimical to me because my inner self is at such complete variance with it. The inner world is inimical to me because there is no unity in my soul, too many paradoxical instincts, too many personalities at war. Hence I feel like a giant embryo in its ninth month who finds the door to life, to reality, closed and the womb too small to retain it.

If you are not obscene you are not healthy.

Spiritual Sculpture.—I have a mind, a psyche, whose thoughts, emotions and desires are twisted to grotesque, fantastic, unearthly shapes by the poundings of contrary winds and opposing storms, like those curious, bizarre and gnome-like trees that I saw at Point Lobos, California.

C'Est Tout!—God is a metaphysical Imagist. Imagination and Desire are the ultimate Artist. Nothing can exist without Imagination. Reason is the mathematics of the Imagination. Consciousness is the Imagination of Unconsciousness. Animals and insects have Imagination and live through Imagination based on hunger and sex desires. Time and Space are the studios of the Imagination. Every thing that is is provisional and fugacious because it is imaginary and dissolves like an image in the brain— in a little while or that little longer while which we may call a year or a billion years. First the tickle of a need; then an image of the need; then its materialization; then its dissolution in the infinite Ocean of Being. *C'est tout!*

Ladies and Gentlemen—Both Drunk and Sober—Who Are Celebrating on New Year's Day, 2000:
From my ashes (if any) through these words, I, Benjamin DeCasseres, greet you!
I am looking at you, drinking with you, weeping with you, cursing with you, toasting with you, and fornicating with you. Where am I? Ha! Ha! that's my secret.
Since 1927 I notice you've been through the usual hells and joys of life on the old grunting dungball called the Earth. I notice, too, that you are no nearer—farther away, in fact, *of course*— ultimate solutions of the elder mysteries than ever.
You all look, for all your new mechanical geegaws, just as unhappy (except when under the influence of drink or deep in

the functional devices of *amour)* as we did seventy-five years ago. Here's a glass to you—to all of you—trapped in life! The year 2000, my good people, doesn't mean a thing—as New Year's Day 3000 will prove.

Lives I'd Like to Live.—Eternal? Yes, if I could live an infinite series of different lives. I'm a hog for experience. In my next life I'd like to live exclusively a sensuous and sexual existence, as a pursuer and collector of beautiful women, a Don Juan, a Casanova. In another life I'd like to be the slave of mathematics, a Euclid, an Einstein, living entirely in symbols and abstractions. In another life I like to be an ecstatic slave of music, a Beethoven, a Chopin. In still another I'd like to live exclusively for drugs and alchohol, closing the door on Reality completely, living in a fantastic empire. In another as a Napoleon who had conquered the planet and who never had a Waterloo, dictator and moulder of human destinies until death. And so on. Anything that incarnates Power and Beauty; anything but a business man!

Faces.—There are men and women—most of them, in fact—with only one and two-dimensional faces. They have length and breadth. A smaller number of faces are three dimensional; they have length, breadth and depth. When I see depth in a face, I see beauty, character. There is a rare four-dimensional face. It has length, breadth, depth and something else—aura, spirituality, beyondness. Such a face is arresting, never forgotten, ravishing.

Inferiority.—I have a fear of porters, barbers, chauffeurs, waiters and others who take tips. They make me uncomfortable. Have I given them the right tip? Are they branding me mentally a "cheap skate"? Can they tell from my clothes, my walk, my face that I'm poor? They seem always to be spying on me. I treat them with exaggerated politeness for fear that they will hiss an epithet at me.

Wisdom Is Hell!—Why is Wisdom always conceived as being

calm, poised? Why do sculptors always make Wisdom and Wise Men beings that are aloof, serene, old? Wisdom is tragic. Wisdom is disillusion. Wisdom is hell! Wisdom is not Minerva. It is Gorgon.

Criminal Woman.—Woman is a born criminal. She is instinctively a liar, a thief, a murderess, a beast of prey. This is her greatness. She is really the superman, always creating her own values, spinning her own "ethic" out of the hell of her heart.

That is an astonishing sentence of Richard Jefferies : *Man is a supernatural being.*

For a Book.—Huneker: Ironic Ecstasy. Poe: Ethereal Ecstasy. Whitman: Sex-Life Ecstasy. Melville: Sea-Ecstasy. Saltus: The Ecstasy of Negation. Emerson: Spiritual Ecstasy. Clark Ashton Smith: Image Ecstasy.

Fantasia of an Intellectual Faun.—The "Electra" of Sophocles at the Metropolitan Opera House. These Greek tragic-writers lifted humanity to the realm of another dimension. Never a smile, never a quip; no Falstaffs, no clowns, no Poloniuses. Sublime, tearless, irrevocable tragedy. Fatality, Law, the solemn and eternal annunciation of Nemesis. A cosmic dirge. The lowest passions magnified, purified and cleansed by Art. No one has ever touched these great Greeks. They are final.

Don Marquis has dedicated his *The Almost Perfect State* to me with a poem which is the greatest piece of cosmic humor I know. The book blows to dancing, guffawing atoms almost all the "problems" of the hour. Its riant, destructive irony is too fine for these cocksure, smug Americans. It is a mirror of Don's soul itself—careless, sprawling, conversational, Montaigne-like. I'm tickled at the dedication. In Don's lightest and most popular stories and satires there is often a profound wisdom. The universe is a toy-store. Nothing is true. Don capers and laughs in every medium—epigram, drama, fantasy, short stories and poetry. One of the finest and most civilized spirits of the times. My tree is dressed in its first robe of spring greenery. It seems more solemn than it was last year. What have those leaves learned in their sleep? They do not laugh up at my window? They seem reborn under a tragic spell.

My first view of Niagara Falls last week. It exceeded in grandeur all my anticipatory images. I desired to throw myself in with a shout of triumph and go out of this world in its colossal roar and boil. I drank six bottles of real Canadian ale instead—the triumph of Gambrinus over Proserpina.

I had intended to put down here something about "the tragic circus of the Soul" and a bit about "the meditative will," but lethargy has stuffed the vents of fancy and thought; so this fantasia must remain a fugue.

From an Old Envelope.—Nothing so intoxicates me, nothing so quickly sets my brain a-seething or so promptly sets the seminal sap in my mental glands flowing to an itch of creational desire as great epigrams and paradoxes. They sting me like the kisses of nymphomaniacs.

Today I went through an old envelope and found these I had put down some years ago:

"The only thing that excuses God is his non-existence." That is by Stendhal. This is pure "blasphemy" raised to the level of the highest wit. No American or Englishman could ever possibly conceive it or utter it.

"There are relics that are sacred only because they are filthy." Remy de Gourmont has here given utterance to something so profound that the saying is meaningless except to one possessing the subtlest of associative apparatuses. The saints and prophets were lousy and stank. Piggishness and swinishness are akin to godliness. There is an odor of ordure about all orthodox rabbis and priests and the places wherein they worship.

"I do not know how to dissociate tears from music," says

Nietzsche. Simple, beautiful, exquisite.

"Sensations are true hallucinations."—Taine. A German would have used up a volume to say this and ten more volumes to prove it. But in those four words are axiom and proof. I cannot understand how Taine ever became so popular in Germany—he thinks so clearly and economically!

"The eyes never deceive us, as they are the eternal liars,"—La Fontaine. Metaphysical wit also of a very high order.

"Possession".—I desire always to be "possessed", as Baudelaire desired always to be drunk. But "possessed" internally, not by external forces. All great things are accomplished by "possession." Sometimes I am possessed by demons, sometimes by angels, sometimes by swine. I want no Jesus to drive them forth. Let them go naturally. I am not concerned with "salvation" or "redemption," but with *experience*.

Sometimes I am possessed of ideas, sometimes of images, sometimes of celestial transports with unimaginably seductive women.

Meanwhile the rent goes on, and I'm not making it. If there is such a thing as "possession." there is also such a thing as "dispossession"—*quoi?*

An Hour in Eternity.—It is a marvellous thing to be selected by the Spirit of Life to be a frontiersman on the outposts of consciousness, to be one of her lighthouses set on the ultimate cliffs of Space and Time, to be selected to be a diabolical and angelic overtone in her colossal symphony.

Pride compensates for all my pains, for all the hells of paradox, for all the disillusions, for all the tortures and humiliations of my life. I am proud, and thank thee, thou Terrible Presence, for casting my soul, with all its horrors and all its mighty grandeurs, its perpetual crucifixions and its mirific resurrections, in the same matrix and mould with Aeschylus, Plato, Sophocles, Shakespeare, Shelley, Montaigne, Buddha, Schopenhauer,

Balzac, Nietzsche, Chopin, Hu go, Whitman, Beethoven, Goethe, Verlaine, Dostoievsky and Swinburne. I am, like them, one of God's eyes, one of his red-black thoughts, one of his carnival children, one or his revelations to men.

Never, never, had I the magic gift of a Francis Thompson or a Plotinus, could I hope ever to put down here, to catch and trammel in a pencil in all its magic, glory and majesty, the hour that I just passed with the Terrible Spirit of the world, distended and made conscious in my brain, in my whole inner being, to the ultimate limit that man in the flesh may know.

It did not speak, yet I heard It. It did not look at me, yet I was eye to eye with It. My thoughts were Its lips. Thoughts? No, much more. Facets of consciousness that fused and mingled with an almighty Consciousness and caught the terrible music of Its words. My ego mingled with the Eternal Ego. My pride of election opened wide its eyes and received the salutation of light from the eye of the Father of Pride and Power.

"When the symphony of my life on this earth ends where are the andantes, the adagios, the funeral marches, the bacchic chorals, the scherzos, the triumphalis, the con furios, the pizzicatti, and the goblin dances?" I asked.

"In the brain of the Director. The symphony of your spiritual woes and joys, your venoms, your lusts, your gifts are in me," came back the Voice.

I was at peace. It cannot be put on paper—that hour. It was Revelation. It was Power. It was God!

The Mysterious Hour.—I postpone my suicide indefinitely because it is too good to be true. It is like a rare bottle of wine hidden in a secret vineyard for a gala hour, like a marvellous woman of effulgent beauty that one keeps for an unknown wedding night.

Pride is self-pity turned snob. Stoicism is self-pity frozen stiff. Resignation is self-pity in a bromidic sleep.

Reality Through a Chink.—In profound, concentrated intellection, creative or mystical, the body and all its organs are forgotten as in deep sleep. As the mental or emotional concentration begins to decline in power and disperse, the body stirs and we become aware gradually of our organs and members as we do when we first awake in the morning.

As a matter of fact, we have been asleep. The highly concentrated period of intellection, creation or physical ecstasy is a dream, but nevertheless a dream. The difference between the waking dream and the sleeping dream is that in the former the apparatus of association is working, while in the latter it is not.

All action, as a matter of fact, as I have said in some of my books, is somnambulistic. But if that is so, how could the somnambulist know he was a somnambulist, how could he declare, "I am a sleep-walker?" Because there is a Reality behind all illusion, and just enough of it is given to us to allow us to see that we are somnambulists. At such moments we are *awake.*

I dream; therefore I am. This is the formula for Man. God must reverse the formula and say, I am; therefore I dream.

The *I am* is God, of which we all have an atom or two. The dreaming of the *I am* is Man.

Defence of Immodesty.—The immodesty of women today is delightful. It sharpens the battle between the sexes. It almost equalizes the struggle. It increases the charm of woman by whetting to a keener edge the pursuit of man—and the pursuit of man by woman. Woman is now not only romantic but fearsome. She attacks. She invites. She solicits. She exhibits. Her frankness, her de-bunking of herself is adorable. Love declines. Sex-pleasure takes its place. It is a triumph of paganism over Christianity. Isis is unveiled—but Isis is still Isis. She is still beautiful, while the veil was just pretty—nothing more.

Vengeance.—There is no peace, no exaltation like the definite vengeance executed on an enemy. It is health. It is psychic tumescence. It is fulfilment. "Vengeance is mine," saith the Lord. The Lord knows the ultimate pleasure—the slaying of an obstacle in the path of the ego. Yea, we are verily made in Thy image!

When a husband and wife begin to brag of the "sacrifices" they have made for one another, they are getting ready to "bump" one another off—at least mentally.

Genius is the protest of Consciousness against Life.

"The Mysterious Awe of Liberation."—I came across that line in Wedekind's *The Awakening of Spring*. It is one of those magic lines that fill a gap, a hollow, in my thought. An adolescent character speaks it just before his suicide. Its five words frame in gold and ebony the emotion of my soul before the image of the great release. "Awe" is the core-word in the phrase. No other word can take its place. The other words sing around it, sing against each other. Of such is the Kingdom of Poetry, of such is the mightier Kingdom of Words! Here is "liberation" conceived as death. Here are "mysterious" and "awe" placed at the summit of consciousness in the sublimest moment in a person's life, at that moment before he "untrammels," as Francis Thompson says. "The mysterious awe of liberation"—to be done as a nocturne by a Chopin or a tremendous rhapsody by a Liszt.

The Malady of Consciousness.—My consciousness, when full-blown and wide-eyed, when it is aware to the quick of life, is like a physical weight on my brain, heart, lungs; the tiny body of Atlas, the tiny head of Atlas, supporting the Universe; creation pullulating with infinite forms; all of life, spiritual, mental, emotional and physical. I cry out against it. I demand of God, in such moments, a partial or total eclipse of this monstrous sun. I cry for a lid to fall quickly over this uncircumferenced eye.
A deep night's sleep, dreamless and lethal. First dawn of consciousness, a streak of light in the east of my brain. Gradually it widens like a monstrous circular fan, eating up sleep and

happiness till it fills all space. It englobes, engulfs the brain, the heart, the universe. In its blazing light stalk the phantom Hopes, Despairs, Defeats, Memories, Cares.

Knowledge is not power, but powerlessness. Consciousness—which is knowledge—is a disease, a malady. It is the sickness of genius.

I See!—Two instances in two years convince me that I am developing powers of second sight. One evening this thought came into my head: It is about time that I saw the death of Vance Thompson announced. The next morning on opening *The World* I saw the display heading, "Vance Thompson Dies in Rome." I had not read Thompson for many years, never met him, and there was no reason why that thought should have been in my head. I evidently got the cable flash by psycho-radio. Last evening, at about seven o'clock, there wandered into my head with great vividness this thought: I shall read about the death or a disaster to Wells Hawks. This morning Bio called to me from the "den" to the bedroom, where I was dressing, "Wells Hawks has been stricken with apoplexy." It was in *The World*. I was startled out of my socks and told my wife about my thought of the evening before. At almost the same hour that Hawks was stricken while eating in an uptown hotel I got the psycho-radio. This phenomenon will become more and more widespread. The consciousness of the race has evidently reached its physical and cultural limits. It is inventing new play grounds, new dominions, new cultural forms. I am convinced that interplanetary communication will come through psycho-radio channels. Evolution from now on will be psychical.

"The Microscopic. Fulcrums of Destiny."—How can anyone talk about free will when two days' constipation may result in a man murdering his wife and child or five glasses of wine taken by a young girl at a party may result in "illegitimate" twins in nine months? Everything in our lives turns on the trivial, the unre-

membered, the forgotten. My friend Christopher has given me the key-phrase to the universe: *the microscopic fulcrums of Destiny.* The universe is balanced on an atom.

Irony is the belly-guffaw of Rabelais frozen in the brain—or maybe it is only a hard-boiled tear.

A Plea for Injustice.—I just read in the papers that Francis Grierson, that curious exotic soul, was found dead at his piano in Los Angeles at the age of 79. He was in want, and probably had been starving intermittently for thirty years.

Unjust? No. There is no injustice in the world. The world conceived as the product of Law, laws exact and inexorable, is just in its decisions to a hair. Whatever happens happens with precise, geometric justice. It would be unjust to demand a separate law for a Poe and another for a Ford. Only the ethicist, the sentimentalist, the atheist or the Catholic believes that this is an unjust world. The thinker, the sceptic, the realist, the ironist sees that "attractions are proportioned to the destinies," that the death of a Chatterton was pathetic but inexorable and just.

My Memory in Blue.—A sweet, a delicious Memory in Blue. She rose out of my emotional tombs into my consciousness this morning just after waking. I held her there in revery with all the purity and immaculate ideality of my youth of more than thirty years ago. She still bears about her the odor of violets. She is still bathed in effulgent blue. (Her dress was always blue, her eyes were blue and she always wore violets either on her bosom or in her hat.)

How exquisite those moments when I can revive the emotions of those years, when the psycho-sexual fluid held in its depths all the breathlessness, the sweet, unaccountable, fairy-like illusions of Woman! The divine, necromantic power of this fluid, with its mysterious affinities, in those first days of the Awakening!

I became aware that some one was looking at me in a theatre

one night—looking at me intently. I had a sweet, uneasy feeling. I did not know who was looking at me. I could not find the face or the eyes. Some one was gently tapping my nerves and emotions. I left the theatre in a glow. I had not seen the person who was looking at me. The following week there came the same uneasy, sweet inundation after the curtain rose and the auditorium was in semi-darkness. But as the lights went up I caught two eyes fixed on me—two eyes that exhaled violets; two eyes that fluttered and lowered at my gaze. An immense calm filled me. The psycho-sexual fluid subsided to an ecstatic breathless peace in my blood.

We never spoke. For two years, from our theatre seats, we carried on a grave flirtation, a delicious, shy, virginal flirtation with our eyes. Beautiful, slim, graceful, adorable, modest, womanly, with all the lure of first love, she passed—into the tomb of my heart. Where are you now, my Lady Blue? What have the years done to you? Am I, too, a virginal, romantic vision, a dream-lover, in your heart and brain? Do I rise in your consciousness at the waking hour, suddenly, unexpectedly, when spring flushes your blood and the psycho-sexual fluid washes me up over the dikes of your work-a-day life and its *ennuis* and inanities?

Ah! my Blue Lady, my Sweetheart with the Violets, my delicious Virgin, we can never grow old. Like the figures on Keats' Grecian urn, we are caught and eternalized *flagrante delicto* in our youth, in our ethereal desire, with outstretched arms that will never meet, with hungry lips that will never join, with feet hurrying to one another forever stricken still on the threshold of contact.

The God of Poverty.—Mammon is the god of riches, but why is there no God of Poverty? Was the conception too horrible for the Greeks? They personified everything except the most obvious and commonest fact—poverty.

It is probable that their imagination failed them. Poverty is beyond Tragedy, which the Greeks personified. It is something that can only be idealized in stone or poem or realized by a Dore or a Poe. Besides, the Greeks were the aristocracy of the ancient world. The fate of the lower classes and the hordes of morons that littered the earth did not interest their poets, statesmen and myth-makers. The recognition of the poor and poverty-stricken came into the world with Christ. The Galilean is the Christian God of Poverty, as the Buddha is the God of Negation. But Greece would have none of it.

To supply this want Christ made of poverty a virtue. We owe him a debt of gratitude. He was fundamentally a realist. He knew there was nothing comparable on earth, nothing more horrible, than lack of money. Hunger, starvation, the defeated flesh, disease, filth and slavery were to him the hells of the race. He knew that economic freedom was the only freedom worth while. It released the mind and the body. Poverty is a fundamental condition of movement and life. So he promised the poor the felicities of the rich in the country houses and golf-greens of a Beyond, where the landlord ceases from troubling and the belly is at rest.

The Buddha offered a get-a-way into Nirvana, but Jesus insisted on vengeance. He threw Dives out of Heaven and made Lazarus the Lord of Dives' estates. It is probable that Dives was in every way superior to Lazarus. He was probably an art-patron and a lady's man *de luxe*. And it is just as probable that Lazarus did not have, and will probably never have, a pleasure-aspiration above the lowest type of moving-picture. Nevertheless, the gesture was a fine one. Jesus whispered to the human race à la Iago, "Put money in thy purse."

Therefore I salute Jesus, God of Poverty!

To Frederick Nietzsche.
Dear Frederick:
I am reading again your "Ecce Homo"—this time in English. On page 71 you stigmatize all "no-sayers", all "idealists", all

Schopenhaureans as decadents, degenerates, and you glorify all yea-sayers, "Dionysians" and life-lovers as healthy beings. I have gone after you once before on this matter (I believe in my *Sir Galahad*). Why is yea-saying superior to no-saying? Wherein is life superior to death? Why are you an "absolutionist" (ah! an *absolutionist*, Frederick!) in regard to Life? Why do you make an ideal (ah! an *ideal*, Frederick!) of Life? Are you not superstitious, "cowardly," "Socratic" and all that in your frenzied and blind sponsoring of life for life's sake? Why isn't negation as great, as brave, as healthy, as Dionysian (yes, as *Dionysian*, Frederick!) as affirmation? Nirvana is conceived ecstatically. Nihilism is tragically intoxicating.

You were a great poet, a great psychologist, a great writer, my dear Frederick, but you lacked a metaphysical organ. You were as complete a propagandist as Jesus, Buddha, Schopenhauer or Karl Marx. Your "Superman" is messianic. Spurning Idealism, you were the greatest Idealist of your age. You had your beautiful, consolatory illusions. Your soul was soap-boxy in the way you screeched.

For the life of me, Frederick, I cannot understand why life is superior to death, why something is superior to nothing, why somewhere is superior to nowhere. Ah, my beloved and always admired companion, you were, in a word, a very religious, Christian soul!

Benjamin DeCasseres

The Morning of an Intellectual Faun.—A June day fabricated by the Renoir of Heaven. Away! Away! through the morning light—on subway wings—to Van Cortlandt Park. Poe in my pocket—"Ulalume" in the subway!

Exquisite brain, music in the moving sewers and garbage-pipes of New York.

I smell roses. Roses in the subway! I look over the people around me; there are no roses anywhere. I take a long nostril breath.

No, I'm not deceived. I smell roses. Then I remembered that I had had a vivid dream last night of someone pinning a large red rose on my coat lapel. That was the dream-rose I smelled in the subway, although I had been awake for three hours. Dreams are the parents of reality. My day is fashioned for me in sleep.

I am roaming through the silences of Van Cortlandt woods. Nature was my first bride. She will be my last. I am cleansed, released, but melancholy—that sweet and musical melancholy that always envelopes me when satur ated with the eternal and miraculous; the melancholy of a prolonged euthanasia, of a mild Nirvana, of the nympholepsy of Panthea, who rapes my soul, my consciousness. Spring!—my pubic-green Panthea!

Earth and trees, sunlight and forest shade, the calm, ironic blue of the heavens bring Shelley close to me—Shelley whose soul was a diary of an ethereal Pan.

Meditation in the woods: Emotions have no power to refine thought. Thought alone can refine the emotions. A prejudice may deform a thought; but thought alone has power to dissolve a prejudice. It is just for that reason that the mob fears thought and hates and fears the civilized thinker, the intellectual dissolver. The mob does not want its emotions refined and it does not want its prejudices dissolved.

The brain is the organ of humor. It has power to make the emotions smile. It has power to open the mouth of our deepest wound and make it laugh. It has power to strike down the granite wall of our prejudices. And for this reason, too, the humor of the brain is feared and hated by the mob-soul.

Posterity Balm.—Up early this morning. Spirits low, which means I am in a creative mood. The blacker my soul the lighter my thought. The black wings of the crow can out-aviate the white wings of the dove. I am centripetal this morning. All my forces gravitate to the sun of my ego. The pulling power of the external worlds pulls very lightly at me. It will be at least three hours, I can see, before I yawn, before the concentrated essence of my being dissolves into nerve-gas and *ennui*.

What shall I do? Well, I'll address the ladies and gentlemen of posterity. On the waves of a vast number of unborn tomorrows I'll radio a talk. I hear you, the now unmaterialized, say, "Go to it!" To the grandchildren and great-grandchildren of those beings who are born on this day, June 7, 1927: Greetings, and may your colons never be lazy!

To the youth of June 7, 2027, just a hundred years from today, I say unto ye, honor your father and mother, live in the open air, avoid tobacco, rum and loose women, keep your bowels moving and multiply in the manner that Abraham has taught ye. Selah. I hovered over you all and saw all that you did in 2023. I was so happy to hear the school-children chant with their childish voices my *The Shadow-Eater, Litanies of Negation* and *Black Suns* on the greens (how cool it was!) and professors from the University of California to the University of Teheran read from *Forty Immortals* and *The Book of Vengeance*. How delighted I was to see my five hundred statues throughout the world decorated with geraniums and herbs and simples! Then, the bands in Washington that played "The DeCasseres March," a strange mixture of the immortal George Gershwin, Franz Liszt and your own incomparable super-jazz symphonists (I see that only street barrel-organs play Beethoven now, in 2027). Through your trans-material noise amplifiers you can, no doubt, hear my tears of gratitude as I behold the book reviewers of the empire city of Detroit intoning, under the radio arc-lamps, the great prose of my *Chameleon*.

Ah, lads and lassies of posterity, and you old cocks and hens, too, there is no joy on earth or in heaven (so-called) like this posthumous apotheosis. I am here with you, in 2027, side by side with the Lords of this World—I have forgotten whether it is the sixth or seventh dimension—and I thank you for the herbs and simples of 2023 and everything!

Is there anything more silent than thought? Great poetry and great lyrical prose are the silent music of the brain. I alone, at this writing, hear the crash and massed choruses of the logocratic atoms in my brain and the whir and flash of my ironic and cosmic epigrams. Swedenborg said he could hear "the music of the spheres," the rhythmic dance-music of their minuets and waltzes around the suns. Well, I hear the music of the spheres of thought and consciousness in my skull—the rolling, frenetic harmonies of image-worlds as they circle around the sun-atoms. But now you, in 2027, hear me from material orchestras and over your radios. Your great composers have put my essays and poems to music. The colossal sound-architecture that you have built up on the theme of my *Comic View, The Trail of the Worm, Zenith, Litanies of Negation, The Ballad of the Minutes,* my *Nietzsche* and many others! You intoxicate me with glory! You blast me with monumental, co-ordinated sound! But why did you jazz my "Muse of Lies"? Naughty, naughty Gershwins! Selah.

The God of Nietzsche.—The most astounding thing about Nietzsche is his incarnation of ideas. He treats ideas as live things, with blood, bone, eyes, ears, nose, heart, liver, phallus and anus. He talks to them, pummels them, kisses them, micturates on them, crowns them, fights duels with them, copulates with them! Ideas are to him Father, Son and Holy Ghost. His style is the most terrible, brutal, vital, coruscating, dithyrambic, inspired, pulverizing in all literature. No such vitalizer of images and ideas has even lived. Only the furies of Jeremiah and Isaiah can be compared to him.

Yes, Nietzsche was a veritable incarnation. In him, Ideas took on flesh, the Abstract assumed a body, parts and passions. He always regretted that Stendhal said before he had a chance to say it, "The only excuse for God's existence is that he does not exist." So I say this of Nietzsche: The only excuse for Nietzsche's atheism is that it does not exist. His God was the Idea, and what difference is there between the Idea become flesh and the Word be come flesh?

The "Style" of My Books.—My style, whether thunderous and frenzied or coldly ironic and cynical, is a perfect reproduction of my interior being. My books are my guts. If I have been powerfully drawn to Stirner, Nietzsche, Huneker, Saltus, Victor Hugo and Walt Whitman, it is because their minds—and therefore their styles—are like mine. I was born a Fury of the emotions and the intellect.

Ideas and emotions produced earthquakes in me when a youth. I am revolté to my utter atom. My style is my spit, my semen.

Read all my works—including my letters to Bio over a period of seventeen years—in one sitting. I defy you! You will fall dead of high-blood pressure, you will be cannonaded into the grave, you will be flayed to shreds. Huneker wrote me that after reading a single one of my essays (I've forgotten which) he felt as though his skull had been riddled by shot. I exhaust reviewers who try to read *Forty Immortals* in one sitting. I cannot re-read my own works except in bits.

Consider my work up to date as a huge canvas:

> LIGHT.—Through the words, sentences and ideas there streams an unearthly light that dissolves all that it falls upon and transfigures the universe to something new and strange. This light has physical impact. It is perpetual sheet-lightning in the ether beating on Matter and Motion.
> COMPOSITION.—Grotesque, unarithmetical, abysms that are above you and star-glutted spaces that are beneath you. Is there a pattern? Has the Infinite and Eternal pattern?
> BACKGROUND.—The background of my work is the intellect of God—musical, ironic, unhuman.

Thieves.—The fact that I understand a thief, why he thieves and my knowledge that I would do exactly the same thing as a thief does under the same circumstances is no reason why I should not kill a thief who robs me. A man may understand himself so well that he will commit suicide.

Gayety.—Gayety of soul (brain, heart and emotions) is rare over a prolonged period of time. The human has required in all ages and all climes stimulants, alchohol, jokes and witty conversation to induce gayety. Tragedy and melancholy need no external stimulants. They are produced naturally. They are inherent in the nerves, the blood and the psyche.

It is long since I have been gay. That is because I have had no alchohol for a long time. I have felt joy in music, a great book, my night wanderings (thou dark, friendly and mysteriously joyful darkness!), baseball and the glamor of the psycho-sexual fluid; but gayety—no. Gayety is complete abandonment, Dionysian, lawless. Joy is enveloped in a subtle shadow of foreboding. Gayety is sexual, alcoholic, a silver sun that eclipses the black planet of the heart.

The Lighter Moments of Your Faun.—The Ouija board... The Yankee Stadium... The movies... Conversation with the janitor... Stroking Mrs. Mandeville's cats... Reading the hogwash of theatrical and motion picture press agents in the daily papers... Hot-dog sandwiches on Fourteenth Street... Bathtub revels in the morning... Shopping for lemons and gluten-bread on Third Avenue... Contemplating with orgiastic joy my next souse, which I eternally postpone, as I do the reading of Shakespeare's *The Winter's Tale*... Wandering through the department stores on the hunt for beautiful, sexy women for my cerebral gallery of tantalizing delights... Cup custard and pineapple at midnight with Bio... Paying a fortune-teller fifty cents to tell me how famous I am going to be... Riding in the subway... Eating in the automat... Watching the disappearance of my belly under the influence of my diet.

"There is, brethren, a condition wherein there is neither earth nor water, nor fire, nor air, nor the sphere of infinite space nor the sphere of infinite consciousness, nor the sphere of the void, nor the sphere of perception nor non-perception; where there is no 'this world' and no 'world beyond' ; where there is no moon and no sun. That condition, brethren, do I call neither a coming nor a going nor a standing still nor a falling away nor a rising up. It is without fixity, without mobility, without basis. THAT IS THE END OF WOE."

—*Buddha*

"How much longer will man continue to pimp for the gluttony of Death?"

—*Shelley.*

"The Universe was created in an act of hate. To dissolve it would be an act of love."

—*Marcel Schwob.*

FINIS

In the last months of his life, the twilight time when all action recedes and life becomes luminous in silence, Benjamin De-Casseres wrote these four essays.

Alive with the poetic flavor of his word-mastery, here is illumination of the uttermost self, a book that is at once a breviary of philosophic fearlessness, a hymnal of the eternal verities.

Before his day had completely receded, *"One last ecstatic glow that stains a hemisphere",* had arched itself above him and he penned the lines which have become the seal of his life's work.

—Bio DeCasseres.

TWILIGHT

The day is dying.
The night, with soft impeachment
Stands in the shadows.
The sky is dismantled,
All its bright colors are folded in chests of silver;
And the clouds have fled
To deck the brows of distant dawns.
The laughter of the rivulets is hushed;
The wind's sweet importune to the field's last blush
Falls broken in the grasses.
The sea strains at its leash of silence,
And the hills—the catacombs of all dead days—
Stand bleak, and dark, and chill.
The expectant faces of happy flowers
Have drooped, and some have shut themselves in
Alone with their sorrow;
And there are only dim hauntings
Of all the rapturous lessons of the air;
The swift tracery of the gull in its ellipse,
The swallow with its parallelogram,
And all the spiral joy of the skylark
Have been stayed. And from every tree
And brake and bourne
Stand watchers in this sacred hour.
One last ecstatic glow that stains a hemisphere,
A sigh, hollowed from a diapason of sound—
The day is dead!
And all the grass, and trees, and tender things
Are wet with tears.

—*Bio DeCasseres.*

FOREWORD

I entitle this book FINIS not because it is necessarily my last book but because it expounds my conception of the END for which this universe exists. For, it seems to me, that if there is one ultimate fact that can be affirmed without contradiction by a human mind it is OBLIVION.

FINIS, in a manner, is a summation of all my books, of my lifelong beliefs.

FINIS has never appeared in any form before. I am having only a limited number of copies printed for distribution.

If any one should care to purchase one they are priced at one dollar apiece.

—Benjamin DeCasseres.
New York, 1945.

THE IRRELATIVITY OF ALL RELATIVES

Whatever is is relative.

The Absolute cannot be conceived or imagined (imaged). It can only be inferred.

What we mean by a relative universe is that one thing (any thing) can only be known (we can only become conscious of it) through some other thing.

Black is known because of white, I because of you, water because of land, pain because of pleasure, etc., etc., *ad infinitum*.

The external universe is only known because it is related to an internal universe—the brain, the consciousness, the emotions.

All, then, is relative. All is interdependent.

But to what is the *sum* of all relatives related?

The sum of all relatives is whatever exists, whatever is perceived, thought, imagined, felt, smelled, seen, heard, tasted.

It is Space and Time and Consciousness and all that they contain.

But to what is this grand total related?

If it is related to an Absolute that we are compelled to affirm as an hypothesis, then all relations are illusions.

And that is precisely what all relations are—illusions.

They are *irrelevant* and *irrelative*.

But suppose there is no Absolute? Suppose that that, too, is a fiction, an illusion?

Then the Relative becomes the Absolute, which is a contradiction in terms.

We are forced, then, again to predicate the existence of an Irrelative Absolute.

In this Absolute no relative can possibly exist.

Therefore (using the logical method) we, you and I, who are made up of a complex and nexus of relatives exist really in the Absolute.

That is, *we have no existence at all.*

We are provisionally only a series of opposites and contrasts which we call "relations."

Therefore I say that all that is in Time and Space is related to the Absolute—that is, to NOTHING.

FINIS

THE DEVALUATION OF ALL VALUES

As the sum of all relatives are irrelative, as all relations lead to the Absolute, which so far as the human mind is concerned is equivalent to NOTHING (*no thing*), as we do not live in a world of substantials, but in a world of pure relations, which are the uniting link of cognition between illusions—it follows that all our values, ethical, spiritual, mental and emotional, are also *valueless*.

Nietzsche said he had transvalued all values.

In transvaluing them he merely substituted a new value for a former value, believing in the substantiality of his new value (the Will-to-Power) with the same fanaticism and certainty that the announcers, theological and philosophical, of all former values believed in *their* ultimates.

He, like Jesus, Buddha and Spinoza, sought for and affirmed an ultimate value—the Kingdom of Heaven, Nirvana, God.

Of the three men mentioned above, it was Buddha who came nearer to devaluing all values in his annunciation that the Universe is inherently evil (the fabrication of Maya, or universal Illusion). Indeed, he was called "The Shadow-Eater."

But even Buddha had certain earth-values, for he taught humaneness, goodness, gentleness, pity, which have only relative values and are therefore not ultimates, for humaneness, goodness, gentleness and pity are not found in cosmic nature but are purely the products of utilitarian evolution.

There are, in fact, as many values as there are human beings.

Some believe that money is the ultimate value, some love, some action, some love of God, some contemplation, some self-sacrifice, some art, some crime, some self-culture, etc.

Nietzsche came nearer than any one else in affirming a universal earth-value in his Will-to-Power. But as an ultimate value it is valueless, for what is the aim and meaning of Will-to-Power even in "God"? WHY?

Omnipotent Power is a form of boredom. All these values are ruses to dodge the irrelativity of all things and the great Devaluer of all values—*personal and cosmic extinction*, which follows us like an enormous shadow.

This, then, is an essay on the *devaluation of all values*.

Just as there is no ultimate relative, just as all relatives are solved in the Irrelative, so all values, human and (so-called) "divine" are dissolved in the *Valueless*.

For *what is of value in eternal Time and infinite Space?*

This has always been sensed by certain supreme minds : Buddha, Spinoza (whose God negates all human values), Koheleth ("vanity of vanities: all is vanity"), Omar Khayyam in his philosophy of transitory sensations, Rabelais with his "Do as thou wilt" and Jules de Gaultier, who said, "Even the atheists make the sign of the cross when they see me."

Man will, of course, continue to "transvalue" his values until the Earth falls piece by piece into Space because Maya rules the temporal order.

But as with relations so with values "by which we live."

They all disappear into the Irrelative and the *Valueless*, into the Absolute—that is, NOTHING.

A universal law is not an ultimate one.

A universal law is war—"war is the father of all things", said Heraclitus.

Nothing can exist except through struggle, conflict, opposition.

But it is not an *ultimate value*, for it is still relative to total existence, which is not related to anything.

Therefore we come to pure Nihilism and a perception of the meaning of the profoundest of all sayings: *Ex nihilo nihil.*

THE EVOLUTION OF OBLIVION

"Tout lasse, tout casse, tout passe".

Life is the evolution of Oblivion.

What we call Change is nothing but evolving Oblivion.

Oblivion is the final blotter of all values and all that is relative.

It is said that negative words like *oblivion, inexistence, forgetfulness* and *nothing* are merely the reverse, the idea-foil to *present, existence, memory, something.*

Oblivion is, however, not a negative idea or word, but a positive idea or word.

On the contrary, all that was, all that is and all that will be are negative.

For Oblivion is the one positive, continuous FACT in the universe and all that exists either of matter or mind, star or flea, empire or space-time itself are but flitting shadows on the white background of infinite and eternal Oblivion.

Life, organic and inorganic, is thus literally the evolution of Oblivion.

Any particular thing—a human being, an ant, a sidereal system, a conception of God—from the moment of its appearance in time and space begins a steady and inevitable ascension to Oblivion.

No matter how high or complex the evolution of the temporal order it is followed by the Shadow of Oblivion.

Memories, identities, acts, deaths are dissolved in perpetual Forgetfulness.

Oblivion—a constant dissolution—is in the blood, brain, bones, heart, nerves of all that lives on any star.

It is the soul of whatever is.

Oblivion is the one universal law of which *there is no opposite.*

For the existence of things in space and time is not an opposed law to Oblivion.

It is confederate, the technique itself of Oblivion. Matter and Mind are the looms of inexistence.

Yesterday is eternal.

The Present and the Future are both myths.

Oblivion is an infinite number of yesterdays—and all our todays and all our tomorrows are already dissolving yesterdays in the eye of Oblivion.

Oblivion has no body, nor does it exist in Space or Time, being the ultimate dissolver of Space and Time.

The Universe, then, and all that it contains, as Shakespeare says, shall not leave a "rack" behind, for all of mind and all of matter and space and time and all that has ever existed or that ever will exist are such "stuff as dreams are made on"—and the extensionless Dreamer is Oblivion whose other names are *Timeless Eternity* and *Spaceless Infinity.*

THE PRESENCE:
Hymn of a Nihilist to OBLIVION

"The mysticism of the voluptuous joy of Eternal
Emptiness."

—*Nietzsche.*

1.

Being is Thy Space, Will is Thy Time, and all matter and mind is
but an atom in the iris of Thy luminous eye, O Presence!

My pain and my pleasure are unknown to Thee as a moth is
unknown to the lamp, O Presence!

Black with despair or rubescent with joy, I walk in Thee, O
Presence!

Sleeping, I drift in Thee like a blind fish. Waking, I sail the
boat of my soul on Thy Being, O Presence!

When I have acclaimed Thee there is no applause. When I
have cursed Thee there is no frown, for Thou knowest me not,
O Presence!

Thou dost miraculize my days and translate the most familiar objects into the thrill of eternal mystery, O Presence!

2.

Thou pourest from all crannies and all nooks of life like light
from a hidden Sun.

Thou art like the air through which I walk, unseen, transparent, sustaining.

Thou art behind me and before me, on top of me and under
me—a sunken boat am I suspended in the middle of Infinite
Waters!

Thou art the wisdom of my ignorance and the culminant
beam of my knowledge.

I retreat in Thee and win all battles. I advance in Thee and
lose all my gains.

3.

My many words and reveries die in Thee, O Presence, like the murmur of muttered dreams in the night.

My frets and hates are caught in Thy glowing laughter like the tears of little children in the sing-song of their mother.

My pride swells in Thee like the imperial rose in the dawn of June—to drop petal by petal into the abysms of Thy eternity.

4.

Good is finite and Evil is infinite. And still, O Presence, Thou knowest naught of these measures.

All that lives must die and dissolve like a dream of fair women on a battlefield. And still, O Presence, Thou knowest naught of these processes.

For, O Presence, Thou art like the sea: perfect evil and perfect good simultaneously. Being both, Thou art neither, O eternally virginal One!

5.

Thou art the humor of my tears, the humor of my doubts, the humor of my desires.

I seek to decompose Thee, to analyze Thee in the crucible of my brittle mind—and Thou dost laugh with Thy all-enmeshing Silence.

Silence is the mirth of Thee—silence delicate and 'whelming.

The night is in the Sun, my No is in my Yes, and my little all is in Thee. In the Presence there is no seam.

6.

I lay down my will before the Presence as I lay down my shoes before going into my bed.

I enter Thy abode as Thou dost enter the sea-drops and the dew on the meadow—silently and without motion.

My breath mingles with Thine and my eyes are tiny suns that move in Thy spaceless ether.

Lapped in Thee, I have nothing of self, being the All.

DE CASSERES DIES; AUTHOR, COLUMNIST

Was Editorial Writer for The Mirror—Started Newspaper Career at the Age of 13

Benjamin De Casseres, author, columnist and editorial writer, died yesterday in his home, 593 Riverside Drive, at the age of 72. Ill since February, he had continued his work as editorial writer for The New York Mirror.

Born in Philadelphia, a son of David and Charlotte Davis De Casseres, Mr. De Casseres was a collateral descendant of Benedict de Spinoza, the philosopher. He left school at 13 to work on Philadelphia newspapers. He was a proofreader on The Philadelphia Press from 1892 to 1899, when he came to New York and took a similar position on The Sun.

In 1903 he transferred to The New York Herald, where he worked until 1919, with an interval of one year (1906-07) when he went to Mexico City to found and edit El Diario.

Wrote Book Reviews

Since 1912 Mr. De Casseres had been contributing book reviews to The Sun, THE NEW YORK TIMES, The Bookman and other publications. He became a special Sunday writer for THE TIMES in 1919. Meanwhile, he wrote many articles for popular magazines and New York newspapers, particularly The World, and contributed articles to the Mercure de France.

In 1922 he became drama critic of Arts and Decorations, where he remained until 1933, when he became affiliated with the Hearst organization as "March of Events" columnist, editorial writer and literary editor, first for The American, then The Evening Journal and later for The Mirror.

Mr. De Casseres also had done drama criticism for several motion-picture magazines, having served for five years on the editorial staff of the Famous Players-Lasky Corporation and one year with Universal Pictures.

BENJAMIN DE CASSERES
1933

Long List of Works

His published works included "The Shadow-Eater" (poems) (1915), "Chameleon — Being the Book of My Selves" (1922), "Mirrors of New York" (1925), "Forty Immortals" (essays) (1925), "James Gibbons Huneker" (1925), "Anathema!" (prose-poem) (1928), "The Superman in America" (1929), "Mencken and Shaw" (1930), "The Love Letters of a Living Poet" (1931), "Spinoza" (1932), "The Muse of Lies" (1936) and "Don Marquis" (a parable and a tribute) (1938). In 1939 he compiled an edition of his own works in three volumes.

An outspoken foe of communism, Mr. De Casseres wrote in The New York American that "the Russian reactionary experiment in communism is the greatest failure in all history."

He leaves a widow, the former Bio Terrill, whom he married on Oct. 12, 1919, and a sister, Mrs. Irving Lehman.

Obituary from the New York Times, December 7th, 1945.

FINIS

www.ingramcontent.com/pod-product-compliance
Lightning Source LLC
Chambersburg PA
CBHW031128090426
42738CB00008B/1011